Gampopa Teaches Essence Mahamudra

INTERVIEWS WITH HIS HEART
DISCIPLES, DUSUM KHYENPA
AND OTHERS

BY TONY DUFF
PADMA KARPO TRANSLATIONS

First edition, November, 2011
ISBN: paper book 978-9937–572-08-8
ISBN: e-book 978-9937-572-09-5

Janson typeface with diacritical marks
Designed and created by Tony Duff
Tibetan Computer Company
http://www.pktc.org/tcc

Thangka images of Gampopa,Dusum Khyenpa,and
Lord Phagmo Drupa © Shelly and Donald Rubin Museum,
Himalayan Art Project, with permission.

Produced, Printed, and Published by
Padma Karpo Translation Committee
P.O. Box 4957
Kathmandu
NEPAL

Committee members for this book: translation and composition,
Lama Tony Duff; editorial, Tom Anderson.

Web-site and e-mail contact through:
http://www.pktc.org/pktc
or search Padma Karpo Translation Committee on the web.

CONTENTS

INTRODUCTION

This book focusses on the way that the most essential teaching of Mahamudra[1], called Essence Mahamudra, was transmitted in the very early days of the Kagyu lineage in Tibet. It introduces the subject by presenting two small texts which contain hallmark teachings of Gampopa in relation to the Kagyu teaching of Mahamudra. It then presents records of personal interviews and teaching sessions given by the early Kagyu lineage holder Gampopa to four of his outstanding disciples.

1. Points of Interest

There are many styles of teaching used in Buddhism. In traditions that emphasize practice, the interview in which the disciple comes to the teacher and presents his doubts or the state of his practice is important—the teacher uses the opportunity to take the disciple further in an atmosphere of personal contact with the teacher, something which is of prime importance within Buddhism. Re-

---

[1] Skt. mahāmudrā, Tib. phyag rgya chen po: Mahamudra is the name of a set of ultimate teachings on reality and also of the reality itself. The name and the teaching are explained at length in the book *Gampopa's Mahamudra: The Five-Part Mahamudra of the Kagyus* by Tony Duff, published by Padma Karpo Translation Committee, 2008, ISBN: 978-9937-2-0607-5.

cords of these sessions can be very important for later practitioners because of the very practical nature of the instruction contained in them. That is very true here—the interview texts presented are full of the blessings of the early Kagyu masters and their particular way of presenting Essence Mahamudra. The result is a book with a unique quality, one that fits with a practitioner's mind.

In terms of time, these interviews are records of the very early Tibetan practitioners of the Kagyu lineage. They are very important to present-day practitioners because they clearly reveal the mode of teaching Mahamudra that was present in the early Kagyu, very shortly after it had come from India. They also contain a wealth of firsthand information about noted people of the time told by the people themselves.

In terms of the place, the Kagyu teachings came from India into Southern Central Tibet via Marpa the Translator who lived in that region. His main disciples, including Milarepa, were from that region and spent their lives there. Milarepa's main disciple, Gampopa, who is the source of the teachings in this book, also was from Central Tibet and established his teaching and retreat centre at Dvag Lha Gampo, some distance south of Lhasa. Thus, this book contains historical information about the early spread of

Figure 1. Marpa the Translator

Kagyu dharma as it occurred in the Central Tibetan region. Histories of the Kagyu lineage from the time it arose in ancient India to Gampopa can be read in the books *Gampopa's Mahamudra* mentioned above and *Drukchen Padma Karpo's Collected Works on Mahamudra*[2].

In terms of the dharma presented, these interviews are mainly concerned with the teaching of what has come to be known as Essence Mahamudra. There are many important points in connection with this. For example, the style of the teaching at that time is clearly evident in the interviews. And, the content of the interviews shows that Essence Mahamudra was very much the heart of the Kagyu teaching before the many Kagyu sub-sects developed. This latter point is particularly important because it shows that, although some sub-schools, such as the Drukpa Kagyu, do not explicitly teach Essence Mahamudra, it was a core teaching of the Kagyu lineage when it came from India.

In terms of the disciples whose interviews are presented here, this book is about four of the eighteen disciples who were foremost among Gampopa's disciples. Two of them, Lord Gomtshul and Yogin Choyung, might not be known to Westerners, but the other two, Dusum Khyenpa, the first Karmapa, and Phagmo Drupa, the source of many of the Kagyu sub-schools, will be known to many. The interviews of all four disciples are packed with both historical information and dharma teaching.

2. About the Teacher, Gampopa

Gampopa lived from 1079–1153 C.E. He was born in Central Tibet in the district called Nyal[3]. At the age of seven, his parents sent him to study medicine, which he did for twenty and a half years. He studied with doctors from Indian, Nepalese, Chinese, and Tibetan traditions and by all accounts became a very expert

---

[2] A book by Tony Duff, published by Padma Karpo Translation Committee, 2011, ISBN: 978-9973-572-01-9.

[3] Tib. gnyal.

doctor. After that, he gave his whole attention to Buddhism for the rest of his life but, because of his skills as a doctor, was always known as "Lhaje" which is a highly honorific title for a doctor.

Figure 2. Lord Gampopa

Later in his life, he moved to the area called Dvagpo[4], so was called Dvagpopa, the Man from Dvagpo, and then was also called Dvagpo Lhaje, the Doctor of Dvagpo. Dvagpo is near the Gampo Hills because of which he was also known as Gampopa, the Man of Gampo. Nowadays, this name Gampopa is the name by which he is most well known amongst non-Tibetans. However, Tibetans mostly refer to him as Dvagpopa or Dvagpo Rinpoche and usually very affectionately.

In his early teens, Gampopa heard a great deal of Nyingma dharma from the Nyingma teacher "Barey". After that, he heard the Kadampa teachings called "Stages of the Path", which are the essential teachings of the Kadampa, initially from Geshe Yontan Drag.

Gampopa married when he was sixteen. At the age of twenty-five, his wife and son both died from a contagious disease. This affected him profoundly and he resolved to give up worldly pursuits in favour of Buddhist practice.

At twenty-six, he took full monk's ordination from the Kadampa Geshe Lodan Sherab and was given the name Sonam Rinchen. This name too is found commonly in Tibetan literature. On his

---

[4] Tib. dvags po.

first meeting with Milarepa, when Milarepa asked his name, he gave this name and Mila replied, "Merit [sonam], merit, you come from great merit and are very precious [rinchen]." Milarepa predicted that Gampopa would be greater than himself in the sense that he would go out and reach many more people. Time has shown that Milarepa became very famous for his practice and realization but that Gampopa became the means by which Milarepa's lineage of teaching spread widely, something that did not happen directly on Milarepa's account.

Although Gampopa became very well known amongst Tibetans, he has not been well known to Westerners, except through his *Jewel Ornament of Liberation* text which was translated many years ago when Tibetan Buddhism was first coming to the West and his *Life Story* which was translated in the 1990's. Given his importance to the Kagyu, I took a personal interest in him and read his *Collected Works* in Tibetan. Having done so, I saw it important to bring his works to the attention of Kagyu practitioners by publishing as many of his works as possible.

Gampopa spent the years after his wife and child's death staying with Kadampa teachers. He heard their teaching, studied it, and practised it to the point of being very adept in it. When he was twenty-eight, he went off with his friend Gongton to Uru Jang to be with the very famous Kadampa Geshe Nyug-rumpa. He and his friend stayed with the many geshes there and heard large amounts of the Kadampa teaching from those various geshes, but especially from Nyug-rumpa. Gampopa had good meditation experiences— or so he thought at the time—but something was nagging him and when he heard Milarepa's name, decided that he must go to meet him.

Gampopa travelled south in his thirty-first year and met Milarepa. Milarepa himself said that they had an excellent connection and accepted him as his student. Gampopa absorbed all of the teachings Milarepa had to offer. He not only learned them but practised them to the point of final realization and in doing so became the foremost of Milarepa's disciples and his main lineage holder. Not that this came easily. He underwent great hardships in his pursuit of meditation and realization. A good account of his time with Milarepa is found in the *Kagyu Ocean of Dohas* which has been translated into English and published under the title *Rain of Wisdom*[5]. I recommend reading the section in it on Gampopa, and even the whole book if possible—doing so will give you more feeling for Gampopa and the Kagyu dharma to which Gampopa is so important.

When it was time for Gampopa to leave Milarepa, Milarepa told him to establish a hermitage in Central Tibet in the Dvagpo region. Gampopa followed the command, went there, and established a monastery and hermitage called Dvags Lha Gampo. He had become very famous and many people came to study with him, both monastics and tantrikas, and his lineage of teachings spread far and wide.

Gampopa had many monk disciples who were great tantric practitioners but, and in accordance with the style of his forefather gurus, the Indians Tilopa and Naropa and the Tibetans Marpa and Milarepa, many of his greatest disciples were laymen who followed the yogin's way of life. A few of these are well-known nowadays as great beings of the Kagyu lineage, most notably Dusum Khyenpa who later was recognized as the first Karmapa and founder of the Karma Kagyu lineage and Phagmo Drupa whose students founded nearly all of the other Kagyu lineages. However, there were many more—at the time, it was considered that there were eighteen highly accomplished disciples, not to mention the many other worthy ones. A list of the eighteen disciples and their ranking according to people of Gampopa's time is contained on page 247, at the end of Yogin Choyung's interview.

---

[5] Translated and compiled by the Nalanda Translation Committee and published by Shambhala Publications, 1981.

Gampopa met with his disciples and spent time personally with the advanced ones, ensuring that they had answers to their questions. Fortunately, some of these interview sessions with their question and answers were recorded in writing and later included in the *Collected Works* of Gampopa. There are four interview texts in the *Collected Works*, one each for Lord Gomtshul, Dusum Khyenpa, and Phagmo Drupa who were three of the four disciples regarded as main lineage holders, and one for the Yogin Choyung who was regarded as one of two very special practitioners with high accomplishment.

Gampopa's *Collected Works* comes in two large volumes. It was originally published in Dvag Lha Gampo though that edition has been lost. Today there are three main editions: one made in Hemis Monastery, Ladhak, in the nineteenth century; a copy made from that published in February 1982, in India; and the Derge wood block edition. It is very hard to get the Ladakh edition, though it is said to be a good reproduction of the original. The copy made of it and published in India was a xylographic copy typical of the copies of Tibetan texts made in the desperate times after the desecration of Tibet by the Communist Chinese in 1959; I can say from personal experience that it has many mistakes in it. The Derge edition is regarded as the best one available but it is exceptionally hard to get. The translations for this book were made from the Derge edition which I was able to borrow[6].

One of the reasons for translating these particular parts of Gampopa's *Collected Works* is that they are very personal in nature. You get a real feeling of Gampopa and his disciples and how he worked with them. More than that though, there is much story-telling included which gives new information about Gampopa and his chief disciples who were such important figures in the transmission of Kagyu

---

[6] Padma Karpo Translation Committee has made a fully searchable digital edition of the entire Derge Edition of the *Collected Works*. See the chapter Supports for Study for more information.

dharma, especially the first Karmapa and Phagmo Drupa. As you read the interviews, you will hear Gampopa telling the story of how own dharma journey in his own words, emphasising the things that are were important to him on his journey. We also hear about the first Karmapa in stories that are not found elsewhere. And we get a sense of the massiveness of Phagmo Drupa, a rock-like man of massive body, learning, and meditative realization.

3. About the Teaching, Mahamudra

The Combined Kadampa and Mahamudra System

As mentioned above, Gampopa spent his early life up to the time of his late twenties studying and practising with the Kadampa school. This school had only recently developed from the teachings of Jowo Je Atisha [982–1054] and its followers were flourishing in Central Tibet. Gampopa joined them, and became both expert and accomplished in the Kadampa system of teaching and practice. After that, he went to study with Milarepa and eventually became the lineage holder of the Kagyu lineage. Later, when Gampopa started to teach, he did not discard the Kadampa system but combined those teachings with those of the Kagyu system. From Gampopa's time onwards, the Kagyu teaching included the influence of the Kadampa teaching. This combination became known as The Combined Kadampa and Mahamudra system of teaching.

The interviews in this book were opportunities for Gampopa to teach Mahamudra to his disciples. However, you will see how he frequently mixed the Kadampa and Kagyu Mahamudra teachings together to make his points about the dharma path in general and about Mahamudra in particular. For example, he frequently uses the Kadampa teachings to compare the sutra approach to that of Secret Mantra; this is particular evident for instance throughout part six of Dusum Khyenpa's interviews. Gampopa also gives Secret Mantra instruction which has been obtained from his Kadampa geshes, though this is less frequent, with most advice at this level coming through Milarepa and the Kagyu lineage gurus before that. Gampopa also gives general and really excellent advice on the dharma path that comes from the Kadampas, for example, this little gem found in Dusum Khyenpa's interviews:

> Potowa said, 'If you want to know dharma, meditate!'
> Drepa said, 'If, compared to listening for three years, all of you were to meditate for one year, you would have a very great samadhi; it is so true that it can't be discussed even! Individually-discriminating prajna even greater again would happen.' Having heard that, the geshes went to places like the mountains and got on with meaningful accomplishment.'

Essence Mahamudra

The Kagyu tradition has two main teachings on the practice of Mahamudra. One is a gradual approach called the Four Yogas of Mahamudra, the other is a sudden approach called Essence Mahamudra. The interview texts are notes of the instructions given in interviews or private teaching sessions where the instructions are mainly concerned with Essence Mahamudra, though there are a few explanations of the Four Yogas approach, the most extensive being on page 208.

The Tibetan name for Essence Mahamudra is "ngo bo phyag chen". The last part "phyag chen" is the Tibetan for Mahamudra. The first part "ngo bo" imeans "entity"—what something actually is. Thus the term "Essence Mahamudra", although it has become popular in the West, is incorrect. The name in fact is "Entity Mahamudra" meaning "Mahamudra itself, what it actually is".

The name Essence Mahamudra is given in contrast to the Four Yogas of Mahamudra. The Four Yogas of Mahamudra, because they are a graduated path, do not simply and directly point at Mahamudra itself. Instead, they successively teach one-pointedness, freedom from elaboration, one-taste, then non-meditation; at the very end of non-meditation one finally arrives at the very entity of Mahamudra. Essence, or we should say Entity Mahamudra, by-passes all complexity and indirectness contained in any graded approach and teaches the entity of Mahamudra, that is, what Maha-mudra actually is. Thus, this is not Essence Mahamudra but Entity Mahamudra—Mahamudra exactly as it is, what it is, without any frills sidetracks or provisional approaches to it.

You will see in the interviews that "the entity" is referred to time and again. This is the language of Entity Mahamudra; it is short-hand for saying "Mahamudra itself, what it actually is".

The key point about Entity Mahamudra is that it aims only at the ultimate, all the time, twenty-four hours a day. Thus, that is the great theme that runs throughout all of the interviews and teaching sessions. You will see this key point made over and over again by Gampopa in the interviews—again and again his disciples veer into duality in their approach to dharma and again and again Gampopa leads them out of that, back into non-duality.

Despite the fact that Entity Mahamudra is correct, I feel that it would be too radical to change the reference at this point, so the book continues from here to use "Essence Mahamudra", though note that "entity" alone is used frequently in the interviews with the meaning given above and this has not been changed.

Essence Mahamudra and Great Completion

The Kagyu lineage holds the teachings of Mahamudra. It does not hold the teachings of Mahasandhi, known in Tibetan as Dzogpa Chenpo and in English as Great Completion[7]. The teaching of

---

[7] The original name "mahāsandhi" is an Indian word meaning Great Completion, not Great Perfection as is commonly translated. A full

(continued...)

Mahamudra held by the Kagyu lineage is a complete teaching with enormous blessings attached—Gampopa give one explanation of the blessings of the lineage on page 157. According to the early masters of the lineage, this teaching of Mahamudra has everything it needs to stand on its own feet and does not need to be augmented by another system of teaching.

Gampopa not only had a Mahamudra lineage full of blessings but, as he points out to his disciples a number of times in the interviews, the lineage was very short which meant that the blessings were very strong—he says to Lord Gomtshul "There are only four in line between us and buddha!" Moreover, all four holders of the lineage were great siddhas (ones who had attainment) who had provided a complete set of instructions of the lineage which, when applied, worked. Gampopa had all of those instructions and took them to the limit in years of hard practice.

In short, in the Mahamudra teaching of his lineage, Gampopa had a complete, functional, and potent means for the final attainment of enlightenment. Thus, he focusses on that and barely mentions to his disciples the other profound system for gaining the final attainment, Great Completion. As he said to Lord Gomtshul,

> As for a blessing, this is so obvious there's no need to
> talk about it. All the Kagyu gurus and dakinis are right
> behind you in your practice of meditation. You are
> blessed! You will not have obstacles, you will have
> meaningful accomplishment!

In accordance with that, given that this book is meant to convey the Kagyu transmission, there is no real need to discuss Great Completion. Still, since at the time of writing the teaching of Great

---

[7](...continued)
treatment of this issue can be found in most of PKTC's books on Great Completion.

Completion has come to the fore in the Tibetan Buddhist world, some readers will be wondering whether there is any relationship between Mahamudra and Great Completion, so I will say just a little about it.

As mentioned above, there are two types of Mahamudra teaching in the Kagyu lineage. Of them, the Four Yogas of Mahamudra teaching is slightly lower than the Great Completion teaching because it is a graded approach which includes much non-ultimate teaching, whereas the Great Completion teaching consists only of ultimate teaching. On the other hand, the Essence Mahamudra teaching is ultimate from beginning to end so is on the same level as Great Completion.

The Great Completion teaching has several levels. The most profound, called "innermost unsurpassed Great Completion", has two main practices: Thorough Cut and Direct Crossing. Essence Mahamudra purely taught is basically the same as Thorough Cut. (I say "purely taught" because, as you will see in the interviews, Gampopa sometimes teaches Essence Mahamudra in conjunction with the Four Yogas approach. When taught that way, Essence Mahamudra is basically the same as, though not equivalent to, Thorough Cut because the mixture makes it slightly less than ultimate.)

Thorough Cut Great Completion and Essence Mahamudra are not only basically the same but are very closely related. One way to know this is through the style and terminology used to give the teaching—both are taught in a very similar way and use much of the same, unique terminology. Someone familiar with Thorough Cut will immediately recognize many of the special words used in Gampopa's explanations of Essence Mahamudra and will find it easy to understand the teaching, and vice versa.

Historically, those who have purely followed the Kagyu with its Mahamudra lineage of teaching have not denigrated the Great

Completion system, but they have tended to pass it off as something of no value to themselves. For them, their Mahamudra
teaching was, as you will see Gampopa continually refer to it, "the
single solution" and "the universal panacea" to the whole samsaric
problem. The teaching and practice of Great Completion was
simply un-necessary in their eyes. This attitude is clearly seen in a
reply given by Gampopa to Dusum Khyenpa:

> On one occasion many of the best type came before
> guru Mila, at which time I asked, "What is this Great
> Completion about?" He replied, "I heard guru Marpa
> say, 'There is talk that it is not dharma but that is not
> so. It is a dharma that goes from the sixth and seventh
> bodhisatva levels on up'. It would be something like
> pointing to a child of about five years and saying that
> Great Completion practitioners are like this, then this
> child saying, 'I have the abilities of a twenty-five year
> old.' Great Completion practitioners are said to speak
> of becoming buddha now, but that talk of theirs has no
> meaning."

In the centuries following Gampopa, the Great Completion teaching started to enter the Kagyu lineages and people who previously
would have been pure Kagyu followers practising only their own
Mahamudra teaching became what are now called Kagyu-Nyingma
followers practising both systems. These people then made the
positive statement that is commonly found amongst Kagyu followers these days about how the two practices complement each other
which says that Mahamudra and Great Completion are like the two
eyes of a person. It is further explained that Mahamudra and Great
Completion work together as a pair, fully complementing each
other, with Mahamudra placing more emphasis on the vividness of
appearance and Great Completion placing more emphasis on the
luminosity causing the appearance. Nowadays, this positive acceptance of how the two practices can be done by one person in a
complementary way is widespread, with many Kagyu practitioners
being Kagyu-Nyingma.

The beauty of the teachings in the interviews with Gampopa is that they show clearly the original approach of the Kagyu lineage, which is that Mahamudra is a single sufficient solution and that Great Completion, while not to be denigrated, is something that is simply un-necessary.

4. About the Texts

Two Prefatory Texts

Gampopa's interviews with four of his disciples form the body of the book. However, I have added two more texts from Gampopa's *Collected Works*.

The Four Dharmas in Brief is the root of Gampopa's most famous teaching called the Four Dharmas of Gampopa. This teaching, as Gampopa's seminal teaching, makes an ideal prologue to his teachings in the interview texts. Moreover, *The Four Dharmas in Brief* should be of particular interest because it shows Gampopa's own understanding of the Four Dharmas teaching, which is sometimes different from what is taught these days.

Note that the eighth section of Dusum Khyenpa's interviews contains a further explanation of the Four Dharmas which should be read because it gives a slightly different explanation of the Four Dharmas than *The Four Dharmas in Brief*.

This text brings us to a very interesting point with the Four Dharmas of Gampopa. The usual translation of the third Dharma of Gampopa in Western publications until now has been "the path dispels confusion". However, all of the many Kagyu teachers whom I have attended have pointedly told me that this is incorrect. All of them have explained that it should be "the path's confusion is dispelled". The first meaning, that the path dispels confusion, seems straightforward to most Westerners—they assume that it means that the path of dharma, when utilized, removes the confusion of samsara. The meaning of "the path's confusion is dispelled" is less obvious but a key part of the teaching of the higher tantras. It is said in these tantras in the context of teaching the ground condition of beings that a being who loses connection to the ground condition of full knowledge and thereby enters the deluded condition of samsara is a being "who has fallen onto the path". This phrase means that the being has fallen into a position where there is no choice but to make a journey back to his original condition of full knowledge. The path's confusion is then the confusion condition of the being who has to make a journey to get back of the path. These ideas of path and path's confusion in relation to the pristine ground of being is a major point of understanding in the tantras.

I had hoped that looking at *The Four Dharmas in Brief* and the interviews would reveal proof of this point. Unfortunately, the wording in *The Four Dharmas in Brief* shows both the possibilities of "path dispels confusion" and "path's confusion is dispelled". Nevertheless, Gampopa's explanation of the Four Dharmas in the interviews clearly shows it as "the path's confusion is dispelled". Rather than impose one view or another on these records of Gampopa's explanations, I have simply translated them as they stand in the Tibetan.

It is a major point both of translation and also of understanding the ground as it is taught in the tantras, so I must say that I have investigated this very carefully with many very well educated Kagyu masters. In fact, while translating for some of them, they have made a point of explaining the matter to the audience and we have had extensive discussions about it in private. Thus, there is no doubt in my mind that the accepted lineage explanation is that "the path's confusion is dispelled".

Well then, what is the confusion dispelled by? By the correct practice of the path of Buddha's dharma of course, which is a point so obvious that it does not need to be said. The point here is not that the practice of Buddha's dharma does what it by definition does, but that a being has fallen from enlightenment and now that condition forces him to take a journey—which the tantras have called 'being on the path'—in order to dispel the confusion involved and return to his original, enlightened condition. That is the accepted meaning of the third Dharma of Gampopa.

Precious Garland of the Supreme Path records a talk in which Gampopa clearly explains his own, very special teaching of Essence Mahamudra, which he sums up in the phrase "the entity of discursive thought is the dharmakaya". Together with this, he taught that his followers should take the particular approach to discursive thought of not rejecting it but treasuring it as a great friend and something of great value. This "the entity of discursive thought is the dharmakaya" together with the need "to treasure and to welcome all discursive thought" is a very famous teaching. For example, it appears in the *Short Great Vajradhara Prayer* which many Kagyu followers recite every day, in the last verse which starts: "The entity of discursive thought is dharmakaya, as is taught".

This teaching brought criticism from others who misunderstood it, thinking that Gampopa was saying that dualistic discursive thought is the dharmakaya. His teaching is much more subtle than that and, when you read the criticisms made against him, you get the impression that his detractors were simply not thinking or that they did not know the profound aspect of the Mahamudra teachings, which is very possible in some cases. The most famous criticisms were made by Sakya Pandita and the arguments that resulted from his many mis-informed criticisms of the Kagyu lineage and its teachings are a well-known part of Tibetan history. Later, Padma Karpo of the Drukpa Kagyu wrote a number of texts in which he very cleverly showed how mistaken Sakya Pandita was and very strongly put him back in place[8].

---

[8] You can read two different criticisms and their refutations in *The*

(continued...)

Precious Garland of the Supreme Path is a very important part of this book because it focusses only on this, Gampopa's hallmark approach to Essence Mahamudra, and lays it out in detail. Appropriately, it has been placed after the sutra teaching of the Four Dharmas and ahead of all the interviews with their teachings on Essence Mahamudra.

The Interview Texts

The interview texts are, generally speaking, records of interviews made either by the disciple who was having the interview or someone else who was present at the time. In many cases the records are notes written as reminders of the important points of teaching received.

I would like to emphasize the point that, for Kagyu practitioners, these teachings contain a wealth of information on the actual practice of Essence Mahamudra as it was transmitted in the very early days of the Kagyu. Although interviews are a class of text that is commonly found in the collected works of great teachers, I have not seen anything like these particular interviews anywhere else in Kagyu literature, so I will yet again emphasize their extraordinary value for practitioners.

Repetition Within the Interview Texts

After reading the interview texts, I realized that there were sections of one of Lord Gomtshul's interviews that were repeated in one of Phagmo Drupa's interviews and likewise sections of one of Dusum Khyenpa's interviews that were repeated in Yogin Choyung's interview. I uncovered all of these repetitions then identified them

---

[8](...continued)
Bodyless Dakini Dharma: The Dakini Hearing Lineage of the Kagyus by Tony Duff, published by Padma Karpo Translation Committee, second edition, 2010, ISBN 978-9937-8244-8-4, and in *Drukchen Padma Karpo's Collected Works on Mahamudra* cited earlier.

in the translation by enclosing them within unobtrusive marks like this: » text « then cross-referenced them for convenience.

Phagmo Drupa writes at the beginning of his seventh interview that the interview is actually an interview of Yogin Choyung. However, much of the interview is also included in one of Lord Gomtshul's interviews. My conclusion after becoming very familiar with all of the interview texts is that all three disciples—and possibly others too—were there on that occasion, asking questions.

Yogin Choyung's interview is, except for the colophon and one short phrase, made up of pieces which are either the same as or very similar to pieces of one of Dusum Khyenpa's interviews. In this case I believe that both disciples were present in the same interview and that Dusum Khyenpa included the questions and answers of Yogin Choyung in his own notes but without marking them off as such.

5. Interview Text: Lord Dvagpo's Personal Advice and Lord Gomtshul's Interviews

This text is in five parts. The first part consists of notes written down by Lord Gomtshul following a number of interviews with Gampopa; it is not a record of one interview but notes from several interviews written together.

The second, third, and fourth parts are very short. The second is Gampopa's reply to a question, not recorded, of Lord Gomtshul. The colophon tells us: "This question and answer between Lord Gampopa and Lord Gomtshul was written down by Langben Dharma Kumāra at the mountain hermitage". The mountain hermitage referred to is Gampopa's retreat place at Dvag Lha Gampo. The third is a reply given by Lord Gomtshul to a question posed by his eldest son, Dampa Baggom. The fourth is advice heard from Tsultrim Nyingpo by, we assume, Lord Gomtshul. (Tsultrim Nyingpo was a contemporary of Gampopa. His eldest son was Lama Zhang, who went on to found one of the eight Lesser Schools of the Kagyu.)

The fifth part is of medium length. It appears not to be an interview but personal advice given by Gampopa to a group of his disciples, including Lord Gomtshul who then wrote it down. The presence of this section explains the first part of the title of the text "the personal advice of Lord Dvagpo".

One of the interesting things about these interviews as a whole is that there are several places where the yogin disciples ask for advice about how to proceed with their lives. Should they stay in the mountains? Should they work a little? What should they do about having an income, if anything? These interactions are reminiscent of the questions I have often heard Westerners asking in dharma assemblies. The answers are very interesting, with Gampopa telling us of Marpa and Milarepa's advice on these matters.

6. Interview Text: Dusum Khyenpa's Interviews

This is a very long text in fifteen parts, with many of the parts containing several interviews or teaching sessions. It is a treasure trove of instructions, histories, personal stories of realization, and more.

The first four parts of the text are arranged in chronological order and hold together as a section in their own right. This section contains significant portions of teaching on Essence Mahamudra but is equally interesting for all the historical information provided in the form of stories personally told. We hear both Gampopa and Dusum Khyenpa tell about their dharma journeys in their own words. This biographical material is unique material not found elsewhere; there are official biographies of Dusum Khyenpa and Gampopa, but they do not have the quality of these first hand accounts given in personal interaction.

The first of these four parts details the time when Dusum Khyenpa came to Gampopa and gives insights into Dusum Khyenpa's

personal journey. It sets the ground for the rest of the teaching in the text by dealing with the more important aspects of Gampopa's teaching of Mahamudra. The second part chronicles a period after that when Dusum Khyenpa has done some practice after receiving the instructions to begin with; it is a long interview packed with instruction on the practice of Essence Mahamudra. The third part

Figure 3. Dusum Khyenpa

records an interview in which Gampopa tells the story of his own journey. Gampopa tells the story at length in his own words, including his time with the Kadampa geshes and then his times with Milarepa. The culmination of it is a long statement given by Gampopa of his final realization—what it was and how he experienced it. It fills me with devotion, every time I read it. The blessings in this third part are particularly strong. The fourth part was written by Dusum Khyenpa after the death of Gampopa; it gives another account of Gampopa's life-story in Gampopa's own words as a way of remembering and honouring the guru. This biography is a little shorter than the one in the third part but is not repetitive and gives another account of his attainment of ultimate realization. This account is more technical in nature than the one in the third part but very interesting in terms of the instruction revealed.

The remaining eleven parts hold together as a second section of the text. This section is teaching only, without personal stories and histories. This section begins with the fifth part, a very short piece by Dusum Khyenpa in which he shows the essential teachings of the Kagyu lineage in verse by quoting the teaching of the lineage gurus starting with Vajradhara and going down to his personal guru, Gampopa. It acts as a preface to the remaining ten parts all of which are notes of interviews or private teaching sessions. Most of these remaining parts contain not one but several interviews or teaching sessions. Altogether, this section of the text is very long and filled with teachings on Essence Mahamudra. Kagyu practitioners will find it to be a cornucopia of profound teaching! Note that the seventh part has several sections, some of which are difficult to understand because they are written as very terse notes on technical points.

7. Interview Text: Phagmo Drupa's Interviews

This also is a long text, though not nearly as long as Dusum Khyenpa's interviews. Arranged in chronological order, it tells the story of Phagmo Drupa and his development under the care of Gampopa in nine records of interviews. The text is short enough that I was able to write a little about each of the nine interviews here in the introduction in order to help the reader get a better feel for them.

Interview 1: the beginning

Phagmo Drupa, affectionately known as Phagdru in the Tibetan tradition, arrives before Gampopa, probably for the first time. Phagdru has come far from Kham (East Tibet) where he is already renowned as an accomplished master. He is already called guru by his disciples and given several other titles of a great practitioner, too.

He asks a variety of straightforward questions for the purpose of finding out what Gampopa knows and how he teaches his students. At the end of these questions, Gampopa chides him, first by calling him "The Swami from East Tibet", a very high title, and then by telling him that his questions are not very good, which implies that he is not really such a great practitioner after all. Gampopa follows that up immediately with a comment to the effect that perhaps he

 does have a bit more realization than that and probably has quite a bit of merit already accumulated, too. In other words, he is saying, "Well, you probably are a smart person who is not just wasting time here; you are at least being humble in the way you ask your questions". Implied in this also is that Phagdru is, in fact, asking intelligent questions.

Figure 4. Phagmo Drupa

All in all, this clearly shows how a prospective student approaches a prospective teacher in the Tibetan system. You politely ask questions to find out what the teacher knows, how he relates to you, and how he teaches. At the same time, he will be examining you as a prospective student.

In this interview, Gampopa provides some very clear and useful definitions of the path—for example, he makes a clear distinction between what is Mahamudra and what is co-emergence. He also very clearly sets out how he chooses to lead his disciples: he would prefer to teach them Fierce Heat[9] first if possible, so that they are well prepared for Mahamudra practice, but, if that is not possible, they could immediately go to Mahamudra practice, though there is some danger to doing so. His lineage coming from Milarepa, with the great emphasis on Fierce Heat, is very obvious.

---

[9] For Fierce Heat, see the glossary.

Interview 2: Phagmo Drupa asks for the introduction to reality

Phagdru has obviously gone away and thought about what Gampopa has said, and probably has had more meetings with him in the
meantime. At some point he has decided to accept Gampopa as a
vajra master and has now come back, asking for the key thing needed to enter the vajra path, the introduction to the dharmata[10], more
commonly called the introduction to the nature of one's own mind.

In reply, Gampopa instructs him, with a very nice teaching of the
path of Mahamudra. First, he gives him a very pithy introduction
to the nature of mind. Of course, you cannot get this from reading
the words on the page. Those who have been with their own guru
and had this introduction will remember the kind of atmosphere
that must have been present. It must have been very strong, too, I
think—Gampopa was a very highly accomplished master.

Following the introduction, Gampopa gives Phagdru a very pithy
instruction on what to do next—basically to dump all cares of life
and go off into the mountains into retreat. Phagmo Drupa later
followed this advice and went to the nearby mountains where he
practised Mahamudra according to the five-part approach taught to
him in this interview with the words:

> You go to congenial places—mountainous areas, and so
> on—where disenchantment can be produced and
> experience can develop. There, you arouse the mind[11]
> thinking, 'For the sake of sentient beings, I will attain
> buddhahood.' You meditate on your body as the deity.
> You meditate on the guru over your crown. Not letting
> any thought spoil your mind, not altering mind in any
> way because it is nothing whatsoever, put yourself in a

---

[10] For dharmata, see the glossary.

[11] For arousing the mind, see the glossary.

cleared-out purity, vividly present, cleaned-out, wide-awake state!

Phagmo Drupa gained great realization through this approach. After that, his fame spread and he attracted many disciples. This particular five-part approach was the source of his realization so that is how he taught his disciples in general. The approach then spread through the Kagyu schools where it became known as "The Five-Part Mahamudra"[12].

Next, Gampopa gives Phagdru a particularly clear exposition of the Four Yogas of Mahamudra, as Gampopa understands them through personal practice of them. You will find it interesting to read this and Gampopa's other presentations found here—for example in the very next interview—of the Four Yogas of Mahamudra and compare them with the extensive explanations of the same given by Padma Karpo[13], one of the greatest authors of the Kagyu School in general.

Interview 3: Phagmo Drupa asks for follow-up dharma

The next interview sees Phagdru asking for some follow-up instruction. It seems that he has already been given quite a bit of instruction on the path of method, including Fierce Heat, and probably also on the first yoga of Mahamudra.

Gampopa begins by saying, "Well look, it seems as though you do have some experience now at least of threefold bliss, luminosity, and emptiness that is such an important feature of the first yoga. On top of that, you are in an excellent position, having had introduction from myself and having all the things on your side that you

---

[12] For a complete exposition of the Five-Part Mahamudra, see *Gampopa's Mahamudra, The Five-Part Mahamudra of the Kagyus* cited earlier.

[13] ... in *Drukchen Padma Karpo's Collected Works on Mahamudra* mentioned earlier ...

have going for you. But look out! Your mind is probably not strong enough yet that you can go wandering into town, as a lot of yogi-types would, drinking liquor and womanizing, and trying to incorporate that into your practice. Instead, and until you have advanced far enough that you can actually take these things onto the path, you should be practising!

It seems that Phagdru has been doing these things because Gampopa then pointedly asks him just what are the certainties—meaning the things that you come to a final certainty about through attainment of the practice—of each of the four yogas of Mahamudra? The implication is that Phagdru has gone beyond himself and could not actually answer these. You can almost hear Gampopa saying, "Just what have you actually realized of this path that allows you to run around playing at yogi practices? Hmm?!"

There's no answer from Phagdru, and Gampopa goes on by smiling at him and pointing out that there is someone here—Gampopa himself—who actually does know the answers through direct experience. Gampopa is talking about himself, which could be odd but he couches his claims in interesting language. He refers to himself as "the spiritual friend" which is a very low way of talking about someone who has very high Vajra Vehicle realization. And he continues on immediately to say how what he does know is just nothing compared to the realizations of the certainties involved in the Four Yogas that his guru, Milarepa, had. He then points out that lots of people are coming to see him but that no-one seems to get the main point, which is the direct practice of Mahamudra that follows on from the introduction to the nature of mind. He points out that nearly everyone who comes to see him in his hermitage comes with extensive knowledge of dharma that they then discuss with him or comes asking only for the method path—the instructions of all the things like Fierce Heat, Bardo, and so on—which is not the main point. He says that even when he openly gives them an explanation of the meaning of Mahamudra and gives them the introduction to it, most of them still don't get it.

So he says to Phagdru, "Look here, this spiritual friend who actually knows these things through direct experience makes it really simple for everyone: he tells each person it's like this, then tells them to go and practise it, and then has nothing more to say."

Gampopa follows those words with a very unusual description of the path to follow after receiving the introduction to the nature of mind. It is a description of the Four Yogas of Mahamudra but one that comes directly out of his own experience and does not follow the usual wording of the tradition. One senses that the successive realizations that he lays out as the certainties of this path were being manifested in the atmosphere of the room for Phagdru's sake and, that way, he was yet again giving Phagdru the introduction. Having given it, it would be Phagdru's job not to have any further discussion but to get on with practising it. As Gampopa has just said, "I tell them it is like this, and then I say, now go and make it one with your mind—that's how I bestow the introduction and instruction."

Again, the reader would find it interesting to compare this explanation of the Four Yogas of Mahamudra with the explanations given by Padma Karpo in his works on Mahamudra mentioned above.

Interview 4: Gampopa teaches how the innate is brought into manifestation

Now that Gampopa has provided the necessary introduction to the nature of mind—which is what is required before embarking on the practice of Mahamudra—this next interview sees Gampopa giving the instructions of the path to be followed when practising Mahamudra. Note how his teaching, which is Essence Mahamudra, corresponds to the Four Yogas of Mahamudra, which is the other main teaching on Mahamudra found in the Kagyu lineage. He starts with shamatha, then moves to rigpa, then moves to unifying appearance and emptiness, and ends with Mahamudra as such. These four steps correspond to the yogas of One-Pointedness, Freedom from Elaboration, One Taste, and Non-Meditation respectively.

Note also how Gampopa's explanation of shamatha is different from that given in the sutras. In the sutras, shamatha is explained through the nine steps of developing equipoise and the practice always has an outwardly-directed consciousness. In one-pointedness as taught in Mahamudra, the emphasis is on an internally-directed consciousness, with the practitioner using mind as the basis for the development of one-pointedness. You might say, "But using the mind as the basis for the development of one-pointedness is also in the sutras" and this would be correct. There is a difference though in how the shamatha is developed using the mind as the basis for the one-pointedness and this can be seen in the particular way that Gampopa speaks of it. In this practice, the shamatha is developed in such a way that it naturally becomes the vipashyana of the second yoga (which, in this teaching of Gampopa, arrives in the form of a discussion of rigpa).

Interview 5: Gampopa teaches mindness

Next, Gampopa focusses on the core issue of the practice of Essence Mahamudra, called mindness. Mindness is a path term for the innate nature of mind, wisdom; it is the key point of the practice. In this interview, he explains clearly the difference between mindness and consciousness, the first of which corresponds to the enlightened type of knowing of nirvana and the second of which corresponds to the deluded type of knowing of samsara. Much could be said about mindness and mind but these instructions are only given in private so no more will be said here.

Note the pithiness of this instruction; Gampopa is giving instructions for practice, not for theoretical understanding.

Interview 6: Questions whose answers reveal that meditation on the entity is the one antidote for all

We can tell from the content of this interview that Phagmo Drupa has gone off and practised the instructions given to him, and is now asking questions that come out of his practice. The answers come in the form of foremost instructions[14] which highlight some of the key points[15] of the practice of Essence Mahamudra. You will see that Phagdru raises one important issue after another and that Gampopa answers with the appropriate foremost instruction for each issue.

Many of Phagdru's questions come from a dualistic understanding of dharma. Gampopa's foremost instructions always lead Phagdru back to the ultimate, non-dual understanding.

This interview is much longer than the previous ones. It contains a wealth of instruction that makes the fine distinctions needed for proper progress on this path. It also contains a relentless insistence on drawing Phagdru back to the ultimate, non-dual understanding.

Interview 7: Yogin Choyung has an interview included here that makes important points about livelihood and what is needed for practice

This interview provides proof that some of the interviews presented in this book have more than one of Gampopa's foremost disciples present. This interview had Yogin Choyung present as well and his questions to Gampopa and answers received are included. This section is repeated in the records of Lord Gomtshul's interviews, so he was probably present as well. This is not a repeat of the material found in the text of Yogin Choyung's interview, so this interview gives us a second interview of Yogin Choyung with Gampopa.

In this interview, initially we get a personal sense of Yogin Choyung and his concerns about which direction to take in his life. After that, as with the previous interview with Phagdru, Yogin Choyung presents a dualistic form of understanding in a series of

---

[14] For foremost instructions, see the glossary.

[15] For key points, see the glossary.

questions which Gampopa answers by relentlessly drawing him back to the ultimate, non-dual view.

Interview 8: Phagmo Drupa tries to find out why he is not understanding and gets further instruction on Mahamudra

In this interview, Phagdru gets down to business. He clearly states his problem and Gampopa nails down his mistakes. Gampopa uses very polite language; that might not be so obvious in the translation though I have done my best to bring it out. Nonetheless, he is very cutting in his replies to Phagdru, telling him that he is stuck in a dualistic framework of mind that has come from listening to the dualistic instructions of other teachers rather than listening to the foremost instructions of his own guru, who is seated right in front of him. Gampopa's comments are tantamount to this: "Phagdru! Forget all of this other, concept-based dharma that you have heard from so many other sources! Listen instead and practice according to the foremost instructions of a non-dual yogin, the one who happens to be sitting right in front of you!"

In this last paragraph, Gampopa very cleverly turns Phagdru's own words that he seems to have said to someone else and which Gampopa has heard of, back on Phagdru. Gampopa is saying to him, "Look, you yourself have said that you have tasted mindness and have a guru who can lead you to the ultimate realization of it. You yourself have said that you do not need to return to East Tibet and stay with your former teachers there! So take heed of your words!"

Interview 9: An overview of the entire path

In this interview, Gampopa gives Phagdru another summary of the entire path of Essence Mahamudra. The overview in the third interview had the quality of basic instructions on the path given to someone who was about to start the practice, whereas this interview has the quality of a reminder of the whole path given to someone who knows the theory and who has been practising for a long time.

It presents all of the most important key points, going from the beginning to the end of practice.

This is the end of the text containing Phagmo Drupa's interviews with Gampopa. Although there must have been many more interviews, this text functions as a complete teaching that shows, from beginning to end, how a disciple will come to a master of Essence Mahamudra and be trained in it. As explained earlier, Phagmo Drupa later went to practise in the mountains and gained great realization. He was particularly effective after that, with his disciples going on to attain their own realization and then establish most of the Kagyu sub-schools that appeared after Gampopa.

8. Interview Text: Yogin Choyung's Interview

Yogin Choyung was one of the highly accomplished yogin disciples of Gampopa. The text contains a single interview and the wording of the colophon clearly indicates that it is a record of one and not several interviews. A second interview for Yogin Choyung is found in interview seven of the interviews with Phagmo Drupa. Again, the teaching concerns Essence Mahamudra.

9. Other Points

Terminology

The interview texts contain the special terminology of the Vajra Vehicle in general and the unique terminology of Essence Mahamudra in particular. In order to clarify this unique terminology, I have provided ample notes and a glossary.

Consistency of Terminology

An important point to understand when reading these texts is that their style of composition is not like that of English. In English, it is good form not to use the same word repeatedly but to change to similar words in order to give a greater feeling for the meaning and more elegant style of composition. However, in Buddhist literature, it is the opposite. Each concept has a technical term for its expression and each term is used consistently when that meaning has to be expressed. One of the features of our translations is that this very important aspect of the language is kept intact. As a matter of interest, the English equivalents of the vocabulary and use of language are maintained across all of our translations of these texts, making them very fruitful to read.

Technical points

There are many technical points raised in these texts that will leave some readers unsure of the meaning. Many footnotes have been provided to assist with understanding the terminology, but no attempt has been made to explain all of the technical details.

There are two issues here. Firstly, many of the technical points raised in the texts require extensive explanation of subjects that are secret—for example, the details of wind, channels, and drops practice—and it would not be appropriate to try to explain them. Secondly, texts like these are intended to be a basis for oral instruction, not complete, do-it-yourself manuals.

Traditionally, when it comes time to teach these subjects to a disciple, the guru will use texts like these as a basis for providing the profound oral instructions needed to understand and do the practice. Therefore, while I have provided copious notes and an ample glossary, I have not attempted to explain every last detail of these teachings.

Notes in the Texts

Some of the texts have notes within them, similar to the way that footnotes are provided in English texts. These notes are rendered simply with parentheses, right in the text. Square brackets are used to indicate the few additions I have made to the texts for clarification.

Sanskrit and diacriticals

Sanskrit terms are properly rendered into English using diacritical marks. However, we felt them to be a distraction in a book like this which is primarily concerned with practice so have not used them except when they are used in one of the original texts.

Further Study

Generally speaking, Padma Karpo Translation Committee has amassed a range of materials to help those who are studying this and related topics. Please see the Supports for Study chapter at the end of the book for the details.

What is required to read these texts

The teachings of Mahamudra say that the subjects discussed in this book are secret and should not be shown to those who have not been properly prepared for it. It is popular in the West at this time to teach anything without observing these restrictions, the teachings themselves make the restrictions clear and, in the past, these restrictions were always observed. Therefore, for the sake of your own spiritual health, please obtain instruction in Mahamudra from a qualified teacher before reading this book.

Tony Duff,
Swayambunath,
Nepal,
September, 2011

Plate 1. A thangka of the Dharma Lord Gampopa with the early heads of the Drukpa Kagyu lineage. The Drukpa Kagyu appeared through the teachings of Phagmo Drupa.

Text 1

The Four Dharmas in Brief

The Four Dharmas in Brief

Namo Guru[16].

He said the following.

"It is necessary for: dharma to turn to dharma; dharma to turn into the path; the path to dispel confusion; and confusion to turn into wisdom.

"Now to say more about that. For dharma to turn to dharma: through meditating a great deal on impermanence, both outer and inner, you come to understand that you will have to leave all personal items, utensils, relatives, and everything else you are connected with behind and go alone to your death. And you understand that, when that has happened, anything that is not dharma is of no use. If you do not give rise to the mind that there is nothing else to do except for dharma, then dharma turning to dharma will not happen. Your death, furthermore, has no specified timing. You have not the

---

[16] Tibetans kept some Sanskrit in their writings as a way of keeping the blessings of the original language of dharma in their writings. In conjunction with this, it was very common in earlier writings to have the requisite homage at the beginning of a text written in Sanskrit. You will see this throughout the texts in this book. "Namo guru" means "I prostration to you, O Guru!"

slightest control over whether it will happen tomorrow and so have no control over whether it will happen next month. Having thought about that, the next point is that, when you have died, your self-knowing wisdom is accompanied only by karma, virtuous and evil[17]. It is impossible to connect with karma that you have not made and it is not possible that what you have made will be of no account. If, due to non-virtuous karma, you are born in the three types of bad migration, the degree of unsatisfactoriness which you will experience there will be worse than that of gods and men. For men, there is the unsatisfactoriness of birth, old-age, sickness, death, not getting what you seek, protecting what you do have, meeting with hostile enemies, and separating from friends and close ones. And for gods, there is the unsatisfactoriness of death and transference, which is greater than that of Avichi and the other sixteen hells[18]. No matter where you are born within the six classes, there is only unsatisfactoriness. For as long as renunciation has not been taken to its full measure, dharma turns to dharma does not happen.

"For dharma turns into the path: if there is the rational mind of loving kindness and compassion that cherishes other more than oneself—the fictional enlightenment mind—and then on top of that the understanding that all phenomena, outer and inner, appearing as the coming together of interdependency are illusory, then the primal dharma turns into the path.[19]

---

[17] When you die, your person sinks back into its most fundamental aspect, self-knowing wisdom. The only part of your former self that continues on with that self-knowing wisdom is your karmic baggage. Everything else has dissolved and is gone forever.

[18] In fact, there are eighteen hells and one would expect this to say seventeen but the text clearly says sixteen. It is of no significance.

[19] For rational mind, fictional enlightenment mind, and enlightenment mind, see the glossary. He mentions rational mind first because the

(continued...)

"Having understood that, the path is to be used to dispel confusion. First, meditation on impermanence dispels the confusion of clinging to this life, then meditation on karma and effect dispels the confusion of bad views, then meditation on the disadvantages of cyclic existence dispels the confusion of attachment to cyclic existence, then meditation on loving kindness and compassion dispels the confusion of the Lesser Vehicle, then meditation on appearances being dream-like, illusory, dispels the confusion of grasping at conceived-of things[20]—overall, confusion has to be dispelled from top to bottom.[21]

"Then, confusion is to be made to dawn as wisdom. If, the force of meditation done on all phenomena being free from birth and cessation in superfact causes whatever appears, whatever is known, to be resolved as its own entity[22], then confusion has dawned as wisdom."

---

[19](...continued)
first step is to develop the dualistic, fictional level of enlightenment mind. After that, one develops the superfactual understanding of emptiness and interdependency which is the superfactual enlightenment mind (for which see the glossary). Primal dharma means dharma of the superfactual level.

[20] For conceived-of things, see the glossary.

[21] See the comments about this third one in the introduction on page xviii.

[22] The own entity or actual entity of any given phenomenon is wisdom, so if phenomena are seen that way, even confusion will, on the spot, dawn as wisdom.

Text 2

One Talk of the Dharma Lord, The Dvagpo Doctor, called "Precious Garland of the Supreme Path"

One Talk of the Dharma Lord,
The Dvagpo Doctor, called
"Precious Garland of the Supreme Path"

Homage to the gurus
Who are realized in the state of dharmata and
Who, by their actions of eliminating every point of deviation,
Do the deed of showing the authentic meaning.[23]

There are four conditions—causal, governing, referential, and immediate—and because of them an unqualified spiritual friend has confusion and attachment to hope and fear whereas a genuine spiritual friend has non-confusion, absence of hope and fear, capability in making supplications, capability to change adverse circumstances, and capability in relation to opening the door of understanding.[24]

---

[23] "Do the deed" is the formal phrase used in the Great Vehicle to indicate the works done by enlightened beings for the sake of others, the sentient beings. The gurus, with their realization, teach dharma that removes every point of possible deviation on the path and thus perform the enlightened work of showing the true meaning of reality to others.

[24] This first paragraph deals with the guru needed for the spiritual journey of Essence Mahamudra. The four conditions were taught by the Buddha in the Abhidharma; they are the conditions needed to produce consciousness of an external object. A spiritual friend who is
(continued...)

There are the characteristics of knowledge, difference, function, and essential nature[25]. The characteristic of knowledge is as follows. Through prajna you are to recognize the characteristic of mind[26]. The characteristic of mind is to be known as the four kayas[27] like this: rational mind that investigates the three kayas comes to see them as birthless dharmakaya, stoppage-less sambhogakaya, and abiding-less nirmanakaya[28]. That mind would like to express them in words, but their very essence is the svabhavikakaya which, divorced from identification[29], is beyond the objects of rational mind. The characteristic of difference is as follows. Any discursive thought that arises is mindness[30] so, through not reject-

---

[24](...continued)
not fully qualified to be a spiritual friend at this level will be subject to that dualistic process—he will live in dualistic consciousness rather than wisdom. A true spiritual friend for this path will not be subject to that process—he will not have samsaric confusion but will live in three characteristics and hence will be able to do whatever is required to take the student along this particular journey.

[25] This paragraph deals with four key aspects of the person who undertakes the journey of Essence Mahamudra.

[26] "Characteristic of mind" does not mean the characteristic of samsaric mind but the characteristics of the inner disposition of samsaric mind also called mindness and wisdom.

[27] For kaya and four kayas, see the glossary under kaya.

[28] These "three characteristics", as they are called, of the innate disposition of mind is one of the core teachings of Essence Mahamudra. Being stoppageless is the prime feature of the sambhogakaya aspect of mind—see stoppageless in the glossary.

[29] Identification is the specific way in which rational mind knows its concepts of objects. See under conceived-of thing in the glossary.

[30] For mindness, see the glossary.

ing it, it will be taken into the four kayas. The characteristic of function is as follows. Thought is the four kayas but, there being no agent causing its function, it turns to being part of the dharmata's[31] illusions. The characteristic of essential nature is that thought is primally spontaneously existent as the four kayas.

When you have understood in that way that all phenomena never depart from those four characteristics, you have the armour of the view, which is that, every one of them being known as an object of prajna, every one of them is constrained, like a bird that has had a rope tied to it.

The armour of prajna is that, with the legs crossed up in vajra posture, the hands in equipoise, the body straightened, and the eyes settled onto the tip of the nose, prajna looks at the characteristic of mind and, having done so, expresses it three times in words[32], which is the prajna of hearing. Based on those words, there is intellectual understanding of the meaning which is the prajna of contemplation. Knowing the fact[33] of thoughts is the prajna of meditation. When in that way you have, through prajna, gained full and direct personal experience of mind, you will be called "a realization-manifested buddha".

In terms of taking refuge, if you realize such meaning and fully take it in, then you have taken refuge in buddha. All phenomena are just

[31] For dharmata, see the glossary.

[32] It is expressed in words, as was done just above, as having a threefold character.

[33] "Fact" throughout this book can sometimes refer to a conceptual fact known to mind but, as is the case here, is mostly used to refer to a fact beyond concepts known to wisdom. Thus, "the fact of thoughts" means thoughts when they are facts known by wisdom.

that[34], so if you make realization of it into the path, then you have taken refuge in dharma. A preceptor who has taken that kind of realization as the path courses in baseless knowing, therefore, having un-hindered prajna[35] is to have taken refuge in the sangha.

For this path with that sort of special feature[36], any thought that arises becomes part of the path of Paramita. It becomes the method aspect because thought, as something not deliberately produced[37], turns into an assistant as follows: knowledge of the characteristic of any given thought is prajna; through all thoughts having arisen as the path there is absorption[38]; through as much thought as is produced being produced as the path there is the perseverance of thorough preparation[39]; through not being afraid of the fact of the profound dharmata there is patience; through there being no seeds of the afflictions in that kind of absorption there is un-outflowed discipline; and, through the practice of that interdependent connection of method and prajna, compassion automatically arises for sentient beings who themselves have not realized such, so whatever

---

[34] ... meaning realized and taken in ...

[35] Baseless knowing is knowing without the solidified ideas that go with dualistic knowing. Unhindered prajna is prajna that is not held back by dualistic ignorance; when a practitioner has that kind of prajna, he will have baseless knowing and will have become part of and taken refuge in the noble sangha.

[36] ... that takes refuge in the ultimate way as just described ...

[37] Where deliberately produced means that they are not part of spontaneous existence, the realm of wisdom, but are part of cause and effect, the realm of dualistic mind.

[38] Skt. dhyāna, Tib. bsam gtan.

[39] "Thorough preparation" is the term for production of buddha fields by a buddha in training. It is one of a set of three activities of a bodhisatva as taught in the Prajnaparamita teachings.

is done turns into something done for the aims of sentient beings, which is generosity.[40]

This path, which has that feature, has eight sections, and these, when taken along as the tools of a practitioner of it, lead to the attainment of non-reversibility as follows[41]. 1) Mind and thought being taken as not-different and carried into the four kayas makes for knowledge of all aspects[42]. 2) Everything known as the path makes for knowledge of the path. 3) It is not that the practitioner has done it by becoming expert at method. Rather, knowing that thought's own characteristic is that way primally makes for knowledge of the basis. 4) Training in cause, path, and fruition as the

---

[40] The point of this paragraph is that he has established that this path of Essence Mahamudra about which he makes the contentious statement that discursive thoughts are said to be wisdom, does conform to the path of Paramita and is a valid path to enlightenment.

[41] Now, if it is a valid path conforming to the paramitas, it will necessarily have the eight sections of meaning explained for the Paramita Vehicle in Maitreya's explanation of the Prajnaparamita to Asanga, written down as the *Ornament of Manifest Realization* (Skt. Abhisamayālaṃkara). It does have them and he shows how they are utilized by a practitioner of the path of Essence Mahamudra. When he mentions "non-reversibility" this shows that Essence Mahamudra does not merely accord with the second turning teachings of Prajnaparamita, but that it also accords with the final turning teachings of luminosity. This in turn touches on issues of self and other emptiness which has always been a major point of the view in the Kagyu school. See the Supports for Study chapter for texts on the Kagyu view of self and other emptinesses.

[42] Knowledge of all aspects is the omniscient knowledge of a full buddha and the first of the eight section of the *Ornament of Manifest Realization*.

same entity makes the complete[43] all aspects manifest . 5) In that way, knowing brings sharp prajna and the training up of the capability of the prajna[44] is[45] without hardship, relatively speaking, making for Peak. 6) Gradual accomplishment without abandonment of thoughts in that way makes for the gradual one. 7) In any given moment of prajna, the equality of all phenomena is known, making for enlightenment in the instant. 8) Everything being partaken of as part of the enlightened activity of the dharmakaya makes for the total completion of that kaya.

This special path, when seen from the perspective of having the five types of path in it, is as follows[46]. Thought turning into an assistant of the spiritual path makes for the Path of Accumulation. Reliance on thought itself produces a path of special features, making for the Path of Connection. Thought itself experienced as the four kayas makes for the Path of Seeing. Any thought produced being not separate from the four kayas makes for the Path of Meditation. If certainty in just that is produced, then there is no other, more excellent path to be trained in, which makes for the Path of Graduation[47].

That path turns into the thirty-seven dharmas of the side of enlightenment as follows[48]. As much mentation as comes up turns

---

[43] ... understanding of ...

[44] ... in this case of this special path ...

[45] ... therefore ...

[46] Now he shows how this special path of Essence Mahamudra does contain the five paths as taught in Prajnaparamita.

[47] Path of Graduation is another name for the Path of No More Learning.

[48] The thirty-seven dharmas of the side of enlightenment is another
(continued...)

into the path making for the close application of mindfulness. Not rejecting thought, there is knowledge of the characteristic realized through prajna and in its path of authentic abandonment[49] every miracle arises making for the four legs of miracles. Faith makes the cause. Mindfulness makes the path. Perseverance produces assistance. Those three are method, yet those three known like that makes for prajna. An interdependent connection of method and prajna is created whereby everything arises as samadhi which makes for the fruit. The five faculties[50] taken into practice like that results in the training up of prajna's capability and of enlightenment mind[51] being without hardship, relatively speaking, which makes the five forces. By bringing on an interdependent connection of method and prajna in that way, the capability of the prajna is trained up and, within that, the enlightenment mind is aroused, whereby all thoughts and knowers[52] turn into assistants of enlightenment, making for the limbs of enlightenment. With everything being known as a limb of enlightenment, you use discursive thought but, because it does not shroud you, it turns into the path, making for the Eight-fold Path of the Noble Ones.

Thus the armour of the view causes the dharma to be honed in on and through that all points of deviation are constrained. Then the armour of prajna carries thought onto the path, but, at that time, will prajna do the enumerated dedications shown for that path

---

[48](...continued)
major formulation taught in the Great Vehicle sutras.

[49] One of the sixteen moments of the Path of Seeing.

[50] The five faculties are a subdivision of the thirty-seven dharmas and have just been mentioned one by one—faith, and so on.

[51] For enlightenment mind, see the glossary.

[52] For knowers, see the glossary.

shown above[53]? There is no fault here for the path is followed only within the prajna of meditation and the prajna of meditation is beyond words and rational mind.

Well, then, how is thought taken onto the path[54]? For the basis used to take it onto the path, it is taken onto the path on the basis of realization—prajna takes charge of thought and turns the thought into prajna. For the attitude to take towards the thoughts, a thought should not be rejected by rational thinking but viewed from the heart as being nice, necessary, and a great kindness. You might ask, "And what happens if I do view it that way?" The answer is that every good quality is inherently present in a thought because the thought[55] belongs to the essential nature!

By viewing thoughts that way, thought's own characteristic is recognized and then the four kayas arise because they are the thought's essential nature. Taking thoughts onto the path in this way does not involve pacifying them—if thoughts of desire or aggression come up, do not try to quickly rid yourself of them but use the armour of the view described above to pinpoint what they really are. By doing so, thought goes on to self-pacification, self-purification—like ice that melts off a lake goes or clouds that

---

[53] Dedications are another essential part of the practice of the Paramita path, therefore he mentions dedications here. However, the usual type of dedication is an enumerated dedication meaning one done with rational mind. Doing dedications like that could be seen to be a contradiction to the path of Essence Mahamudra. However, he says that there is no problem here because, for Essence Mahamudra, everything is done within the sphere of prajna, and hence that problem is solved before it even starts.

[54] Now that the theory of the path has been clarified, how does one actually take thought onto the path by seeing it as the dharmakaya?

[55] This is a nice way of saying that the thought belongs to the svabhavikakaya, emptiness.

disappear from the sky go—then every one of the good qualities, asserting themselves as phenomena, arise of themselves without stoppage. If you attach yourself to those qualities, that will cause them to be stopped. If that happens, do not remain in that state but know the temporary fruition[56] and that will train the capability of the prajna steadily higher.[57]

That capability of the prajna causes discursive thought to be tamed into the four kayas, therefore, this is also known as "Taming". Prajna causes the thought to be seen as dharmadhatu, therefore this is also known as "Valid Cognition". The root of prajna's thoughts is recognized bringing separation from every extreme, so this is also known as "Middle Way".[58]

This authentic foremost instruction of the identification of the innate is to be kept secret.

---

[56] The temporary fruition is one that comes in any given moment from prajna seeing the four kaya. This is Essence Mahamudra talk.

[57] The comments in these last two paragraphs are very famous within the Kagyu lineage. They show Gampopa's own approach to Essence Mahamudra. It is noteworthy that some others, such as Sakya Pandita, strongly objected to this approach of Gampopa which is summed up in the axiom "the entity of discursive thought is dharmakaya", but their complaints were made through a lack of understanding. Within the Kagyu school, this approach to Mahamudra practice is treasured.

[58] He shows again how his teaching of Essence Mahamudra conforms to the sutra paths: Taming is Vinaya, Valid Cognition is Pramana; and The Middle Way is Madhayamaka, all of which are essential features of the sutra path to enlightenment.

Text 3

Lord Dvagpo's Personal Advice
and
Lord Gomtshul's Interviews

Lord Dvagpo's Personal Advice
and
Lord Gomtshul's Interviews

I take refuge in the precious guru.
Please grant your blessings.

I have recorded here, as a set of notes to jog my memory, answers
that the Lord gave when asked about the entity[59].

I asked, "Furthermore, what are these two, self-knowing rigpa and
other-knowing rigpa?" The reply came, "They are not two.
Naturally, in the state of rigpa, there is an indeterminacy, and that's
what they are."

I asked, "Which is it—emptiness having an experiencer of a very
pure empty quality, emptiness having a thinker with the thought
"this is emptiness", or emptiness which is freedom from elaboration?" The reply came, "The first two are not it, freedom from
elaboration's emptiness is it." He said, "The two—rigpa itself and
that freedom-from-elaboration emptiness—co-emergent is co-

---

[59] "The entity" is used frequently throughout all of the interviews in
this book. It refers to Entity Mahamudra, both the practice and the
reality reached through the practice. See the explanation in The
Dharma Taught, Essence Mahamudra section of the introduction.

emergence. That is primordially present and the recognition of it is wisdom[60]."

I said, "I would like to ask about the measure of merging equipoise and post-attainment. Is all conduct possible within an equipoise that remains un-separated from one-pointedness? In post-attainment, is discursive thought present as an assistant? Is post-attainment dreamlike, illusion-like? In post-attainment, should discursive thoughts that have appeared as ordinary[61] ones be cut following their appearance?" The reply came, "If the first possibility occurs, it is good but is just becoming[62]. What you describe in the middle ones will suffice[63]. In the last case, if discursive thought that comes on as ordinary discursive thought is not cut after it has arisen, equipoise and post-attainment will not be merged.[64]"

----

[60] In other words, co-emergence is the primal condition of mind in which rigpa comes at the same time as its knowledge of emptiness. When that primal condition is recognized in direct perception that direct knowledge is called wisdom. Thus, wisdom as a term is not used to refer to the innate condition before it has been recognized but after it has been recognized. This is an important distinction to understand.

[61] Meaning that they have not been turned into wisdom but are ordinary samsaric thoughts.

[62] For becoming, see the glossary. It means here that the meditation is good meditation but still is within samsaric existence.

[63] The middle two are how appearances should turn out when the path instructions are applied. What Gomtshul describes is not final but is sufficient in the sense of being a sign that the path is being fulfilled. The last means that the continuity of ordinary discursive thought has to be cut. One thought leads to another and, if that is not cut, then one will be remaining far away from equipoise, let alone merged equipoise and post-attainment.

[64] The last means that the continuity of ordinary discursive thought has
(continued...)

I asked, "Does wisdom wind have movement in it or not?" The reply came, "All movement is karmic wind. When every subtle movement of such wind has been purified, wind goes on to being wisdom wind solely and, when it has, that is buddhahood."[65]

I asked, "Is the wisdom wind interrupted or uninterrupted? Does samsara have a beginning and end or not?" The reply came, "Dharmakaya is beyond both interruption and non-interruption. Co-emergence's wisdom, which is experience beyond rational mind and is on all the time[66], is the dharmakaya. The two form kayas are in own appearance interrupted and in others' appearance un-interrupted[67]. As for samsara's beginning and end, there is nothing which can be pointed to and said, 'It is this'."

I asked, "What is the measure of view and meditation that will purify birth in the bardo?" The reply came, "Those of best faculty purify birth in the bardo. Those ones of best faculty do it with their

---

[64](...continued)
to be cut. One thought leads to another and, if that is not cut, then the practitioner will be remaining far away from equipoise, let alone merged equipoise and post-attainment.

[65] Wisdom wind is said to move but that is not the same as having movement occurring in it. Movement in the wisdom wind would mean movement of discursive thought which is contradictory to its being wisdom.

[66] Wisdom being on at all the time or being something which covers all times is a theme in these teachings and is described further in various places in the interviews.

[67] Own appearance and others' appearance are an important pair of terms with deep understanding involved. Very briefly, there are appearances that only occur to oneself and not to others, and there are appearances that are shared by others. This theme is also described further in various places in the interviews.

true realization of the entity; for those who realize it like that then meditate on it as well, it is so true that there is nothing to discuss[68]."

I asked, "If entity meditation does not happen in dreams, could it come at all in the bardo?" The reply came, "Even if meditation on the entity does not happen in dreams, it certainly will come in the bardo."

I asked, "Will entity meditation purify the karmic winds or not?" The reply came, "It will."

I asked, "Does wind meditation train the entity?" The reply came, "It does." He said, "My guru Mila meditated solely on Fierce Heat[69]."

I asked, "Which more easily purifies wind: entity meditation or wind meditation?" The reply came, "Entity meditation does it more easily."

---

[68] "Realization" in "realization of the entity" is a special use of the word realization found in Essence Mahamudra. It means that the entity is seen nakedly and clearly. It does not mean that the initial realization of the entity in direct perception has been developed with practice. Thus, there is realization and there is realization which has been developed through meditation on it. This kind of realization alone is potent but when developed through meditation is very potent indeed.

[69] Skt. chaṇḍālī, Tib. gtum mo. Fierce Heat is one of the Six Teachings of Naropa.

I asked, "When the entity has become the yoga of continuous flow[70], is there enhancement[71] to be done or not?" The reply came, "There is not."

I asked, "Is there a difference between the entity when realized and not realized and the entity when being habituated[72] to?" The reply came, "Except for shortness of duration, there is no difference[73]." He said, "Having realized the entity, other than the amount of meditation needed to bring it to continuous flow, there is no amount of meditation can be done to improve it." He said, "There is nothing better or worse about the entity whether it is of a person who has realized it in meditation on the present moment, of a bodhisatva[74] of the ten bodhisatva levels, or of a buddha."

I asked, "If I die with the entity realized but not having reached continuous flow, will the karma of former lives up to this one, which is karma to be experienced in another of many[75] coupled with

---

[70] Yoga of Continuous Flow is the name for the final level of attainment in Mahamudra. It is explained in various places in the interviews.

[71] For enhancement, see the glossary.

[72] For habituation, see the glossary. Here he is asking about the entity at the time when it simply has not been realized—as in the case of a normal, samsaric person, at the time when it has been realized—which here means that it has been directly seen, even if for the first time, and at the time when it has not only been seen but is now being habituated to by a yogin.

[73] He is saying that the entity itself is not different in any of the three cases but that the length of the period for which it is seen is different in each case. He uses "shortness" rather than "length" because for the three cases mentioned, shortness of duration is the salient feature.

[74] For the spelling of bodhisatva, see bodhisatva in the glossary.

[75] This is a particular classification of karma; it is karma which is
(continued...)

evil deeds done in this one, harm the future one and so does this have to pursued or not?" The reply came, "It will not, so it does not have to be pursued. A disciple of mine from Tsang developed an approach earlier in life of tripling the value of things he was selling that stayed with him till we met again later. Here is the story of how he worked at meditation and produced it. I told him that he had to clear his evil deeds. I told him that there was a method for it, which was that he had to write out and offer many copies of *The Heart Prajnaparamita*. He asked, 'Are you sure that will purify it?' I told him it would, so he said, 'All right, I'll have to do it!' Later on he appeared before me with his unhappiness gone. He told me, 'I have no evil deeds to clear off *per se*.' That was his way of realizing the entity."

»[76] I asked, "For purifying evil deeds of the past which of the two, laying aside[77] via the four powers and meditation on the entity for a short while, is stronger?" The reply came, "Meditation on the entity for a short while is stronger." «[78] He said, "Consider the person who realizes then meditates on the entity. From the aspect of the nature of the samadhi, he has arrived on and is treading the Path of Meditation. From the aspect of appearances' signs, he is treading on the greater Path of Connection yet, because he is someone who has the entity, if you comply with the paths and bodhisatva levels, you have to say that he treads the Path of

---

[75](...continued)
created in one life but which will not be experienced either in that or the following life but in an unknown number of lives—two or more— later. In this case, it means karma from past lives that, not being experienced in this life could affect the next life.

[76] The text from here down to the next ending brace is also found in Phagmo Drupa's interviews, starting on page 230.

[77] For laying aside, see the glossary.

[78] End of first section of repeated text.

Meditation. The nature[79] has more influence in this." He said, "All of appearances' path signs are provisional meaning[80] explanations. They do not arise for everyone. They are merely appearances in others' appearance. So, if you meditate to produce the path signs of winds and channels, signs that are in direct agreement with the path will occur, though all of them will be ordinary siddhi and will not help towards becoming a buddha. In the Maitreya Dharmas[81], and so on, there are many explanations of the occurrence of signs. Signs appearing to their full extent without the presence of realization is explained. Realization without the presence of signs is also explained. Presence of both realization and path signs is also explained. The uncertainty of how it will happen for some people is also explained."

I asked, "Is the cause, accumulation of merit, the cause of the fruition, wisdom? Is it the cause of its production? Is it the cause of its abiding and increasing? From the start and up to buddhahood, is joining to unification[82] needed or not?[83]" The reply came, "What invokes the fruition—wisdom—is the entity. It does not have sometimes abiding and sometimes not. It does not have

---

[79] For "the nature", see the glossary.

[80] Provisional meaning is for the purpose of leading students along, where definitive meaning directly shows the actual thing itself.

[81] These are also known as *The Five Dharmas of Maitreya*.

[82] Joining to unification is a path term. It is similar to "unification" but not quite the same. It is when you are still making an effort to get to the unification. The unification itself is something that comes spontaneously as part of the entity.

[83] Here production means "production of the entity" which is the wisdom as first seen on the path, also called "realization of the entity" and "birth or production of the entity". He is asking whether accumulation of merit contributes to the initial sight of the entity, and following that, to being able to abide in and develop it.

increase and decrease. The entity not being known is the cause that
makes it be known. It is said that when entity has been known to
start with, if merit is accumulated and then it is meditated on, it will
become clearer. For myself, I have found that I have accumulated
merit but did not sense it becoming clearer."

I asked, "Entity meditation causes the dharmas of the eighty-four
thousand afflictions and evil deeds, all of samsara and nirvana, to be
purified in their own place. Thus, if it ends all the discards[84], they
must end in the ending place, and have gone to the gone-to place.
If you were to pull something out from that as a separate item then
do laying aside on it, you would be not seeing the central whole,
would you?" The reply came, "Precisely! Entity meditation alone
is sufficient."

»[85] I asked, "Having mentally cast aside the world, one wanders
mountain tracts, but to do so requires food so should one take care
of oneself by maintaining a simple level of possessions, or should
one do Essence Extraction[86], or should one earn a little money? Or
perhaps these are wrong and one should meditate without concern
for whether one dies or not?" The reply came, "Guru Milarepa
said about this, 'If you abandon all of your possessions and leave
yourself empty-handed, it will not work. You need to maintain
enough so that you have what you need at least for your own
livelihood'. To do that, then to leave everything else aside and just
meditate is what is important. The dakinis will help with livelihood. Don't do Essence Extraction—you don't have any accomplishment in it! Chongzhi is for the purpose of curing sickness;
don't rely on it even a little. I also would not advise you to practise

---

[84] Each step of the path to enlightenment has specific afflictions and
obscurations to be discarded. Discard is the technical name for them.

[85] The text from here down to the next ending brace is also found in
Phagmo Drupa's interviews, starting on page 230.

[86] For Essence Extraction, see the glossary.

austerities; doing some simple work as needed to earn what you need will not be contrary to your aims."

I said, "May I ask, should I meditate in a place where someone has attained siddhi, or in deserted rocky mountains, in an isolated place, or in a valley?" The reply came, "Meditate where you find it comfortable. If it suits you, then meditate for longer periods. If you become unhappy, meditate for short periods."

I asked, "If one really does not want to engage in virtue-producing activities of body and speech, can one put them aside and do entity meditation alone?" The reply came, "Guru Milarepa said, 'If you think, 'I do not need that', then that is the very marrow of need itself! When you are free of both thoughts of needing and not needing that is not to be needing!'"

I asked, "What about if I stop the mind that concerns itself with others' aims then meditate?" The reply came, "By your thinking about it, sentient beings are not abandoned and through that the two types of form kaya for others' sakes do get accomplished. It is all right to prepare it with thought like that then abandon it."

I asked, "If you take refuge while in the entity, the refuge gains dharmata. If it is vows, then they become the un-outflowed ones. If it is compassion, it becomes the non-referential one. If it is arousing the mind[87], it becomes the superfactual one. If it is samaya, it becomes the primordial keeping[88] of it. By doing it within the entity, anything becomes a part of the entity and is complete in every way, so nothing else is needed, isn't that correct?"

---

[87] For arousing the mind, see the glossary.

[88] Samayas are vows that one keeps. The ultimate keeping of vows is not protecting them with dualistic mind but staying in the entity which contains the vows within it and which itself is the great or ultimate keeping of vows.

The reply came, "Everything else is false. Meditate solely on truth."

I asked, "What is the difference between the two, alaya consciousness and the entity?" The reply came, "The inner nature of the alaya consciousness is the entity. The pair ignorance and co-emergent wisdom, are like turning the hand over. For as long as the entity is not realized, it is the root of samsara; when realized, it is the root of wisdom."

I asked, "Which one of these two is it: the entity sticking out clearly while one-pointedly on it or rigpa with deception[89]?" The reply came, "It is both. There is no saying 'It is this' that can be done for the entity. All appearance is mind. All mind is rigpa. All rigpa is the entity."

I asked, "What kind of behaviour goes with the entity? Should the eyes be open or closed?" The reply came, "Any of the four types of conduct[90] are fine with this meditation. For some things it is more comfortable to have the eyes not closed. After you have completed training, having them closed is more comfortable. «[91] Overall, it is easiest to keep them closed. For Luminosity and Fierce Heat meditation each of the channels first has to be cleaned out and a certain posture has to be taken for that."

I asked, "How did confusion first happen? How does appearance appear? How does realization work? How does liberation work?" The reply came, "It is not possible to point out something prior to confusion and say, 'This is it'. It is the primordial great confusion.

---

[89] Rigpa with deception is rigpa running in the samsaric mode of ignorance.

[90] The four types of conduct is an ancient Indian formulation intended to mean all types of conduct.

[91] End of second section of repeated text.

Appearances' illusions are latencies[92] appearing in various ways. Realization is realization in which you recognize the dharmakaya that exists in you[93]. Liberation is, moreover, self-liberation. At the time of realization being its own cause, the fruition abides there because of which that itself is buddhahood." He said, "You can also understand this from looking at the main texts. It is not necessary to ask the guru about it."

I asked, "When entity meditation has been done and mind is turned inward, which mind should there be: compassion meditation, or having turned outward, the two meditations, or fictional level 'where does mind abide?' meditation, or what?[94]" The reply came, "Channels and winds meditation, outward-turned, and close-and-far kinds of things[95] are all covered by entity meditation—the entity

---

[92] For latency, see the glossary.

[93] This neatly defines the use of realization in nearly every case in this book. Realization of the entity has this sense of actually recognizing it. Beyond that, there is nothing further to realize, only the work to do of habituation oneself to it.

[94] He is asking which kind of meditation should be done with the mind, as opposed to the mind's entity, once the entity has been engaged and mind has been turned away from dualistic externally-directed looking to non-dual, internally-directed looking. He offers several alternatives: internal compassion meditation, or the two meditations of loving kindness and compassion which look at an external object again, or at the fictional level of truth with investigations of mind such as where does mind come from, where does it abide in the interim, and where does it go to when it ceases type of meditation. The answer is that none of it is necessary—one should continue to habituate oneself to the entity.

[95] Close-and-far refers to the fourth of the Four Limitless Ones meditation and hence to all types of loving kindness and compassion meditations connected with the development of fictional enlighten-
(continued...)

pervades everything throughout all directions, it is on all of the time." He said, "Mind, which is a stream of wind-mind, is the wind-mind that abides as one entity that can be liberated internally. Externally it abides up to thirty-two fingerwidths in distance. Thinking of something far away, mind has already gone there. When it is thinking internally, it is appearances[96]. For mindness, there is no 'It is present within this, it is not present within that' that can be done."

I asked, "Does entity-only meditation have points of deviation distinguished for it or not? If birth in the bardo is not purified, where will the next birth be?" The reply came, "Entity meditation has no points of deviation. Are there any in your experience of it?! It depends on nothing and hasn't a single point of deviation. Through meditation on the entity, instead of seeing the bardo, you obtain buddhahood, and if not, you are born as a noble one in pure abodes of the noble ones where, by prodding the mindstreams[97] of the buddhas and gurus there, you go to buddhahood. Except for that, there is no other destination."

»[98] I said, "I have mentally rejected grasping at a self. In the current life, wandering mountain tracts and meditating on the entity is for me. Please give me the oral instructions needed for this. If I go to

---

[95](...continued)
ment mind.

[96] Here Gampopa is drawing quotes about mind from all over the place to make the point that mind is something that has location. Mindness can't be said to have such. Each sentence about mind has no bearing on the others (and hence they do seem disconnected) except for the fact that they are all statements that imply a location for mind.

[97] Prodding the mindstreams means that you rouse their compassionate activity so that they aid you on your journey.

[98] The text from here down to the next ending brace is also found in Phagmo Drupa's interviews, starting on page 232.

terrifying places and meet wild demonic ghosts in empty valleys and empty mountains or if spirits make obstacles there, what should I do?" The reply came, "For mountain tracts, you must have the three assurances of view, meditation, and the deity's essence mantra and nothing else." He said, "If, in a terrifying place, wild demonic ghosts start to create obstacles, offer torma to those living there and they will not make obstacles or do any harm. Offer torma to the dharma protectors. Supplicate the dakinis, dharma protectors, guru, the Jewels. If you recite a great many of the yidam's essence mantra, obstacles will not come. There are only four in line between us and buddha[99]. That means that the dakinis and dharma protectors are right behind whoever is meditating, following along like dogs, so no obstacles occur for the disciples who meditate." «[100]

»[101] "On the basis of entity meditation, gods will not trouble you. Demonic ghosts will not affect you. Gods and demonic ghosts know the meditation of things being empty in that they know how to send off various emanations but they have never realized the entity and do not know how to meditate on it, so the entity has never become an object of theirs. Entity meditation is preferable." «[102]

I asked, "What is the difference between gentle wind and rough wind in Fierce Heat?" The reply came, "None except for the winds being pressed down strongly versus weakly. Such things as the visualized object and the letters and fire light can be done in any way and it does not affect which type of wind it is. For both, not

---

[99] The four in line are Tillipa, Naropa, Marpa, and Milarepa. His point is that the lineage is very short so the blessings are very strong.

[100] End of third section of repeated text.

[101] The text from here down to the next ending brace is also found in Phagmo Drupa's interviews, starting on page 233.

[102] End of fourth section of repeated text.

restraining the lower wind is guru Mila's way. If your training is done as a pressing of the winds, the lower wind becomes a little bound. Note that what is really important for Fierce Heat is Luminosity[103]."

I asked, "Will the ordinary siddhis come because of entity meditation?" The reply came, "They come and that is explained. Usually they come from doing Fierce Heat meditation. Leaving the entity aside, they will come even for a person who has an abiding[104], though buddhahood will not[105]."

I asked, "What do you have to do to eat that food of samadhi?" The reply came, "The woman Chana Dakima brought food and drink for a party for Guru Mila. He said, "I don't need to eat food, it will make my stomach roil and I'll vomit." The non-distraction that comes with one-pointedness that is essentially an abiding brings with it a lack of need for food but does not bring the fruition of buddhahood."

»[106] I asked, "For entity meditation is there experience or not?" The reply came, "There is experiencing of it, and that could turn

---

[103] Here Luminosity specifically means the Luminosity which is another of the Six Teachings of Naropa.

[104] Abiding here means simply the ability to stay concentrated. Any serious meditator, Buddhist or not, can do this.

[105] In other words, the ordinary siddhis will come just through the levels of one-pointedness practice that are part of the Fierce Heat. Fierce Heat at the higher levels is mixed with Luminosity practice; it is these levels that lead to enlightenment. Without freedom from elaboration there is no transcendence, but many attainments that would be remarkable to worldly people, such as flying, and so on, can be obtained.

[106] The text from here down to the next ending brace is also found in Phagmo Drupa's interviews, starting on page 233.

to pride and attachment. What could also come is totally casting off clinging to the world. It could also turn into dropping all other dharmas as just the outer husk. It could also turn into a happy mind of trust in yourself. For the entity, experience and realization can come." «[107]

I asked, "Birth in the bardo having been purified, at the time when rigpa has separated from the body, does the entity as itself go on to dharmakaya or, as a different possibility, does that rigpa go to Akanishtha[108]?" The reply came, "When rigpa has departed from the body, there is no Akanishtha at any level that transcends the peak of becoming[109]. This rigpa as itself is the dharmakaya beyond rational mind which is called "Akanishtha". For rigpa, there is no going and staying. For the entity, there is no going and staying. For the entity, there is no equipoise and post-attainment."

I asked, "Is discursive thought that comes up mind or mental event arising from mind? If it is mind, it has gone into being various discursive thoughts but also the entity. If it is mental event, and one meditates based on the various discursive thoughts, since it is movement over the basis, if one were working at the development of one-pointed meditation, how would that be?" The reply came, "At the time of its determination, there is no equipoise and post-attainment so you do have the sort of thing where it has gone into being discursive thought but is also the entity. At the time of its practise to gain experience of it, it is not meditated on as discursive thought. It is movement over the basis so this is meditation only on one-pointedness."

---

[107] End of fifth section of repeated text.

[108] Akanishtha is the name of several different fields, at least one of which is in samsara and many of which are differing levels of buddha field. Here he uses it to mean the highest level of buddha field.

[109] The peak of becoming is the highest level of existence in samsara.

I asked, "At the time of realization of the entity, not-rigpa[110] is purified. That causes purification of wind but the movement that comes from the wind's making the realization is a superfice on the entity, a superfice which is thought. Does that produce no virtuous or non-virtuous fruition at all?" The reply came, "That's how it works. Dream-like, illusion-like wind is dream-like, illusion-like realization, so its fruition does not have the capacity to produce full-ripening[111] at all."

I asked, "Will the meditations of Illusory Body, Luminosity, and Fierce Heat[112] cause the wind to go inside the Dhūti[113] or not? Will progress of the mindstream occur or not[114]? If the lower wind is drawn up, will it still be possible or not?" The reply came, "In the meditation of combined Luminosity and Fierce Heat, there is no difference in the visualization of the heating fire. The wind is put into the Dhūti without change to the visualization. All of gentle wind, rough wind, and drawing up the lower wind are done in Luminosity and in Fierce Heat."

I asked, "If the holding of the wind falters, is it a little bit let out and the pressing done again? Or is it that, having sent it in, the breath is pressed?" The reply came, "If you do the latter, it will harm you."

---

[110] ... that is, ignorance ...

[111] Full-ripening is one of the categories of karmic ripening. It refers to the production, through the ripening of a karmic latency, into an actual samsaric existence.

[112] These are three of the Six Teachings of Naropa.

[113] Dhūti is an abbreviation of Avadhūti, the central channel.

[114] Will there be progress towards the realization of Mahamudra, rather than just the various path signs associated with the various practices mentioned?

I asked, "Please discuss the view in terms of points of concurrence and superiority." The reply came, "The entity view concurs with Mind Only in everything being included in mind. It is superior to Mind Only in that Mind Only asserts mind as superfact whereas Entity asserts that mind is birthless. It concurs with Middle Way in freedom from elaboration. It is superior to it because of the wisdom it asserts. Mantra vehicles do not assert true superficies[115]. They concur over the path of complete liberation but mother tantra meditates making bliss the object, Great Completion meditates making emptiness in the object, and Mahamudra meditates making equality the object. Now the Secret Mantra vehicles are done with rational mind; meditation on the entity cannot be done with rational mind because it involves meditation on actuality, and that makes the entity superior to all of them. You can understand the factors of concurrence by looking for yourself. Overall, if you understand the points of concurrence with entity meditation practice, that has great blessings with it."

I asked, "What is the difference between the two, mind's entity and fact's entity[116]?" The reply came, "Mind's entity is un-stopped luminosity[117], its characteristic is movement into various discursive thoughts. Fact's entity is the nature of mind's entity, the ground awareness, its characteristic is birthlessness."

---

[115] True superficies is a feature of the Mind Only school's presentation.

[116] Mind's entity here means samsaric mind's entity. The fact's entity is wisdom's entity.

[117] Samsaric mind is simply, stated, a knower that is always on. There is nothing special about that; it is just how it is. Wisdom is the nature of that samsaric mind, which is the ground awareness. Samsaric mind has thoughts moving out from it; wisdom mind is unborn.

»[118] I asked, "How are those two knowledges and five wisdoms possessed at the time of buddha?" The reply came, "All such explanations belong with rational mind. If we too look into the terms using rational mind, we can connect them with dharmakaya and two form kayas. Yet in fact[119], the operation of buddha is beyond rational mind; the dharmakaya is co-emergence wisdom and the two form kayas appear primarily in others' space as things made up by their rational minds." «[120]

I asked, "Do the five signs, eight qualities, and so on connected with purification of wind[121] come from entity meditation or not?" The reply came, "They do. If the abiding in the entity is continuous, they come continuously. If you are sometimes putting yourself in the entity, that sporadic placement will not bring them on."

I asked, "In the case of entity meditation, is it that the wind is inserted into the Avadhūti then there is purification or is it that there is purification without the insertion?" The reply came, "Having gone inside, there is purification. They are inserted, so-to-speak, but what happens is that the insertion simply occurs."

I asked, "All rigpa is pervaded by emptiness. Is all emptiness pervaded by rigpa?" The reply came, "All rigpa is pervaded by emptiness. All emptiness appears and so it is pervaded by appearance."

---

[118] The text from here down to the next ending brace is also found in Phagmo Drupa's interviews, starting on page 234.

[119] "In fact" meaning "in the fact which is the reality of non-dualistic mind".

[120] End of sixth section of repeated text.

[121] The five signs and eight qualities are signs of progress in the practice of Fierce Heat.

»[122] He asked, "If you do wind meditation with a consort, and make a point of sitting up and not lying down, will it work or not?" The reply came, "It will work, yes. It is explained[123] that always sitting up and with the legs simply evenly arranged, your intestines can go bad. It is explained that there are many good qualities associated with having the legs crossed-up so that is preferred[124]." «[125]

I asked, "Equipoise is luminosity now but if the rigpa comes to appearance as something moved by wind and wind in general is not purified, won't the same sort of thing happen in the bardo?" The reply came, "It will not. Marpa maintained the following: 'When death has started, the elements gradually absorb then, at the time of consciousness dissolving into appearances, thirty three instances that have come from anger cease. At the time when appearance dissolves into flaring, forty instances that have come from desire cease. At the time when flaring dissolves into attainment, seven instances that have come from delusion cease[126]. Then attainment dissolves into luminosity and if, at this point, the luminosity is recognized and so met, then, it remains permanently present without need of deliberate rousing. If at this point it is not recognized, well, cold passes can't happen in the summer[127].' Guru Mila

---

[122] The text from here down to the next ending brace is also found in Phagmo Drupa's interviews, starting on page 234.

[123] ... in the medical texts that Gampopa was expert in ...

[124] In other words, if you are going to stay sitting up, don't do it with the legs just arranged loosely, do it with proper vajra posture of the legs both crossed up; the former can make you sick, the latter will bring many good qualities with it.

[125] End of seventh section of repeated text.

[126] These instances are the eighty instances in total of thought. The dissolution process is discussed at length on page 77.

[127] The axiom means that it is too late, it has already happened, and

(continued...)

said to me, 'When luminosity abides continuously, because of that the city of the bardo[128] is not seen.' All my Kadampa gurus also meditated on mantra and they all said to me, 'Best is to become buddha in this life, middling is to do so in the bardo, and least is to do so in the next life after this. If buddhahood does not happen then and the being of that time does not stay on the mantra path that is one thing, but if the being does, corruption of samaya can send the person immediately to Avichi. Interdependency is very powerful!'" He said, "In that latter case, even if the wind was purified now, the body that will rise then will have the five elements.[129]" He said, "One does not arise in the bardo without a body. You do not need to ask the guru about this; cut the exaggerations of rigpa internally and that will do it.[130]"

I asked, "Is this how to see it: karmic winds are indeterminate, discursive thought is illusion-like, and all sights and sounds of the five objects, and so on, do not exist separately from mind, so all

---

[127](...continued)
there is no further chance for it to come this time around.

[128] The bardo is often referred to as a city. It is a place with many different inhabitants in differing phases of activity.

[129] You become buddha in this life, the bardo, or the next. If not, you return to samsara where it is easy to go to Avichi hell if you have entered the Secret Mantra vehicle and corrupt your samaya at that later time. On top of that, despite having purified your body in this life, you will have a body with the five impure elements again; you are right back where you started. It is best to practise the entity and get to enlightenment in this life or in the bardo or in the next one after that.

[130] Either you recognize the luminosity and become liberated or have to take a bardo body which leads on to the problems just mentioned. Stop asking about working on the problem with external cutting of exaggeration and get on with solving the whole problem by internally cutting exaggeration through the most direct practice of all, the entity, rigpa!

equipoise and post-attainment is mindness alone?" The reply came, "Precisely! Everything is mind. Everything is mindness, something that goes on at all times. The emission of discursive thought itself is rigpa and emptiness in non-duality, thus, when the rigpa emits as discursive thought[131], that thought is being emitted as mind's stains or mind's latencies. The thought is self-starting, self-appearing, and self-purifying[132]. There is nothing to do other than being undistracted from mind's state all the time. At the time of any given habituation, there is no need to be un-distracted using mindfulness. If you can manage that, the karmic winds will be purified into indeterminacy so themselves become wisdom winds and, because of that, discursive thoughts do not come as bearers of the stains of latencies, in other words, mind would not be emitted. There is no need to rely on mindfulness and no need to practise the kind of non-distraction that goes with it."

I asked, "At sleep time, there is the presence of no-thought and rigpa is there latently—is that equipoise or not? If at the time of dreaming time the presence of rigpa is there as no-thought, it would mean that rigpa has no-thought inherent in it, so could that be the yoga of continuous flow or not? If not, are Luminosity meditation at sleep time and Illusory body meditation at dream time needed?" The reply came, "At sleep time, rigpa is not latent. Rigpa is there very purely and with that there is no-thought which is the cause of it not being sensed. Luminosity and Illusory Body meditations are not necessary. At the time of sleep and dreams, luminosity existing there inherently is sufficient. That which has not been apprehended by mindfulness is looked at after waking and, by doing so, trust comes that it is not other than luminosity, which in turn leads to continuous flow."

---

[131] ... apprehended in a dualistic mind rather than in the entity ...

[132] The abiding rigpa begins to move, gets up as an appearance, then ends again all in a self-performed process which is not the dualistic, cause-driven process of samsara.

I asked, "Should one seek bardo advice or not?" The reply came, "What will bardo instruction do for you? Both at present and at death, bardo meditation is not necessary. Meditate on luminosity alone. Luminosity is something that is on at all times so, by it, the bardo will not be seen. For example, if you are in a place where there are no enemies, fear of an enemy and an escort are not required."

I asked, "Which is preferable: meditating clearly on whatever you shift to from a referenced object or meditating by coming back from it then continuing?" The reply came, "Both. You meditate undistractedly with the understanding that this is both mind and mind's light, which is how to hold close to being mind and mind's light undistractedly at all times." He said, "Now you do not need to ask the guru questions! All your doubts about rigpa could be cut! Questions are not necessary; cut the ties to this life and meditate! I am with you definitely, at all times."

I asked, "Now if there is any meaning that could be improved or any instruction that is incomplete please provide it for me." The reply came, "Now there is nothing to improve in the meaning and there is also no instruction that is incomplete. There is no cause for buddha[133] so you must rely on your own experience! Whether I die or not is beside the point; get it with your own mind! As for a blessing, this is so obvious there's no need to talk about it. All the Kagyu gurus and dakinis are right behind you in your practice of meditation. You are blessed! You will not have obstacles, you will have meaningful accomplishment! Get on with it and meditate on your own precious mindness!"

---

[133] Meaning that there is no cause that can be created by yourself or another; buddhahood comes only through revealing one's own entity by one's own effort.

That is the end of honing in on the entity with the precious guru, done in question and answer sessions, that dispelled all the tough spots in experience and meditation.

❋   ❋   ❋

This oral instruction is for those few karmically fortunate ones who will find it pleasant to listen to and who, having heard it, will have devotion and realization shine forth. It is to be kept secret from those without the necessary karmic fortune and who have wrong views.

> There is not an iota of permanence anywhere in all the
>   containers and contents[134], great and small.
> Practise view and meditation undistractedly with the
>   king, mindfulness!
> Not letting your aim be changed by this or that,
>   persevere at the practice!
> Seek nothing other than continuity of un-distracted
>   mindfulness!
> Having become the garbha of the conquerors of the
>   three times[135],
> Doing what is meaningful for myself, effortlessly brings
>   what is meaningful for others.
> E MA how amazing this is so look at your own mind!
> Seeing mind there is complete liberation, the palace of
>   the conquerors of the three times.

---

[134] For containers and contents, see the glossary. Here it is plural because the Buddha taught multiple universes, not one.

[135] That is, having brought the sugatagarbha from its state as potential for enlightenment into its fruitional state of the enlightenment of the conquerors of the three times ...

This question and answer between Lord Gampopa and Lord Gomtshul was written down by Langben Dharma Kumāra at the mountain hermitage.

❀   ❀   ❀

The elder son of Dvagpo Gomtshul, Dampa Baggom said, "Generally, the sacrifices in regard to food and clothing that have to be made to do the practice mean that you have to be prepared for some suffering. You have to give in to being a beggar. You have to give up on what you want for yourself. That means that your ideas will no longer fit with the rest of the people who are concerned with looking after this life. Then how could having the intention that there is nothing to do except benefit sentient beings be of any help?! What we have to give our mind over to does not get them what they see as best, namely, constant happiness!"

Acharya Dvagpo Gomtshul said,

> Try to remain unseparated from the mind knowing all
>   as illusion
> In the deity's body where there is no clinging to the
>   appearing mind.
> Seek to be unseparated from a faithful, respectful mind
> Towards the Jetsun who gives introduction to the three
>   kayas.
> Seek to be unseparated from the mind that sees nakedly
> The nature, unborn luminosity.
> Seek to be unseparated from the experience of dharmata
>   experience
> In conduct that is self-arising and without stoppage.

That was spoken by Acharya Dvagpo Gomtshul.

❀   ❀   ❀

I prostrate to the realized gurus.

A yogin wanting to realize Mahamudra
Sets himself unmoved by anything, like a ocean,
Sets himself in luminosity without nature[136], like space,
Sets himself in experience without impediment, similar to wind
    in the sky,
Sets himself through samsara and nirvana being non-dual in the
    state of dharmata.

The nature of the three times is the dharmakaya;
Know it through mindness, co-emergence!
The nature of dharmata is not tainted by discursive thought;
Know it through it being unaltered, liberated in its own place.

E MA HO
All phenomena's co-emergence state,
The nature not referenced, no meditation to be done state,
The nature of samsara, free of root, the innate state,
Complete purity, birthless nature, the dharmakaya state.

Not thought of, spontaneously existing, the dharmakaya,
Appearing equally throughout the three times, the innate's path,
Its nature freed of elaborations, the yogin's mind,
Three kayas shining forth as itself, the enlightened mind.

All samsara and nirvana dissolved into the space of the innate,
All grasped-grasping[137] vanished into the birthless expanse,
All conceptual activity of accomplishment used as the path
    through no alteration,

---

[136] Nature here means a solid nature as seen by dualistic mind.

[137] For grasped-grasping, see the glossary.

All fruition shining forth in absence of attainment—

It is the Mahamudra called "inexpressible".

I heard Jetsun Rinpoche Tsultrim Nyingpo speak this.

❋   ❋   ❋

I heard the precious Jetsun say this.

"You meditators gathered here, if you do real practice, you cut the ties to this life then put your body and life in a deserted place. You make the sacrifice of not eating better food, then get on with practising to gain accomplishment.

"To do that sort of thing, you have to stay in mountain places. The best person will be like a lion gone into the snow mountains; middling like the Indian tiger who has gone to the forests; least like a vulture who has gone to the rocky crags. Do not be like the charnel ground foxes who live around the cities.

"Overall, we have to have food and clothing, but we are ones who have little in the way of livelihood so for us the yogin's ability to wear a cotton robe only is important. If you are going to eat just lower quality food and make a practice of not concerning yourself over whether there is more or less of it, you need the thought, 'Better and worse, it's all the same'.

"Overall, if you do dharma, don't place great hopes in anyone else, don't be easy to please, don't be quick to revenge, and don't look for kindness—and then things will go well. I have never looked for kindness, though I think you are very kind.

"Overall, the students disgracing the guru and the guru disgracing the students works both ways, equally. In that regard, all those who have become my disciples will, in this best case of those of you who are here, reach unsurpassable enlightenment. So do not beat yourselves about the head but accept yourselves and be certain that that is exactly how it is.

"Generally, when doing dharma, do not fall into dharma that is just talk, do not fall into dharma that takes the easy way out, do not fall into dharma that is for just a specified time[138]. You think, 'Humans do dharma so I do dharma too' then, because death is an ever-present danger for a person engaged in negativity, the Stages of the Path of the Three Being's[139] meditation on death and impermanence meditation, and the meditation of karmic cause and result are important. These are the goads of perseverance.

"Overall, in terms of people who have entered the door of dharma, the best ones should be joyful, smiling, and truly delighted at the time of death; they should only go from bliss to bliss. The middling ones should not be adversely affected when death comes. The least should have no regrets of 'Oh, I did this, I did that' over anything done with body, speech, or mind.

"Meditators must rely on mountain areas. They want to practise one-pointedly in isolation away from all distracting activities, so

---

[138] Thinking that you will practise for say one year and it will be enough is not all right; you have to practise it for as long as it takes, with no time limit put on it.

[139] The core teaching of the Kadampa is called "Stages of the Path". It sets out three levels of dharma practice that correspond to the practice done by beings of three, increasingly greater levels of capability. This system of dharma lays special emphasis on the meditation on death, and teaches the meditations of karmic cause and effect, and so on.

they rely on mountain areas. If you want distraction, spend your time in villages and populated places and that will work. If you do stay in the mountains, do not involve yourself in more distraction than a villager, persevere at your spiritual practice! Then, if you are successful, that's it! Spiritual practice is an unending great treasure. It is a precious, wish-fulfilling jewel extremely important because it creates the merit for all future lives. Even if your spiritual practice is initially successful, the work of habituation to what you have produced still needs to be finalized; it has to be taken to the finish with view and meditation. That sort of thing is what can help others. If you have not achieved that, doing something to help others is going to harm you. It is difficult to help others, so first finalize the work being done for your own sake, then care for students.

"To finalize your own purposes, it is important to roam mountain areas. Regarding that, I have heard from a Kadampa teacher, 'For the person who roams the mountains, there are five dharmas.' He said, 'This is what is needed: for discipline, nothing hidden; for the antidote, one that actually works as such; for oral instructions, ones that have been fully absorbed and as such are effective; faith that will restore you as needed; and the ability to dispel the subtlest harm by others who are capable of harming you.'

"Dewar Shegpa Rinpoche said to me 'There are four dharmas for a person who lives in mountain areas.' He said, 'He needs to have assurance about the oral instructions. He needs to have assurance of capability. He needs to have assurance of experience. He needs to have assurance of view. As he uses those, he also needs to keep close a perception of his guru as buddha. He needs to supplicate the guru without interruption and should stay in the guru's presence for a long time. It is not good enough to fly in and fly out. Moreover, it is important not to become overly familiar with the spiritual friend and be on his level, not to become resistant to the oral instructions, and not to let faith grow old.' He said, 'You have attained a precious human body, now enter and stay within the precious teaching, hear the precious dharma, meet a precious, authentic spiritual friend, and ask for the precious oral instructions. These are the connections that will give you the independence needed to practise to gain accomplishment. They must be brought together and then, on that basis, you must meditate. If, at that time, you meditate, it is not possible for meditation not to occur. If it does not, it means that you have not meditated!' He said, 'Pleasing the guru is done best of all with the service of your own practice, middling with the service of body and speech, and least with the service of offering this and that. If, based on that, you have done real dharma, it will be a source of all benefit for yourself and others. You will be happy in this life and all future lives. Happiness is something you do for yourself. A person who makes a prayer, has a prayer fulfilled. If you don't do what I have just said, then, as is said, a person who moves along on his belly like an animal will become an animal who moves along on its belly. You will make your own suffering. The result will be birth in the three bad migrations.

"If you think from the depths of your hearts, 'I am going to do dharma', then you must develop your strength of perseverance, of antidotes, and of faith and respect, and not be a disgrace to your guru and friends, not be a cause of evil sentient beings' evil deeds, and in short, must not, please, under any circumstances, fall into doing any of the extreme karmas[140]."

---

[140] The *Illuminator Tibetan-English Dictionary* explains that this phrase is coined in the Buddha's teachings on precious human rebirth. Specifically, it is coined in the section on the five personal connections where it means a person who has not done or caused someone else to do one of the five immediate types of karma.

Plate 2. An ancient modern thangka showing Gampopa (left) and Dusum Khyenpa (right) surrounded by the 1002 buddhas of the fortunate aeon

Text 4

Dusum Khyenpa's Interviews

Dusum Khyenpa's Interviews

[Part one: the beginning.]

I prostrate to the holy gurus.

Dusum Khyenpa said, "I asked the precious guru for an oral instruction. I went away and meditated on it and then an experience of an all-encompassing, cleared-out luminosity arose that lasted for some days." Rinpoche said, "That is the universal solution[141]! It will come tomorrow, the day after, and always—that is how it is! So take heat as your back rest[142]! Wear thin clothes and meditate! Live making consciousness into your servant!"

Then, not having a woman partner, Dusum Khyenpa went off to look for one and did not meet again with Gampopa for three months. After that, Dusum Khyenpa went to live at Olka Srub. After arriving there, he meditated for a few days and a genuine

---

[141] A synonym for Mahamudra.

[142] Heat throughout refers to the heat that comes from Fierce Heat practice. As Gampopa says in one interview with Phagmo Drupa, he prefers to teach his disciples by giving them Fierce Heat practice to start with followed by Essence Mahamudra.

experience of bliss, luminosity, and no-thought[143] arose. He asked
Gampopa about it and he replied, "You looked directly at it so now
your meditation is good. Now, where does its root come from?"
Dusum Khyenpa didn't know, so Gampopa said, "Well, you need
to continue to meditate just like that."

He meditated for a few days, following which he got the idea that
the bliss-luminosity[144], no matter what he was doing, was mind. He
reported this with, "I now have discursive thoughts coming to be
known, at least a little bit, as mind." Rinpoche said to him, "No
matter what it is that arises—bliss-luminosity, heat, or whatever—
you meditate for not long at a time and again and again."

He meditated again for a few days and reported that an unbearable
heat had arisen below the navel. Rinpoche said, "The winds are
now slightly inserted; because the wind has come inside the channel
you have developed discursive thought about it, so do not meditate
on Fierce Heat for a few days."

After that he reported, "I did not meditate but just remembering
Fierce Heat caused the same thing to happen." Rinpoche said,
"That's all discursive thought! Hold the gentle wind down below
the navel, meditate on Mahamudra, and let the winds go their own
way!"

Then he reported that, on one occasion, there was a very pure rigpa
with none of the appearances in view of meditation in which there
is both something to be cultivated and a cultivator of it. Rinpoche
rebuked him strongly saying, "This Mahamudra is stated to be 'like
the dream of a mute' and 'like the bliss of a young woman'—your

---

[143] For bliss, luminosity, and no-thought, see the glossary.

[144] Bliss-luminosity is a feature of the combined practice of Fierce Heat
and Luminosity. As Gampopa said to Lord Gomtshul, these two
practices have to go together.

giving an explanation of it shows that you have no understanding of it! On top of that, you make out this on the basis of what you know through one meditation! Please! No matter what bothers you and makes you want to ask a question, stay firmly in your retreat!"

Then, one night Dusum Khyenpa dreamt that a monk explained a dharma to him that he had not heard before. He reported to the guru that it had been very clear. Rinpoche asked, "Did you like that?" He did, so the guru rebuked him strongly again then said, "You have all sorts of marvels actually happening! If you understand all of them as illusory, they will turn into the path; if you hold them to be true, they will be obstacles! Whatever comes up in mind, do not hold any of it as good and worthy, do not reject any of it as bad. All of it should be understood as non-dual. If you do not understand it that way, then, whenever something happens to you that you do not want, it will turn into an obstacle."

Then, Dusum Khyenpa meditated again on Fierce Heat but, when he produced the warmth, found himself caught by affliction. He told this to the guru and Rinpoche said, "It is supposed to be expansion of enlightenment mind, so you have to carry it into bliss! You spread it upwards from the vajra's jewel and then, starting from the crown, meditate that you have brimmed over with bliss. If the semen is about to be lost down below, think that there is an orange-coloured drop at the crown. Think that your two eyes are at your navel looking up at it and, keeping your awareness unwavering on it, stay in bliss-luminosity. Then, for each discursive thought that arises, know it as mind and that will prevent the discursive thought from continuing on."

Dusum Khyenpa asked, "If sights and sounds are known as mind would that prevent them from continuing on?" Rinpoche said, "Yoginī Gagādhara said to Yogin Vajra Shrī, "Son of the family, do not look at objects, look at mind! Do not engage in many activities and separate yourself from anger and desire! Do not be anxious, do not bind yourself with doubts! Let go by letting mind do what it likes!" When Vajra Śhrī attained accomplishment, he said,

> A non-dual awareness like water and milk merged has
> Experiences which, like clouds, are all right no matter
>   what shape they take.
> A yogic awareness which realizes like an elephant
>   comprehends[145],
> Like space, pervades all.

> Not losing rigpa by following discursive thought,
> No matter what discursive thought arises, know it as
>   mind!

> It does function so the cleared-out rigpa
> Similar to space has to be known as mind!

> Everything arises known as mind;
> It functions as the cow out on the plains but with nose
>   rope in hand[146].

> Discursive thoughts are like clouds.
> Each one has its own way and
> How each will come is uncertain.
> All of them are experience[147] functioning.

Whatever arises, know all of it as mind and meditate that way!"

Later on, this thought occurred to Dusum Khyenpa: "My rigpa is cleared-out luminosity; there is nothing at all, from the peak of

---

[145] An elephant in India was regarded as a seer of all; its height allows it to survey all at once.

[146] It is completely free to do as it wants but at the same time is self-restrained into its own sphere.

[147] ... meaning the experiences of the enlightened mind ...

cyclic existence down to the wind zone[148], that is not present as my own mind." He reported it to the guru who replied, "It is stated in *Hevajra* that the entity:

> Has not a viewer of absence of visual form,
> Nor a hearer of absence of sound,
> Nor a smeller of absence of smells,
> Nor a taster of the absence of tastes.

It operates just like water put into water and just like butter put into butter so relax your body-mind as a whole with mental relaxation! From the three existences down to the wind zone[149] everything known by you is mind. There is nothing existing by way of a nature[150]."

Then again, Dusum Khyenpa asked, "Sir, is the functioning of the luminosity what is referred to as, "All dharmas are known as mind?" The reply was, "Everything is that way. When that has been understood, then for us[151], that self-knowing rigpa is a luminosity which is un-stopped and without birth or cessation, and that is the functioning of luminosity."

Later Dusum Khyenpa offered this, "When staying alone, I just want to laugh from deep down. At midnight I laugh so much that others cannot sleep." The reply was, "That is bliss growing, so it is good."

---

[148] In Buddhist cosmology, there is a zone of wind that underlies the entirety of existence. The meaning here is "in existence from top to bottom".

[149] The three existence are the desire, form, and formless realms. This again means "in all of existence".

[150] Existing by way of a nature means existing by way of a solid, real nature as seen by dualistic mind.

[151] Meaning for our Kagyu system of practice, the way that we understand it to work.

Then, one day, Dusum Khyenpa requested the path of method. The guru said, "It would be all right to explain all of it to you. However, if you do not meditate, learning the oral instructions of the bardo will not help. If you could meditate still more, the further nurturing of it would be good. Even at the time of the bardo, meditation will be following the luminosity—it is invited by the nature's luminosity." Dusum Khyenpa offered, "If I could meditate further, would that suffice?" and Rinpoche said, "That would be applying the universal solution[152] to it. Even for myself, there is nothing other than that."

Dusum Khyenpa said, "Well then, the cleared-out bliss that I have developed sometimes comes up with distraction. It is clear during the day and not clear at night." Rinpoche said, "You still have one fault. You have the fault that when it is clear, you like it and when it is not clear, you don't! Don't take that approach. Put your own rigpa in cleaned-out clearness then do not follow after discursive thoughts, rather, whatever discursive thought arises, know it as mind. This is done on the basis of knowing mind as birthless. Whatever comes up in mind, you must know it as non-dual. During the day, the luminosity will be the mixing of rigpa with appearances. In the night-time too, there is a pure bliss of nothing whatsoever. When you are among crowds, keep your mouth to yourself and meditate! Whatever you are doing, check to see, 'Is the meditation happening?'" After practising the last instruction, Dusum Khyenpa reported, "No difference between the two is coming, now." "Oh, that's it!", came the reply.

Dusum Khyenpa said, "Previously, I did some small bad actions. When I meditate on karma and effect, just by remembering them, great anxiety arises." Rinpoche said, "All of it, every bit of it, will be purified by one dose of emptiness. For example, a single spark striking a haystack will reduce all of it to nothing and in the same way, these small bad acts that you have done previously are discur-

---

[152] A name for Mahamudra.

sive thoughts, they are mind, so if you make that mind birthless, they will be purified."

Later, Dusum Khyenpa offered, "I now find myself thinking, 'For me, all sights and sounds are mind. They do not come as something else separate.' When I look at the entity of that mind, I do not meet anything. It has become like flourishing a lance in space[153]." Rinpoche replied, "Not letting this mind follow along after discursive thought and not engaging in any alteration of it, put yourself into self-purifying, self-illumination. No matter how disagreeable you find discursive thought, do not get into not liking it but look right at it! It has no colour, it has no shape, it has no identification[154], it is rigpa, your own entity—un-stopped luminosity is exactly that."

"Well then", he asked, "At the time of pursuing bliss, luminosity, and no-thought, you have said, 'not for long times', is that right?" Rinpoche replied, "Unless you do it that way, there could sometimes be experiences not of luminosity alone but of great bliss of body with luminosity to it and no thought to that luminosity. At such times, if you practise for a long time, your awareness can be distracted to the bliss of body, then the winds can be lost out

---

[153] You can hold up a spear or lance and whirl it around in the space above your head but nothing happens because the lance is being flourished within space. It is a metaphor for excellent practice in which the actual state of emptiness has been met. There is a further explanation of these two in a later interview.

[154] For identification, see conceived-of thing in the glossary. In these texts it nearly always is the technical term meaning that there is nothing in the entity that requires the dualistic process of identifying it as this or that or the other.

through the hair-pores, and eventually you will turn cold[155]." Rinpoche also told Geshe Cheng-ngawa's story.

Later, Dusum Khyenpa said, "For me, of the three bliss, luminosity, and no-thought, the luminosity is proportionately greater. At times, if my awareness wanders, things outer and inner become merged then at midnight[156] there is a period where I do not think of anything." Rinpoche replied, "Your staying in cleared-out luminosity like that is at root mind[157] so do not lose that! No matter how much thought arises, make the root mind! Do not engage in manufacturing and alteration, do not engage in examination and analysis[158], but set body and mind as a whole at rest and do the meditation of an idiot! To say more: if water is not dirtied, its pure part which is its nature, remains. If mind is not tainted[159], the luminosity which is its nature remains operative, whereas if you engage in examination and analysis, manufacturing and altering, desire and anger, it turns into non-luminosity."

Later, Dusum Khyenpa said, "One time my bliss went down and the luminosity and no-thought remained equal." The reply was, "There is no worsening of it at all; earlier when the bliss was greater, you meditated for a long period which made it fade."

Later, he said, "One time during a sleep session, everything was crushing me. At the time, an unthinkable suffering like that of the pretas arose." Rinpoche said, "It is a wind fault that brought it on.

---

[155] … which would be to completely lose the heat of the Fierce Heat that he has been practising as a way of developing the luminosity.

[156] For about two hours, the equivalent of one watch.

[157] Here mind does not mean samsaric mind in particular but means mind in the most general way, mind which is the root of everything.

[158] Examination and analysis are events of samsaric mind.

[159] By the functioning of dualistic mind as just described.

All faults are dispelled by this ..." and he showed him one, profound yoga posture which then dispelled it. One person who was inside and saw it cried out and left, and Rinpoche said, "We two are being carried by wind. You listen to dharma, then when you explain it to others, no-one understands it! You have, at long last, reached the point of obtaining true dharma!" Then he said, "The preta-type appearance that happened to you earlier was desire; it did not come from some other place at all, it came from your own mind. Your own mind is the birthless dharmakaya, so meditate accordingly."

Later, following on from recognition of the luminosity, there was an experience of everything sort of dissolving. At that time, he had a sort of experience where not one thought was emitted at all. He offered this to the guru who replied, "Some winds have been inserted into the Avadhūti. That will not go on indefinitely."

Then, one time he dreamt that he had gone deep into the ground. He reported that he had that kind of experience and Rinpoche said, "We take discursive thoughts onto the path[160]. Even very small discursive thoughts operating as mind will prevent this from happening, so, whatever experience is dreamt—whether the suffering of the three bad migrations, or leaping into a fire, or leaping into water, or some other experience of great suffering—or whatever experience arises, it is made into the path by approaching it as something you want to have[161]. Then at last you do get to real dharma. Put greater emphasis on it! When you look at the

---

[160] "We the Kagyus, in our particular way of doing things, take discursive thoughts onto the path because the entity of discursive thoughts is dharmakaya."

[161] Together with teaching that the entity of all thoughts is dharmakaya, Gampopa was famous for teaching that thoughts should be welcomed and cherished rather than seen as undesirable. This was one of Gampopa's biggest contributions to the Kagyu dharma.

suffering of the present, it has no colour, no shape. None of it goes beyond being your own mind. All of it is mind, is birthless mind, so you have to meditate accordingly."

He meditated again for a few days. This caused the appearances of the hells to come into his experience but he was aware of them as mind. He offered this and Rinpoche said, "This[162] Secret Mantra of the Great Vehicle is the profound truth. In it, the hells are not true the way they are for the shravakas. They are not an object like that[163] but are confused appearances of mind, so there is nothing more profound than this carrying of discursive thoughts onto the path. Still, experiences of the hells that do arise must be known as mind, must be known as birthless mind! By familiarizing yourself with that, tomorrow, the day after, and beyond, should the appearances of the hells arise in the bardo, they will be known as mind, so will come to no more than being hit with a ball of silk. Acharya Koṭali said[164],

> In dependence on this awareness,
> The appearances of bad karmic latencies
> Could cause births in the hells but
> Hell itself is also Sukhavati[165].

That is also part of the meaning of its function."

---

[162] This meaning this secret mantra that we are practising here …

[163] … shravaka-style sense object in which the objects of the senses are external and real dharmas …

[164] Acharya Koṭali was one of the eighty-four great Indian siddhas. He spoke very eloquently because of which his instructions are frequently quoted in the Kagyu Mahamudra teaching.

[165] Sukhavati is the name of the buddha realm of Amitabha, a name which means "blissful place".

Then on one occasion, a disease went around the place where the three roots formerly were gathered[166]. His gums swelled and his Brahma aperture swelled too, and he did not want to eat. Rinpoche said, "It is a little sickness of the elements. A meditator's sickness is usually a discursive-thought disease that happens when he thinks about dharma and does not practise it. It is a function of meditating on non-duality and straying into duality."

He said, "All sicknesses are hope and fear itself. Because of hope, there is fear of failure and with that something to prevented. For the sickness of hope and fear look at oneself and, since it is colourless, shapeless, everything is mind. Don't get into fear which is the concern that something will go on interminably and don't get into hope which is the desire for something to get better. You should think to yourself that you have gained understanding through this."

Later, Dusum Khyenpa had a cleared-out experience in equipoise. At the time, he leapt up onto a rocky crag and stayed there for a whole day but, on thinking that it was a dream, fell down from it like a stone rolling over the edge. He asked about it and Rinpoche said, "Your first appearance was a hazy one. The second one was pervaded by luminosity. This third one was abiding within mind. No adjustments are necessary for any of them."

Later, a self-luminous rigpa that could not be hindered by anything arose. In it, there was nothing else whatsoever to see yet each thing just arose. He stayed with that and the elements gradually absorbed. "When the sense objects[167] have been cast off, is that rigpa entity, the dharmakaya?", he asked. The reply was, "Whatever duality of body and mind might be made, they never become a

---

[166] Dusum Khyenpa's body became ill.

[167] Which are the result of the elements.

duality. Everything having gone to luminosity, the absence of conceived-of things[168] and concept tokens[169] is called 'buddha'."

Then again, on one occasion, each time a thought was just starting
to twitter, an absence of thought process would occur. He asked
about it and Rinpoche said, "Oh, that is just being on the opposite
side now of not hankering after something. Previously, your mind
was frequently twisted around by the same sort of events." He said,
"The best shamatha is just the cause of gods and men and that sort
of excellent meditation done on the present moment will disappear
tomorrow or the day after. Rather than sending this rigpa chasing
along after thoughts, one after another, whichever discursive
thought arises, know them as mind! If two arise, know them as
mind! No matter how many discursive thoughts there might be, at
the time when each of these unwanted discursive thoughts comes,
let rigpa deal with it and know it as mind! Or, if you cannot do
that, at least stay relaxed!"

He meditated further and that brought on a sickness of head and
upper torso. He reported this and asked, "Will knowing this as
mind itself be able to solve the problem?" The reply came, "For
that there is a key point. If you have the thought, 'The sickness will
be cured by knowing that sickness as my own mind', that itself is
straying into emptiness being the antidote for affliction at work. If
you look right at the sickness itself, its not existing by way of colour,
shape, or any other entity whatsoever is known as mind's nature
and the alleviation of the sickness that goes with that is the dharmata."

Again, one time something unlike anything before occurred. His
abiding lessened. When he entrusted everything to a pure rigpa,
any discursive thought that arose also went into the state of the

---

[168] For conceived-of things, see the glossary.

[169] For concept tokens, see the glossary.

pure rigpa. As each discursive thought arose, the experience was bettered by it. Then, when he let the rigpa free, internally as well, an experience of luminosity-emptiness without a single bit of 'what is it?' arose. In post-attainment[170], the result was that everything was present as mind. There was nothing at all existing external to mind.

He reported this and Rinpoche said, "Well, that's it! In *Entering the Bodhisatva's Conduct*, it explains that one should 'look one ox-yoke ahead' for awareness that has become agitated; you put an abiding rigpa on a small thing about one arm's length away and then, no matter which unwanted discursive thought arises, you entrust it to rigpa. For awareness that is sinking[171], again, deal with it by entrusting it to rigpa. Later, when the awareness has become workable, it is all right to entrust it rigpa for long periods of time. Stated in terms of shamatha and mindness's fact, there are two abidings, not one. Shamatha is concerned with whatever the thought process comes up with and that is all. For abiding in mindness's fact, which is the context of entrusting to rigpa, any discursive thought that arises proceeds to be part of the experiences of luminosity-emptiness, and that is something that does not require very long periods of looking. That is the how the door is opened to rigpa. It is the starting point from which rigpa is made all-pervasive."

Later, when he was pressing down the gentle wind, there really was nothing to hold down and the heat was great. He reported this and Rinpoche said, "This is a function of the training of the winds to purity. Continuing to meditate in just that excellent way will do nicely. It also will cause the rigpa to remain un-distracted from itself. There is one group who say at this point that, 'Since its

---

[170] For post-attainment, see the glossary.

[171] Sinking and agitation are the two great faults that prevent one-pointed concentration.

abiding doesn't harm me at all, movement can be allowed to start up as much as it pleases.' However, when that is done, harm starts up, too."

"Well then", Rinpoche said, "We two are still amusing ourselves with these stories, so you still have to habituate yourself further."

Later, he asked, "Well, when entrusting to rigpa, will there be a problem if the luminosity-emptiness without conceived-of things in view is looked at for a long time?" Rinpoche replied, "If you force it over a long time it will develop surface faults of being pond-like[172] and stupid. Thus you should find its rhythm—allow it jiggle about and allow it to be relaxed—and then the experience of luminosity-emptiness without outer and inner will arise and you meditate on that again and again."

At that time, a luminosity-emptiness experience without a bit of 'Which one is it?' arose. He reported that, and the reply was, "That is the functioning of wisdom which is not other than the mind of the buddha. Our way is to know through just that."

Later, it happened that there was a luminosity but without entrusting to rigpa it turned into groundlessness. He reported it and the

---

[172] This is an important term in these interviews. The style of Kadampa practice is that you listen to some dharma teaching, then contemplate the meaning of it until you get a correct understanding of it, and then meditate on it by resting yourself in pond-like utter stillness on the meaning you have understood. This is how the teach the classic analytic contemplation (Tib. dpyad sgom) followed by resting meditation (Tib. 'jogs sgom) of the sutra tradition. Milarepa and Gampopa will fault this approach over and over again, because in the end it is really just a type of śhamatha practice that does not arouse the actual vipaśhyanā needed to see reality. In the Mahamudra teachings, there is no mention of this pond-like approach to meditation except to indicate that it is a faulty practice.

reply came, "That is the functioning of superfact[173], the innate, your own entity. In a similar way, no matter which conceived-of thing of sickness arises, by dealing with it by entrusting to rigpa, it turns into groundlessness and is the dharmata. Likewise, no matter what negative force[174], supernatural event, etcetera arises, just that itself is to be entrusted to rigpa to deal with it."

Later again, he asked, "For this entrusting of conceived-of things to rigpa to be dealt with and the like, what are the distances involved?" The reply came, "For an agitated awareness, the awareness is given a closer, smaller thing. For sinking, the awareness should be given a small thing, the height of a hand."

Again, it happened when he was meditating that what he was using as a reminder would sometimes become just empty with no conceived-of thing there at all. He reported this and the reply was, "It is all a facet of the experience of everything. Each teacher has his own way of assertion using the various tenets of the Middle Way, Paramita, Mantra Mind Only, and so on, but the basic thought is the same in every case. There is not one of all the dharmas that there are that is not included within mind."

He thought about that and it occurred to him, "Just by preserving the abiding purely in bliss-luminosity, will that be the certainty of arising as the deity?" He asked about it and Rinpoche replied, "We have this Co-emergent Unification of ours as our most profound oral instruction. Whatever occurrence there is of discursive thought, no matter how much you do not want it, you do the work of knowing it as mind. Whatever arises and whatever it does, all of it is training the mind in mere dreams, illusions."

---

[173] See fictional and superfactual in the glossary.

[174] See don in the glossary.

Later, it happened that he entrusted each conceived-of thing to pure, wide-awake rigpa then set himself into relaxation and was able to dance within the state of no conceived-of thing whatsoever luminosity-emptiness. At that point in time, he had arrived at what he had originally aimed for. He said to Rinpoche that fences and mountains still hindered him in various ways. The reply was, "Oh yes, your experience there is an exceptionally good one. That is the view that things are pure rigpa. That is the great wisdom not apart from the enlightened mind of all buddhas. If you meditate on that basis, you still have a sequence of steps to go through—there are still one hundred, one thousand like that to go."

That was the interchanges between Precious Gampopa and Precious Tshurphuwa[175].

❀   ❀   ❀

[Part two: an interview after practice has begun.]

I prostrate to the holy gurus.
In the hermitage moistened with those with blessings,
Resides the person with winds inserted into the central
    channel
Who has seen the fact which has no-thought,
    luminosity, and bliss inseparable.
I come before you Lord Guru who has realized that
    meaning
With the request to write something small to calm my
    fears of forgetting our interchanges.

---

[175] Tshurphuwa is a name for Dusum Khyenpa.

He said, "My meditation brought to me a place free from all discursive thoughts, whose nature was luminosity, whose entity was blissful, that was all three inseparable, and which could not be expressed. At the time when this arose, the forms of many bodhisatvas appeared in space and with music resounding were saying 'Biritiri'. Sir, what was that?" The Jetsun replied, "It is insertion of winds into the central channel. You were a little forceful in your adjustment of the winds and they have turned into rough winds."

"Sir, what is the difference between gentle and rough winds?", he asked. The reply came, "Rough winds is that the two winds, upper and lower, are held for the maximum possible time, including past the point of discomfort. As with a pipe that fills up with water, then swells and bursts, because of the great overflow, there is the danger of leprosy and other such problems appearing." Then he said, "Take both the three parts of the upper winds and three parts of the lower windows as gentle wind and hold that below the navel. When that becomes uncomfortable, it is gently released. There will be no overflow from doing that, so it is a good way to do it."

Dusum Khyenpa asked what the two visualization systems involved with that were, and the reply was that they were the same. "Well then", Dusum Khyenpa asked, "Are there specific times at which the winds will become inserted into the central channel?" The reply came, "The circumstances of naturally-occurring insertion are listed as four and eight. The listing of four is: insertion at the time of buddhahood; at intoxication, at loss of consciousness, and at male-female intercourse. The listing of eight is those four with their subsidiaries added: at the transition of the winds right and left; the arousal of intense anger; deep sleep; and at the seeing of forms with the eye resulting in lack of grasping. In all these cases, when the fact of how it actually is has not been realized, the wisdom functions as something drab, old, and run down. In relation to this, the guru's oral instructions are used as a condition to make the co-emergence appear, then the disciples are engaged with the three phases—the phase of vase empowerment and the phases of insertion through the force of recognizing dreams as luminosity, meditation on the winds, and so on—then realize the fact of how it actually is, uncontrived[176]."

"Well then", he asked, "Which is greater, the force that comes from the referenced visualization[177] in Chaṇḍālī[178] followed by adjusting the winds or that from meditating on no-thought followed by adjusting the winds?" The reply came, "If it is greater Chaṇḍālī, that is, Chaṇḍālī done undistractedly and with a sharp visualization, first heat is produced with a buzzing sound, then bliss is produced, then no-thought automatically comes. Thus, Chaṇḍālī is the more effective."

He asked, "When you know that the first step of producing heat has happened, do you just leave it at however much bliss and no-thought is known?" The reply came, "When you have not gained the full extent of it—the example of which is ice melting to water in spring because of heat, then sprouts appearing, and ripening into leaves, trunk, flowers, and fruit—the winds and Chaṇḍālī produce heat, then bliss with discomfort happens at the navel. At that time, that bliss is used, within the four chakras, to hold mind. Then the bliss seated there is sent out to pervade the whole body. Then all thoughts automatically stop of themselves. Then there is what is

---

[176] The three phases are the phases of the first three of the four empowerments—which are mentioned in the list he gives. The final realization of the fact of how it actually is, uncontrived, is the meaning of the fourth empowerment.

[177] See referencing in the glossary. A referenced visualization is one done in dualistic mind.

[178] Chaṇḍālī, the Sanskrit name of Fierce Heat, was used throughout this section.

called 'the great bliss without outflow'[179]—from down below the discursive thoughts automatically rise up. Other than with this kind of talk, it is not possible to show you how it actually is. Teaching it is exactly to the point that it causes the winds to be inserted into the central channel."

"Well then", he asked, "Are the no-thought of adjusting the winds and the no-thought of not adjusting the winds, the same?" The reply came, "They are not. The no-thought of unadjusted winds is a neutral feeling, the functioning of a pond-like no-thought. The clearing of faults of sinking, agitation, and so on, by wind leads to true no-thought produced in direct perception."

"Well then", he asked, "Which of these two is it: to stop the six-fold group[180] so that there is no engagement with those consciousnesses internally or, while not attempting to stop the six-fold group, to settle oneself in loose no-grasping[181]?" The reply came, "The internally settled one is to put yourself into a no-thought that includes alaya seeds of thought process. It is not the authentic[182]. The shravakas, tirthikas[183], and others have it too. The one we want is the one in which you are settled in the sixfold group left loose and without being grasped at."

---

[179] For great bliss and un-outflowed, see the glossary.

[180] The sixfold group is the set of six consciousnesses possessed by humans.

[181] Loose here and in other instructions like this means that the sense consciousnesses are left unmodified, untouched, left to hang out, literally, as they are.

[182] The authentic is one of many names for reality.

[183] Tirthikas is a name for the non-Buddhist religious practitioners. For a complete explanation of the name, see the *Illuminator Tibetan-English Dictionary*.

"Well then", he asked, "The fruition of all dharmas is needed at the time of death. At the time of a meditator's death, should transference[184] be done through the process of sequential steps with suffering or through an un-sullied awareness?" The reply came, "Whichever will be more clean-cut. Use either the transference involving twenty-eight HIK or the one where thinking is not appropriate."

He asked, "How are the two done?" The reply came, "The basis for it is, as explained in the *Saṃpuṭa*[185], thinking that, within the spine there are twenty-seven four-petalled lotuses between top and navel, with all the lotuses having one's own awareness bound to them in the form of a letter A. The lower doors of rakshasha, and so on are blocked with the hero armour deities. The upper doors of the mouth, and so on are blocked with the heroine armour deities. The wind is drawn up with a forceful HIK done by saying out loud 'Hikk[186]' while thinking that the A at the navel with a thread tied to it is drawn upwards through each of the lotuses. When you train in transference, the wind adjustment together with the expression of HIK both draws the upper winds inside and prevents the A from being sent downwards. Once you are old, you are not able to train the transference. You draw it upwards with twenty-one HIK's with the KA HIK preventing it from going down, and you do that again and again. At the time of transference, you

---

[184] Tib. 'pho ba. Transference is the practice of deliberately ejecting the consciousness prior to death. It allows liberation in varying degrees according to the person's capability or at least the ability to avoid the death process.

[185] The *Saṃpuṭa* is the root explanatory tantra of Chakrasamvara used by the Kagyus. It is frequently quoted in lineage explanations.

[186] The presence of the extra "k" is not a mistake. The reason for its presence is explained in the oral instructions on transference, and hinted at just below.

draw it with twenty-eight of them then the awareness is sent to the place where it wants to go."

"Will transference happen through that?" he asked. The reply came, "Not quite! The heart pumping causes a pulse to happen. After that, the transference in which thinking is not appropriate should be done. Then it will happen, no doubt."

"Well then", he asked, "Will a meditator who meditates on no-thought do it that way?" The reply came, "My greatest guru said this to me, "If, at the time of death, you eject using the sequential steps with suffering, it is to go up in stages, though there are some who do not like that."

"Well then how is it done?", he asked and the reply came, "At the time of dying, you take up the lion's pose of lying down, lying on the right side. Then you mentally lie down so that body and mind meet, letting the mind place itself where it wants—a joyful mind, and so on; if you can put it into no-thought it will be naturally joyful."

"Will there be transference through that?" he asked. The reply came, "A winter flower has to close! When you meet a flower which has bloomed in autumn, it fades with the others all at once. It is like that. At the time of dying, through the key points of the absorption of the elements, the relationship between body and mind can lead to a quick transference without going through the sequence that has suffering with it[187]."

"Well then", he asked, "There are both rapidly induced and trained transference; how should these be understood?" The reply came, "The rapidly induced one is a person of great evil deeds or a person

---

[187] The sequence which has suffering with it is the normal process of death with its many steps of dissolution that culminate in transference.

of ordinary body and mind who is struck and falls[188], and so on. The trained transference is a meditator who, with seventeen HIKK or six postures or previous training in mixing[189], does indeed do it."

"Well then", he asked, "Using transference, in what way does the bardo occur?" The reply came, "There are three types of bardo. Your present situation in between being born and dying is bardo! Dreaming is indeed the same. By meditating now on the oral instructions of the dream bardo, luminosity can be apprehended when dreaming, which is path. Then in the becoming bardo[190], you mix with the fruition luminosity."

He asked, "Having apprehended it while dreaming, how do you meditate afterwards when awake?" The reply came, "Afterwards, when you are awake, you meditate with the thought, 'What difference is there between this present appearance and the dream offput[191]?' There is no difference, it is one and the same."

---

[188] "Struck and falls" means that the person is stricken with death and falls either into the bardo rapidly or falls immediately into a lower birth without an intervening bardo birth.

[189] Mixing here is the mixing of "mixing and transference". Mixing sums up all the practices done in this life for enlightenment because one is mixing oneself with enlightenment. Transference is the practice done at the end of life in order to avoid the usual transference with suffering.

[190] The term "becoming bardo" is used in two ways. Here it is a general name for the bardo existence in between lives, not the name of the specific phase at the end of between-lives bardo existence in which one takes on a new, samsaric existence.

[191] For offput, see the glossary. Appearance is the offput of the nature of mind as is what is dreamt in a dream.

"Well then", he asked, "Ngog, the lineage son of Jowo[192], said to meditate on sleep as the dharmakaya and to meditate on dreams as the sambhogakaya. Is it so?" The reply came, "Sleep is ignorance, not-rigpa, so how could you possibly meditate on sleep as dharmakaya? That would be to do dharma based on an explanation that is not founded in meditation, not founded in experience! It is true though that, when dreaming is recognized as dreaming and the dharmakaya luminosity is additionally recognized within that, it is meditation. At that time, you are mixing yourself with Dream, Illusory Body, and fruition Luminosity, so it is indeed mixing."

"Well then", he asked, "At the time of death there is the progressive absorption of the elements, followed by appearance, flaring, attainment, and luminosity[193]. How do their signs come?" The reply came, "During the death process, earth dissolves into water with the effect that the body cannot be lifted. Water dissolves into fire with the effect that the mouth and nose become dry. Then there are signs that come as appearances to the dying person: externally there is an appearance like that of the moon rising; and internally like that of fireflies. Of the eighty discursive thoughts, the thirty-three that come from anger cease. Fire dissolves into wind at which time the warmth of the body withdraws. Appearance dissolves into flaring; the external sign is like that of the sun rising and the internal signs is like a butter lamp. The forty that come from desire cease. For the meditator, heavenly beings come to greet and for evil-doers, the messengers of the Lord of Death come. When it is time for the cycle of breath to cease, the expiration of breath gets longer and the inspiration shorter until finally, the breath stops. Attainment of appearance has an external sign like darkness and an internal sign of a butter lamp. The seven that

---

[192] Ngog the translator, one of the principal disciples of Jowo Je Atisha.

[193] These are the principal steps of the death process from beginning to end. There is also a description of the process in Lord Gomtshul's interviews on page 39.

come as delusion cease. At this time of being present just as internal breath, there is the inverted HAM obtained from the father at
the crown of the head and the A stroke with the nature of Fierce
Heat obtained from the mother at the navel. These two letters of
method and prajna meet at the heart centre then the radiance of the
corpse could stay for one or two or three or four or five or six days.
After that, the fruition luminosity comes having an external sign of
the light of the early hours of the dawn and an internal sign of a sky
with all clouds dissolved. At that point, the path luminosity and
fruition luminosity merge as a result of which the luminosity is
naturally illuminating, is divorced of all discursive thoughts, and is
filled with un-outflowed bliss. Appearance also shines forth with a
blissful nature. The appearance of being in hell might arise but no
harm will be sustained; it is appearances seen as suffering that binds.
The appearance of being a buddha might arise but no benefit will
occur; appearance shining forth as bliss liberates."

"Well then", he said, "For how long should these be done: the
present luminosity of the path, and these—-the wind being inserted
into the central channel or the phases of the three empowerments
or dreams being luminosity—and the fruition luminosity which is
the entity sort or fruition luminosity?" The reply came, "Like for
the entity. The present and path and fruition too, like at the time
of inserting the wind into the central channel; for short times. For
example, it comes like the moon on the first lunar day of the month.
After having merged it with fruition luminosity, for long periods;
finally for half a day and four days. For example, like the full
moon."

He said, "At that time, for those with the instructions, bliss is
sambhogakaya, luminosity is nirmanakaya, no-thought is dharmakaya. The three inseparable is the svabhavikakaya, making the four
complete. Thus you have the operation of the bardo in which all

good qualities are complete. It says this in *Expressing the Names*[194] with:

> In one moment, complete buddha
> In one moment, all the details come out.

And, in the Dohas with:

> In one moment of knowing[195]
> Like the mandala of all knowables being pervaded
> With no discursive thought, all is perfectly known."

"Well then", he asked, "How do the two form kayas for the sake of migrators arise within that?" The reply came, "Without any thought of something to do and the doing of it, Vairochana adorned with the signs and marks appears to the tenth level bodhisatvas purified of karma. Appearing as the six Capable Ones[196] in tens of hundreds of millions of Jambudvipas, and so on, it acts for their benefit."

He asked, "Which acharyas make those assertions?" The reply came, "Naro's lineage, guru Tiphupa, guru Adul Vajra, and myself, too, assert the present path luminosity and the bardo path and the fruition mixing. Guru Balpo speaks of the present, self-fruition." Gampopa said, "Thus we have a history now for many days of the two of us debating arguing again and again."

"Well then", he said, "If that fruition luminosity is not apprehended, what should be done?" The reply came, "Using the guru's oral instruction to make co-emergence, in the present when the wind is inserted into the central channel, one should recognize the path luminosity and by that it will be impossible not to apprehend

---

[194] Skt. manjushrinamasamgiti.

[195] ... of a buddha's mind ...

[196] For Capable One, see the glossary.

the fruition luminosity. Those who do not have the oral instruction will fear luminosity and so, seeking the wholeness of a body will wander in cyclic existence. If luminosity is not apprehended, then fruition luminosity, operating as the illusory body purified of karma, which is the yidam deity ornamented with the marks and signs, should be made to rise. Tshurton Wang-nge said, 'How I feel compassion for the sufferers! All these others do not want to rely on mind. My deity, Lord Marpa, wants to rely on mind. In the bardo, this mindness is the entity as the deity. It is blissful. The fact operating yet birthless is the ultimate fruition!' Acharya Ngag-gi Wangchug Drag talked of having the seven famed ones. He maintained the ultimate fruition to be buddha's form. I have no argument with that—it is the functioning of their illusory body. It gives one hundred thousand bodhisatvas of the ten directions empowerment and, when they request dharma, it gives it to the ultimate, tenth-level bodhisatvas."

"Well then", he said, "What results of transference are there?" The reply came, "One is that those with great evil deeds who have done the five immediates[197] have a rapidly induced transference then are born in the formless states. Two is Gods and men who have selected a Wheel-wielder's womb then transfer. Three is that those who have trained in transference identify the fruition luminosity then become buddha. Four is those who apprehend luminosity then rouse the pure illusory body and so gain tenth-level bodhisatvahood."

"Well then", he said, "How do beings go on from the luminosity to wander in the six classes?" The reply came, "Those who have no oral instruction fear the luminosity then seek a body. First they

---

[197] Tib. mtshams med lnga. The five immediates are a set of five bad actions whose karmic force is so strong—for example killing a parent—that the person who has done one of them dies and goes immediately to the next birth, usually one in hell, without any intervening bardo existence.

take a mental body in the bardo. That is known as 'the impure illusory body'. Its character has been stated as, 'Having the fleshy form of the previous occurrence' meaning that, from the fruition luminosity the being rises up in a mental body like the former body. It is also asserted by others that it rises up as what will be appropriated[198] in the next life. It has been stated that 'its faculties are complete[199] and it has the quality of being unhindered'. That means that it gets the sensations it had previously and that it is unhindered in respect of the dharmadhatu and a mother's womb other than its impending mother's womb; saying that it is 'not prevented from entering other' does not mean that it is not prevented from entering anything at all. It is stated that 'it is seen by others of the same class and by the pure god's eye' meaning that it is seen by those inside the bardo and seen by the gods. It is stated that 'it automatically has karmic miracles' which means that it does not have wisdom's miracles. How long it can stay there before it has to enter the becoming bardo is seven days or fourteen days or twenty-one days or twenty-eight or thirty-five or forty-two or, ultimately, forty-nine days. Then, at the time of that transference, there is the condition of desiring the father and mother but aversion to entering the womb."

"Well then", he said, "What do Secret Mantra's narrow path oral instructions[200] say to do for the bardo?" The reply came, "One is, 'In the becoming bardo, practise non-distraction from your own mind'. A second is, 'Have the thought, 'I will not go into a parent's

---

[198] For appropriation, see the glossary.

[199] Meaning fully present and fully functional.

[200] The Kagyu distinguishes the narrow path of hearing lineage oral instructions and the highway of the textual instructions of the tantras. The former is more rapid but they both lead to the same place.

womb' so as not to go into the womb.' A third is, 'Recognize the fruition luminosity through which you abide in bliss.'"

The interview. ITHI 𑀩 [201]

❀ ❀ ❀

[Part three: an interview, with Gampopa telling his own story.]

I prostrate to the holy gurus.

He said, "Precious acharya rinpoche, sir, how should one listen to dharma to start with, how should one practise it in the middle, and how should the mindstream turn out in the end? Please express the answer using words that do not belong to the hidden secret[202]."

The unequalled lord replied as follows, "Generally speaking, I do explain the secret; advocating the experiences of abiding is harmful. Once the entity has been produced, it comes with the two of what works and what does not. What I just mentioned could be harmful but will not be harmful; I have the hope that it will be beneficial so I do not keep it secret beforehand. For accumulation there were two things so will I mention that, too: first I trained in medicine, then I heard a lot of mantra from Ngaripa[203].

"At that time my friend Gongton said, 'Acharya bodhisatva, you have the oral instructions of guru Mila. You have told us that Mila

---

[201] A sign of secrecy.

[202] That is, please express it in more general terms rather than through the words of Secret Mantra whose meaning is hidden.

[203] One of his early dharma teachers who was from Ngari, West Tibet.

is a siddha. We request those instructions from the acharya.' He gave us all those instructions and we asked, 'Is there anything else that will help further with what you have told us?' He replied, 'I am familiar with this, given that I have had a good abiding come that lasted for seven days', so we should meditate together. The acharya and the two of us practised meditation together. Gongton said to me, 'If you have something that comes on in a steady way you must tell me!' When I told him that a meditation had happened, he said, 'Either a meditation happens or I die right on this bed[204], there's nothing else!' Then he also had an abiding happen, so he wrote a reminder of it right there on his bed, then said, 'Gongton's samsara has ended here', and sat there. After that, I asked Ngaripa to be my preceptor and in my twenty-sixth year took all levels of ordination at once.

"In my twenty-eighth year, Gongton and I went to Uru. We asked Geshe Nyug-rumpa for the Kadampa oral instructions. We also asked for arousing the mind[205]. From that time on till now I have not been separated from the fictional enlightenment mind[206]. Staying there in that confined place with many people, my previous meditation failed. I was unhappy about it, so the geshe told me to go off to Gyayon Dag, which I did. There were few people there so I was able to generate the abiding again. I meditated there on the Stages of the Path topics, death, karma and results, and the disadvantages of samsara and that brought back the type of experience I'd had previously. This previous one, which had bliss-emptiness with it, now turned into a mind that was easily upset. The mind of disenchantment had become prominent. Gongton asked, 'What has happened?', so I told him what had occurred. He said,

---

[204] In Tibet, practitioners usually do not have a fancy place to practise; they sit right on their beds and do it.

[205] For arousing the mind, see the glossary.

[206] For fictional and superfactual enlightenment mind, see the glossary.

'For me, too, something has happened. I find that this Kadampa seems to come as one thing after another.'

"While staying there for three years, I had been hearing that guru Mila was a siddha, so I thought to myself, 'He is still with us. If you don't go to see him even briefly, you'll regret it later.' So Gongton and I went to ask for leave and were told[207], 'If you stay here, you will be escorted by the method path. If you go, may you end up at the one that has the foremost itself with it[208].'

"We went. When we had arrived at Gurmo, Gongton's help was complete, so I roused myself and went on alone. The morning that I was to meet the guru, the guru said to his disciples, 'Today, a teacher from Central Tibet is coming to see me here. It will be beneficial to migrators', and dispatched one of them to escort me. It was overcast, ready to rain, so we had made our way up to an overhang. I had come a long way and was exhausted, body and mind. He said, 'Hey, are you all right?' I told him how happy I was. He told me what the guru had said that morning and all the exhaustion from before cleared. After waiting there, the guru's disciple Seban the junior teacher came down. He said, 'I am here to help you to request the foremost dharma.' That is how I came to meet the guru when I was thirty-one years old.

"I made many genuine prostrations then said that I had been travelling for four months to see him, so asked him to give me his full attention. He replied, 'Compared to your four months, my teacher had to go all the way to India!' Then he said, 'The two of us have come together as if we were a pair; just considering our

---

[207] ... by Geshe Nyug-rumpa, the owner of the dharma assembly that they have been staying at ...

[208] In other words, "May you find a dharma that has the teaching of the primordial state, which is the foremost of all dharmas with it". That is, may you find the liberation path.

bodies, I am here with someone with whom I have no karma connection. However, it's always the case that Kadampa geshes who are beset by doubts go to straight to the guru like firing an arrow, so in fact there is a very great karmic connection here'. I asked him for oral instructions then said, 'I haven't obtained good oral instruction on enlightenment mind.' I explained my earlier practice of meditation to him and he said, 'That's good, that is exactly what it is.' We had one round of discussion and guru Mila said, 'Don't meditate by having a good session of asking about dharma then going and sitting pond-like in what you have understood[209]; meditate on pranayama[210].' After our round of discussion, Seban the junior teacher and the guru told dharma stories back and forth. Then, with the assistance of Seban the junior teacher, I got this from guru Mila: 'Your system of practising meditation is like this talk! When I have meditated like you, I will then give it to you!'[211] I wondered, 'Does the guru not do meditation like that?'

"I was good at asking dharma questions which led to the guru saying, 'Nobody has come along with more questions than you!' He said, 'When the early part of winter has arrived, you must stay and work hard on your meditation. At that time, it will be good to

---

[209] To do so is to practise according to the Kadampa approach; it develops conceptual realization of the dharma but does not go beyond that.

[210] Skt. prāṇāyāma. This is the practice of working the life energies through various yogic exercises in order to get the mind to meet with reality. It is more often referred to now as "channels, winds, and drops practice".

[211] Milarepa is criticizing him and joking at the same time. Gampopa's Kadampa style of meditation never gets beyond the chit chat of concepts. Milarepa doesn't have any experience of that sort of meditation though he will teach it to Gampopa after he has trained in it—something which is not going to happen.

wear a cotton cloth, if you can.' He said, 'Wearing a single cotton robe then meditating is the very best.'

"After waking from sleep, my body was like a heavy lump, so meditation wasn't coming. I meditated that summer, which brought on the heat one time. We shifted through three valleys and one village. I was staying there wearing an tattered old cotton cloth when the guru came and asked, 'Has that made heat?' 'There is heat now.' 'Will it work for the whole winter?' 'Yes.' 'Now you are better than me', he said.

"I finished my stay after thirteen months and came down in my thirty-second year. He told me, 'After you have gone down, watch out for obstacles.' At this time pretas[212] were a menace, so I did a lot of recitations of 'guru know me'. Then I went to the place where Gyayon Dag was and he[213] asked, 'Where have you been all this time?' I said, 'I decided to stay with my guru for the time; attempting to train when the end of life has arrived is useless!' He said, 'A sick person who I cured gave me one and a half khal[214]. It will last for both of us.' Then Olkar arrived as well and the food was not enough for all of us, so I went to Dvagpo where a new fear hit me. The heat was there, but only as sometimes good and

---

[212] Skt. preta. Pretas are a class of beings in the desire realm below animals and above hell-beings. There are three types of preta. Two types have trouble finding food and water; they do not have the strength to bother humans. The third type does not have those problems and does have the power to bother humans, for instance, malicious ghosts and spirits.

[213] ... meaning his friend Gongton who was staying there ...

[214] A khal is a dry weight. He probably means a large bag full of the roasted barley flour called tampa. Tibetans can live on tsampa and butter for months. As an interesting aside, I have done this myself in Tibet during months of practice. It doesn't satisfy Western taste needs but it does keep the body going quite well.

sometimes bad. I'd had a good meditation previously, but it failed in the face of so many people staying in the confined Kadampa monk's residence. I had been told that it was necessary to stay in isolation and it was so. After the austerities, my body had wasted. Samadhi failed.

"The guru had said to me, 'Butter doesn't come from sand. There's no butter in white mustard. When the body has no vitality, samadhi does not come.' The guru had said, 'You won't find this with my Fierce Heat!' Remembering what he said, I practised and in Sewa district one very good consort appeared; now I had both a meditation with samadhi and the good consort needed. Away from the guru's presence, for three years I developed the heat down on the plains. I didn't meditate for the summer but it still came on. In the meadowlands, no matter how much samadhi I practised, it came on (which is to say that it came on just from the wind-mind being held inside). It came on continuously during a period without sleep and when I looked to see how long it had come for, I found that it had come uninterruptedly for thirteen days. Then that mind failed like grass withering. Then I stomped on all afflictions and that made it come on without identification[215] involved.

"With my mind seduced by the bliss of the samadhi, I found that it did not gravitate at all towards the desirables of the five senses. The teacher Trang said, 'What has happened for you?' and I said, 'This desire by itself is just a cocoon.' I wasn't even noticing desirables of the senses. He asked me how my other half was. I said, 'For me, I do think that there is bliss in a woman and because of that, I do have lust appearing.' I said, 'Even though that kind of thought is happening, I don't recognize it as movement within mentation[216].' Geshe Drewa said to me, 'What is this samadhi of

---

[215] For identification, see conceived-of thing in the glossary.

[216] Mentation is the operation of mental or dualistic mind. Movement
(continued...)

yours like that you say is good?' I told him, 'There is no difference between walking on pleasant grasslands and the samadhi that I have brought forth in my mind! Staying on the plains, I stay cross-legged, use a consort for equipoise, and do wind-mind practice. Through that, I have reduced wind to a corpse internally with the result that no-thought bliss comes. This is no easy thing to do.'

"When I next came before the guru again, I had spent seven years in Sewa district looking and had seen mind's entity just a little. For me, that was something difficult to produce. For you, that can be produced without much difficulty.

"I dreamed a good dream and the primordial spiritual practice was born. Carving gold gets you which basin? I also dreamt that I had the idea that I had to write the *Eight Thousand*[217] out once. Then, when that did not turn out well, a certainty was born. First, a decision on the level of mind occurred: 'If it is not co-emergence, do Fierce Heat meditation alone; everything is thought; thought is adventitious; all that is part of mind.' It all came on automatically within that one thought. Then, the entity of that awareness was known like meeting someone known from before. The entity was seen standing out. Unlike with the previous meditation, it came as something that stood up, was very clean and clear, as something which had always been there. Then, all previous dharma heard and all the guru's dohas appeared vividly, as though the whole lot had been just dumped into my mind. And appearance flashed and flashed illusion-like; sometimes it came like it was just sitting there

---

[216](...continued)
within that kind of mind is what discursive thought is. He is saying that he could have these apparent thoughts but they were not binding because they were not occurring within dualistic mind. It is a very high level of realization already and probably quite shocking to the geshe who is hearing it.

[217] The Prajnaparamita in eight thousand verses.

and sometimes it just came as the awareness's own entity. That itself having become meditation, there was no meditation to do. With no meditator, all previous dharmas became just an outer husk, then the rigpa's entity having gone to being without support, there was no longer a need to focus on rational mind. Sometimes it was empty, sometimes like an illusion. There was no need to apply conceptual analysis and examination to the appearances. Sometimes, I would think that I should extend and extend the experience but that was the experience itself, too. I went to relying on realization. There could be no enhancement practice to make it greater. Well, the elder of Rongphu flew in the sky and this did provoke one enhancement of the realization—the way it was previously where all thoughts came as mist now was gone and I found myself thinking how joyful this was. Then thought went on to being luminosity alone. In that, thought was harmless. Then it occurred to me that none of it could be harmful. Then it went into being luminosity alone and from then on, till now, this has occurred without interruption. Then it was uninterrupted with no difference between night and day. For the yogin there is no dying and not dying. It occurred to me that there was no bardo.

"Later, a happy sensation arose. Prior to this, even if I did a great deal of recitation, harm from dangerous ghosts could still come. Now, even if I didn't do a single bead's recitation, not even a single bit of harm from demonic ghosts could come. Before, whenever I met any of the geshes who were expert in dharma, I would become anxious. Now, even if buddha arrived before me, that would not happen. Now, no matter how expert and intelligent someone is said to be, my prajna has been opened so I have no anxiety in the face of such a person.

"In a dream, I found a rhinocerous horn amulet and the meditator Tray Yung said 'Show me!' but I wouldn't. I told him that Jowo Lord's body relics and the Kadampa foremost instructions were in it. He pressed me hard and I dreamt that I opened it once for him. Now, this small benefit for humans that I will give is benefit that comes in dependence on the Kadampa. There are many explanations of Naropa's oral instructions but ones not connected with the Kadampa are only of small benefit.

"In one night's dream, I gave copper long trumpets to two men then had them blow them. Even in these times, copper long trumpets of that girth do not appear in the whole of U and Tsang[218]. Since then, it has happened just as I dreamt. I went to Olka Srub where I took up residence then dreamed that I slayed a black man. Afterwards I thought, 'Now I cannot be affected by obstacles of maras, and so on', and that is just what has happened. In one night's dream, I dreamt that I cut the head off a child who was there. Afterwards I thought, 'There is nothing more loved in the world than a child, shouldn't I love them equally, with detachment?' and that is just what has happened. Since then, I have not had dreams of striking and killing. All the Kadampas have said, 'If emptiness is realized, it leads to avoidance of karmic results.' I have that absence of karmic result. Now, I have in my own experience, one of the dharmas that came for the Kadampas."

❀   ❀   ❀

[Part four: memories of the guru, Gampopa, after his passing.]

Namo Guru.[219]

> On the water year's summer's middle month's
> Fourteenth night, he was a little sick.

---

[218] Even now, he is saying, in times where there is more wealth and better craftsmen, long trumpets of this size are unheard of in the central Tibetan kingdom.

[219] Dusum Khyenpa tells of Gampopa's death in a short piece of verse. He then recounts what Gampopa has told of his own life story.

"I will not take medicine now", he said.
Due to this condition he
Laughed again and again.
On the fifteenth day he passed away.
We cremated him in a large stupa.
On the eighteenth, when the cremation was done,
A mass of light above Gungthang was seen.
One person from Nyalwa saw spears of rainbow light.
Various rainbows appeared many times.
A wondrous state of mind uninterruptedly appeared.
I prostrate to the Lord whose mind is luminosity.[220]

I heard the following from the precious guru.

"When I (born in the sheep year[221]) was a teenager of sixteen years, I went (in the dog year) before the geshe of Zangkar[222]. I studied the tantra sections of Yoga, Chakrasamvara, and others[223]. In my twenty-sixth year (the year of the monkey), I took ordination at Drongkar, taking it all at once. I took many empowerments of secret mantra from guru Mar Yulwa and the bodhisatva, both, then meditated. A good experience of shamatha arose; appearances shone forth like misty rainbows and no-thought[224], without

---

[220] "Whose mind is luminosity" here means that his guru has passed away and entered the full fruition luminosity of buddhahood.

[221] A number of notes have been added by a later scribe in order to make the original notes of Dusum Khyenpa more understandable. These notes are shown in parentheses in the text itself.

[222] Zangkar is the name of one of the three districts that made up the Western-most province of Tibet, Ngari. That geshe is referred to in the previous part as Ngaripa.

[223] Yoga here means yogatantra.

[224] This is the no-thought of shamatha, which simply means that
(continued...)

identification, arose day and night. When I looked to see how long it had lasted, I saw that it had occurred uninterruptedly for thirteen days. Now I had achieved excellent meditation.

"I thought to go to observe the conference on bodhisatva conduct happening with the geshes at Uru plains which led to hearing the paramita Stages of the Path in the presence of Geshe Nyug-rumpa and Geshe Gyayon Dag. These two had gone to buddha knowledge and experienced the kayas. I felt that the enlightenment mind which I now had roused in my mind was a kindness of those two.

"Then, hearing guru Mila's name, extreme faith arose, and I requested leave of the geshes. In Tsang, I was on the road for forty days. In my thirty-first year (the ox year) I met guru Mila. I offered my earlier experience in meditation to him and he said, 'That's your meditation! It is not the path to buddhahood!' He also said, 'At some point you should stop this kind of pond-like meditation and do pranayama meditation!' Then I meditated for one year on pranayama and by that all the good qualities of wind meditation were completed. He said, 'It seems to me that you have been able to produce bliss-warmth and samadhi in your mindstream without difficulty.'

"I had stayed in the presence of the guru for thirteen months. Now, I decided to go back down (in the tiger year). He put a large white torma on my crown and gave the empowerment of the dakinis and dharma protectors. 'Through you, there will be much benefit for sentient beings', he said. I asked how that would be and he said, 'When you came here, a sign that you would benefit beings arose. After you stayed here, I had a dream in which we had a race and you came first; it says that your benefit for sentient beings will

----

[224](...continued)
thoughts have been stopped within dualistic mind; it is not the no-thought of the entity in which discursive thoughts do not exist within wisdom mind.

be greater than mine. Again, one time I dreamed that you hurled a boulder bigger than a Bra[225] tent to another land and by striking the boulder with both hands it was reduced to dust. Your body also was better than mine; I did not have your capacity. It means that you will not be afraid of external objects.'

"I went down. Then I heard extremely detailed explanations of glorious Dipankara's[226] oral instructions from geshes Drewa, Chag Riwa, Ja Yulwa, and so on.

"The monks there begged me to tell them about the practice I had been doing and what had been produced in mind because of it. I told them the experience of abiding came on when I meditated on the three experiences of bliss, luminosity, and emptiness but not unless I meditated. I told them that this experience of one-pointed-ness is different from that of the four types of conduct; it comes on through a cleared-out purity and with a continued presence of thought process[227]. It can be brought forth with the clear type of knowledge that thinks, 'This is it.' Sometimes the meditation would come on separated from awareness and I would think, 'Is this totally without meditation?' Sometimes not meditating would come and sometimes meditating would come. I did not gain realization but that practice produced a little of the awareness. The

---

[225] A Bra tent is the standard tent of Tibetan nomads made from the very coarse hair of a yak woven into canvas called Bra. It is a very large tent that can accommodate a whole family with kitchen, beds, and all other possessions included.

[226] Dipankara is Atisha Dipankara. His oral instructions are the instructions of the Kadampa.

[227] This means that his one-pointedness developed in meditation according to Mahamudra instruction is different from the ordinary one-pointedness developed in the ordinary kinds of meditation that most people do. It has the special characteristics mentioned.

root is mind so this was somewhat like the moon of the first lunar day of the month appearing.

"It is when wisdom gets started that the path is actually reached and begun. A genuine occurrence of wisdom shone forth; I had an excellent dream then I saw, as though it was standing there, a rigpa which could not be greater, my own entity. It was like meeting a person with whom I was acquainted from before. Now that awareness itself had become meditation, there was no meditation to be done. There was no meditator. Mind shone forth as supportless luminosity-emptiness. I understood that it was being recognized clearly. All dharmas became an outer shell. Nonetheless, I was thinking that, if discursive thought arose, I did not like it and that if there was no-thought it would be proper. If there is no discursive thought, there is no un-interrupted luminosity-emptiness; 'Oh!', I thought, 'that has happened!' That was my view staying in Nyal of Sewa district.

"I shifted to Drongphur where there was a production of realization. Previously, when discursive thought arose I did not like it and when realization arose preferred that. Now at Drongphur, discursive thought shone forth as luminosity, and now, when thought did arise, it was as though it was light coming off the luminosity. The thought arose, 'For the secret mantra yogin, it doesn't matter whether he lives or dies.' For such a person, the appearances of the bardo will not shine forth. The Jetsun guru had said to me, 'Stay constantly in the luminosity. Through that, you will not see the city of the bardo.' I think that has happened to me. I am not harmed by discursive thought so the luminosity is never interrupted by anything. Now I have embraced a continuity of luminosity and luminosity-emptiness arises like the flow of a river. It travels with me as a part of me which is not obvious, and because of it, even the use of my intellect—which also is free from grasping at the luminosity—does not contaminate me in the slightest. For me, mindness has gone onto being dharmakaya."

Following that, he shifted to Zang[228] district where, in his year of passage (seventy-five), he recognized the way in which the three kayas shine forth.

❀   ❀   ❀

[Part five: oral instructions of the lineage gurus written in verse.]

Vajradhara,
Like water poured into water,
Like butter poured into butter,
Himself saw his own wisdom well.
I prostrate here to that good seeing of wisdom.

Tailopa said,

Kye Ho, this self-knowing wisdom
Is beyond the avenue of speech, not the domain of
    mentation.
Thus, this wisdom of suchness is something that
I Tailo, cannot show you at all.

Naropa said,

Appearance's characteristic is that it is birthless.
Samsara's characteristic is being free from ground and
    root.
Mind's characteristic is unification.
Guru's characteristic is to have eight[229].

---

[228] Gampo Zang Valley in Central Tibet.

[229] One description of a qualified vajra master is that he has eight specific qualities.

Marpa said,

> The view is wind-mind non-dual.

Mila said,

> Make efforts not to fall into any side at all and
> Work the key points of pranayama; by it, the all-
>   inclusive result will shine forth for you.
> Divorced from colour and shape, it is beyond being an
>   object of the faculties;
> Having no words or conventions, it is beyond being a
>   sound of verbal expression.
>
> If you realize the fact which is without awareness and
>   also without empowerment,
> The supreme empowerment will have been made.
> If you realize the fact which is without meeting and
>   parting,
> The supreme friend will have been made.
> If you realize the fact which is without birth and death,
> The supreme life will have been made.
> If you realize the fact which is non-duality,
> The supreme view will have been made.

Gampopa said,

> To look at your own mind is the view.
> To realize dharmas as mind is realization.
> To meditate by habituating yourself to that is
>   meditation.
> To experience the entity is experience.
> To stay un-interruptedly in that state is conduct.
> To manifest it is the fruition.
> To show it to others is enlightened activity.

❀   ❀   ❀

[Part six, a collection of five interviews with Gampopa.]

I heard the precious guru say this.

"Generally, there are two ways of approaching dharma: through understanding characteristics and through gaining realization. Hearing and contemplating are method only. What you need is something that does not become an assistant of affliction. That comes with the explanation of awareness's fruition, though that by itself won't help at all. It does come, even if you do not learn the path through the prajnas of hearing and contemplating, by meeting a holy guru then practising his oral instructions. That is what has the capacity to produce realization in the mindstream.

"At the time of putting the guru's oral instructions into practice, abandonment of worldly thoughts is required; that is so true that it doesn't need to be discussed. And the words of treatises have to be forgotten; having heard a lot you will be very sharp on words but very dull over the meaning and your qualities will become faults. If you are going to do practice that becomes real, it is necessary to abide in five dharmas: having the guru's blessings; having decided to sever the ties to the world; knowing that no matter where you are born in the six classes of migrators, it is suffering; knowing that all sentient beings are mothers and fathers, not separating from the mind of enlightenment mind, loving kindness and compassion.

"The paths of shamatha and vipashyana need to be produced in the mindstream. That involves the two distinct phases of putting a lance into a mouse-hole and of flourishing a lance in space[230].

------

[230] You put the lance into the mouse-hole and you cannot move it around because there is no space to do so. It's hard work. That is the practice of shamatha in which you use your weapon to kill thoughts without the space of vipashyana. Then you put the lance up into space
(continued...)

"You must please the guru from whom you receive the authoritative statements on how to practise and merge your mind with his. This Kagyu lineage is profound because of having the command seals. It is not to be given to those who are not capable of accomplishment. If the samaya is corrupted, it is a cause of being cut off from the dakinis. Therefore, having pleased the guru and with samaya un-corrupted, do not talk about the oral instructions but, through his blessings, let realization shine forth from within. The guru is the vajra-holder; never see him as separate from you and in doing so, siddhi will arise."

———— ◆◆◆ ————

"It is very important to make the mind trainings of the three beings of the Kadampa Stages of the Path relevant to your life. If you do not, not only will the innate become blurred, as with floaters[231] in the eye, but because of attachment to relatives, lands, wealth, possessions, it will go down, not up. Therefore, mentally cast aside this life and develop certainty that all dharmas seen and heard are dream-like, illusion-like. If you train the enlightenment mind of loving kindness and compassion, even if you do not have the innate, it will go up, and not go down.

"If the innate really has been produced once in the mindstream, that is enough to start. There are five things related to it. The innate's entity is as follows: it is the fact which is not non-existent but is free from birth and cessation. Its characteristic is as follows: it is not produced by cause and condition; becoming a buddha does

---

[230](...continued)
and flourish it there. This is connected with reaching emptiness through the practice of vipashyana. There is a further explanation of these two approaches in the teachings of part ten of Dusum Khyenpa's interviews.

[231] For floaters, see the glossary.

not make it and becoming a sentient being does not alter it. The fruition is as follows: that, free from birth and cessation, is the dharmakaya; due to its blessings and to merit accumulated, the two form kayas shine forth. The experience is as follows: bliss, luminosity, and no-thought which cannot be shown by any example arises; the experience with those that arises from Fierce Heat is a cause; the cause of the arising of the innate is Fierce Heat. The innate having been produced also is the cause of prajna alone without Fierce Heat. There is a small enhancement could be made because when there is no Fierce Heat, method and prajna are not paired.

"For the Four Yogas, the Yoga of One-Pointedness is that moment of awareness where there is no stoppage of the luminosity. The Yoga of Freedom from elaboration is that rigpa's entity is seen as birthless. With this, there is no hope upwards to buddhahood, no concern downwards to samsara, and in between with no grasping to appearances, no being deceived by other. The Yoga of One Taste is that you realize the inseparability of appearance and emptiness. The Yoga of Non-Meditation is that, whatever comes forth, whatever is produced, it shines forth in one entity thus, everything at the time of the thought process comes as meditation.

"Bardo is as follows. Beings with best faculties have no bardo. Those with middling ones make bardo into the path. Those with least ones take a rebirth. Those with the best have real realization shine forth; the body is that of a sentient being but the mind is that of a buddha. You might ask, 'Then, do the qualities of buddhahood not appear?' and the answer is that they do not but are there; it is like the moon on the first day of the lunar month. You might ask, 'When will all the qualities be manifested?' and the answer is when there is separation from the trap of the body. You might ask, 'For the middling one, how is bardo made into path?' and the answer is that the awarenesses of the three times of the present, dream, and death are mixed with bardo.

"If mind's entity is seen, that is what it is to know self-knowing wisdom. It is called 'seeing truth'. It has been said, 'The body is a sentient being and the mind is buddha'; if everything has been realized as non-dual, even though there are differing grounds and paths, there is no gradual process of opening them up. Without separation from the three poisons, one abides on the level of nirvana. Without engaging in complete purification of the obscurations, the wisdom of knowing everything is attained."

"Well then", I asked, "What is the difference between that person and buddha?" The guru replied as follows.

"New moon and empty moon are the one moon but its qualities are not the same in each case. Similarly, because both have realized the dharmata, they are buddha types but their qualities are not the same. The yogin still has not abandoned discursive thought. He has discursive thought, afflictions, suffering, and so on and because of that the buddha's qualities are not manifest at all.

"You could ask, 'Well then, why did buddhahood take three uncountable aeons[232]?' The answer is that getting to realization is easy but getting to its real form is extremely difficult.

"You could ask, 'Are discursive thought and obscuration gradually cleansed or suddenly cleansed?' The answer is that the sutras and treatises on them usually say 'they are cleansed through three uncountable aeons'. However, there is also sudden purification. A person who has a vast accumulation, who is fortunate, who has greater prajna, and who is interested in the profound and vast can,

---

[232] Shakyamuni Buddha explained clearly that it took him three countless great aeons (the length of time approximately of three of our universes) to become a full buddha.

through meditation on the samadhi of absence of concept tokens[233], have the sudden cleansing; it is said,

> With lack of self of dharmas and the person
> Your afflicted knowables are permanently purified
> Through the absence of concept tokens.

And,

> Just as a small lamp dispels great darkness all at once, so the karma and afflictions accumulated throughout many aeons are dispelled by one moment of realization.

And,

> I, a layman practitioner have a low class body but a mind that is buddha.

The obscuration that comes from having taken birth can be cleansed in one countless aeon or one life or one year or a month, a day, during the dawn, in one session, one moment or a fraction of a moment.

"A guru with realization who instructs a fortunate disciple to mentally cast aside this life first ripens him with empowerment then has the ripened trains in the method that does the liberating, twofold development and completion. Development stage consists of meditation on being an illusory deity. Completion stage with elaboration consists of practising with the channels and winds, and without elaboration consists of practising the mind of luminosity being empty. Undistracted meditation on those produces certainties[234]. If mind's entity is not lost, not even the subtlest discursive

---

[233] This is one of the three samadhis of the Prajnaparamita teachings, also called signlessness.

[234] For any given level of practice, the theory which goes with it says that such and such attainment can be gained through doing such and such. When one has actually practised and gained definitive experi-

(continued...)

thought will become visible; like a cloud in the sky it will proceed to self-pacify itself. If one attempts to practise this state for long periods, the qualities of the entity do not become visible and, on top of that, there is the danger of being born in the formless realm.

"When the two, development and completion, are meditated on like that in isolation[235], eight qualities arise. If the sign which is like smoke arises, then wind and appearances have been stopped and the wind has been inserted into the Dhūti. The whole body will be blissful and mind will be pleased. Body bliss which roils, is only partially there, or is not balanced shows that the winds have become trapped in places which are not their own. If the second sign shines forth, it means that appearances are coming as experience and would no longer be referred to as 'external appearance', rather, they are mindness being experienced. If the third sign appears, it means that no-thought has come into the luminosity, that wind has been put into mind. If the fourth sign appears, it means this view's fact and all dharmas are known-and-illumined and that the four enlightened activities are accomplished. The view's fact is the certainty that in mindness there is rational mind. Known-and-illuminated means all of samsara and nirvana shines forth as luminosity. The four enlightened activities are accomplished is that, without having to do approach practice[236], all are accomplished without difficulty.

---

[234](...continued)
ence of those attainments, one has gained the certainties mentioned in the theory of the practice.

[235] There are three isolations within isolation: isolation of body, speech, and mind. These are fully explained in *A Juggernaut of the Non-Dual View, Teachings of the Second Drukchen, Gyalwang Je* by Tony Duff, published by Padma Karpo Translation Committee, 2011, ISBN: 978-9937-572-07-1.

[236] Tib. bsnyen grub. Approach practice is the general name for development stage practice given because one gets closer to the deity

(continued...)

The fourth is that shamatha has been taken to the end; wind has been put into luminosity. If the fifth arises, it is that the prajna of vipashyana has been produced; the wisdom sign of the body seen as a rainbow or mass of light or empty with nothing to be seen and no seer, comes.

"Generally, the Great Vehicle consists of both Paramita and Secret Mantra. For the first, the path of Paramita, one starts by taking the common refuge then trains in the eight trainings. Then, the special taking of refuge is done as a preliminary, after which one does the arousing of the aspirational mind directed at supreme enlightenment. After that, one studies the five trainings to provide a method by which aspiration could be accomplished. Then one trains in the seven branches. Then one does the arousing of the engaging mind directed at supreme enlightenment.

"One trains in the trainings of the three types of discipline. Via the six minds, one trains in the three types of training. Having trained in those three types of training, one is carried along both by direct full-ripening and indirect correspondence with the cause[237]. On the Path of Accumulation and the Path of Connection, the full-ripened fruit brings a body with freedom and connection[238]. The full-ripened fruition for the Path of Seeing is that one becomes a master of Jambuvipa; for the Path of Meditation it is that one continues in a deity's body; on the tenth level, it is that one arises as a great lord. That is all other's appearance. The fruition of separation on the Path of Accumulation is separation from the eight worldly dharmas. On the Path of Connection, it is separation from the pair, grasped-

---

[236](...continued)
by doing visualization and recitation, which is what is being referred to here. Approach practice is part of Development Stage practice.

[237] These are two types of karmic ripening.

[238] That is, a precious human rebirth that is characterized by freedom and connection.

grasping. On the Path of Seeing, it is separation from the discards belonging to Seeing. On the Path of Meditation, it is separation from the discards belonging to Meditation. On the tenth level, the vajra-like samadhi is obtained which leads to the seeds of karma for becoming[239] on the alaya consciousness being stopped and then, in a sequence of two moments, there is arrival on the eleventh level Total Light, the occurrence without interruption of the great bliss dharmakaya on at all times which has been manifested, like space, pervading everything. Due to prayers of aspiration, the form bodies' appearances shine forth for those of pure karma who are to be tamed.

"Second, the Secret Mantra Path. How is it? First, to ripen what is not ripened, there is empowerment. The vase empowerment generates body, speech, and mind as the deity's enlightened body, speech, and mind. The five afflictions are generated as the five wisdoms. The body is isolated. The secret empowerment does the work of generation of bliss in one's own mind. Speech is isolated. The prajna-wisdom empowerment does the work of generation of un-outflowed bliss. Mind is isolated. The fourth, precious word empowerment introduces mind's emptiness as the dharmakaya entirely freed of the net of elaborations and the great bliss kaya as dharmadhatu wisdom. Then the disciples hear about the root downfalls and hear the *Fifty Verses of Guru Devotion*[240].

"Then, for the path that does the liberating, first, development stage is shown. Then, completion stage with elaboration—the channels and winds, and so on—is shown. Then completion stage without elaborations—the ultimate—is shown. Meditation on those brings samadhi. Then four inner signs come forth.

---

[239] For becoming, see the glossary.

[240] A text by the Indian acharya Ashvagosha used in all schools of Tibetan Buddhism as the basic text on how to behave in relation to one's guru.

Shamatha is taken to the end and by that worldly absorption[241] is achieved. When the fifth sign shines forth, shamatha and vipashyana have been joined in union. The three signs of progress arise: the external one is that one does not sense that one has a body; the inner one is that one does not sense the movement of outer and inner breaths; the secret one is that no-thought bliss arises. That is meditation's luminosity. At the point of death, one relies on the oral instructions for apprehending the bardo; the absorption[242] luminosity and nature luminosity are mixed and that does the work of manifesting the great bliss kaya.

"You could ask, 'What are dharma[243] and dharmata and rational mind?'[244] What dharma is in actual fact is one's own rigpa, the enlightenment mind. What dharmata is in actual fact is being right on that, without moving from it and without creating anything; in the end it does not fall apart due to a condition, it is primordially pure, it is uncontrived, self-arising wisdom. What is rational mind in actual fact? It is, similar to how the view would be realized, staying in no minding whatsoever, no-thought, the state of the great equality, without any contrivance. There is no altering and no meditation to be done. With it, wisdom is abiding in itself. The

---

[241] Skt. dhyāna, Tib. bsam gtan.

[242] Skt. dhyāna, Tib. bsam gtan.

[243] In this paragraph, dharma means phenomena.

[244] Dharma here means phenomena. They are in fact the luminosity of one's own mind. Dharmata is the reality of the situation which includes those dharmas or phenomena. Rational mind usually means dualistic mind and is pejorative. Here he is explaining how wisdom includes the rational mind as a non-dualistic occurrence. There has to be that sort of enlightened rational mind or wisdom would not have the ability to make distinctions between this and that, which is what rational mind does.

trickery[245] of concept tokens might arise from it, but, since in the fact itself there is no movement and no change, there is no suppression or furtherance[246] of it to be done and one meditates staying undistractedly in the self-arising awareness. Even though sinking or agitation occurs, it is a sensation in the state of the equality. Should it happen sometime that there is rigpa's knowing the fact, it is no more than self-knowing. Should that self-knowing come as a thought 'This', there is nothing through that that could be shown to or expressed to others.[247]

"The five introductions are: introduction using the examples of sleep and dream to appearances being mind; introduction using the examples of water and ice to appearances being inseparable with emptiness; introduction using the example of empty space to mindness being empty; introduction using the example of a sugar lolly to many being in one taste; and introduction using the example of a flowing river to the dharmakaya being a flow.

"'There are also five minds of buddha'. The mind of realization come up as wisdom is like a forest fire spreading; the mind which is concept tokens self-liberating is like ice melting into a lake; the mind of inseparable appearance-emptiness is like meeting a person already known; the mind of wisdom as a mass is like the core of the sun; the mind of samadhi that has no arising and entering is like having arrived on an island of jewels and gold.

---

[245] Trickery here means the stuff that comes from the wisdom in a miraculous way. It is trickery because it is illusory, even though it appears, like the trickery of a magician.

[246] For suppression and furtherance, see the glossary.

[247] This section on rational mind is saying that there can be a mind that makes the distinction between this and that which is not the dualistic version that all samsaric beings use but the version that is part of enlightened being.

"The holders of the lineage of Jowo Lord's commands give the four things of luminosity, no-thought, subtlety, and pacification most significance and bliss the least, given their concern that it could lead to attachment. A Secret Mantra person on the other hand uses bliss as a method that will lead to accomplishment given that no-thought can be produced from it. If you train in channels and winds, you gain control over the awareness and so it is possible to augment the inner layer in that way. Bliss, luminosity, and no-thought arises because of it."[248]

————— ♦ ♦ ♦ —————

"I asked Jetsun Milarepa about this and he replied, 'That is how it works.' Doing the channels and winds meditation I have taught you also reduces the afflictions as a side-effect—but that as such does not fulfil the requirements of the path and should not have any great significance attached to it. The thing of great significance is to gain certainty in relation to mindness's entity. If mind's[249] entity of bliss, luminosity, and no-thought is understood to be empty,

---

[248] In this paragraph, he is making the point that those who follow the path of Paramita, such as Atisha and his followers, pick out four features that are important for the development of abiding and de-emphasize bliss for the reason stated. However, the Vajra Vehicle practitioner has the option of emphasizing bliss as the vehicle to an abiding, which has the advantage that it can be also be used to gain control over the innate mind, so that the inner layer, wisdom, is brought forth by working on the outer layer, bliss, and so on.

[249] There is not a mistake here; the previous sentence says and means mindness and this sentence says and means mind. "Mind's entity of bliss, luminosity, and no-thought" means the meditative experiences achieved within dualistic mind which can be penetrated by knowing their emptiness. By doing so, one gets to the entity, mindness. By not doing so, one remains a worldly person, even with the bliss, luminosity, and no-thought which has been developed through meditation.

unchanging, and un-interrupted, then there will be certainty in relation to appearance. When appearance has not been understood as mind, the absence of certainty in relation to it is merely the view of the world. It has been said,

> If mind thinks, 'Now I am happy',
> The cherishing of sadness of heart involved,
> Which is the mere husk of the seed, is painful, yet
> Migrators do this, producing only suffering for
>   themselves.

"Seeing the bliss to be the best then trying to prolong it will bring birth as a god of the desire realm; attachment to the luminosity will bring birth in the form realm; and keeping a pond of no-thought will bring birth in the formless realm. A shravaka will make a ground out of it them and, by doing so, will create dharmas which are the experience of concept tokens. One should not engage in a view of grasping as supreme[250] but view them as empty. The bodhisatva will make a ground out of them then train in samadhi, but the experience that comes from doing so is discursive thought. Discursive thought, one's own mind, is to be taken onto the path as wisdom. The bodhisatva's abiding alone will not fulfil the path—it is also found in fainting and being drunk on beer. No matter which of the various red and white thoughts[251] appear, they are rigpa

---

[250] The view of grasping as supreme is the name of one of the five bad views. It is the view in which a practice of austerity is viewed as supreme in itself without the practice being mixed with other correct understandings such as the understanding that phenomena, including the practice of the austerity are empty, the understanding of karma, and so on. Usually it is used in reference to non-Buddhist practitioners who take a particular exercise in austerity as an ultimate practice but here Gampopa is applying it to the lower levels of Buddhist practice in which there is still grasping at the practices themselves.

[251] Red and white thoughts are the thoughts produced in relation to the
(continued...)

which can be experienced as luminosity. One's own rigpa, given that it does not exist by way of a nature, is, if ascertained, realization. If abiding occurs for someone, meditation but with absence of thought is what has to have its duration lengthened[252]. If you see the entity, and attempt to prolong it, that is a sign that you have not understood the key points involved with its being interrupted and not. Primordially speaking, it never has or will have an interruption of its flow. Someone who has had the realization of ascertaining the entity then takes the approach of knowing appearances as mind then making mind into his reliance through freeing it from identification, which brings an experience of evenness like the centre of space. At that point, meditation associated with concept tokens is no longer necessary because the elephant of mind[253] has been found.[254]

"You might ask, 'How is the investigation for pin-pointing samsara and nirvana done?' A guru with realization introduces a fortunate

---

[251](...continued)
main channels of the subtle body, roughly speaking. The point is that they include all types of mental thought and physical appearance that occur to a being.

[252] Here, "absence of thought" does not mean that there should be no thought but that there should be no dualistic-type discursive thought. In other words, an abiding leaning towards wisdom is what is needed.

[253] In the ancient Indian way of talking, an elephant is used as the example of something which is to be found by searching for it. Thus, elephant of mind means "mind as the thing to be sought and found".

[254] If you look carefully, this has been taught in a progression of the meditation of a worldly person, a shravaka, a bodhisatva working on one-pointedness without wisdom, and a yogin practising Mahamudra. The comments about the yogin's approach are also given in a sequential order.

student to both rigpa and not-rigpa[255]. The student meditates accordingly which leads to the birth of realization in relation to the fact[256] that was experienced at that time. His experience of it is rigpa shining forth in freedom from elaboration, which arises as having un-outflowed bliss. Being unsure of it is what leads to the the certainty that sentient beings do have not-rigpa. The spectacle of mind's illusions seen by sentient beings is not existent because the buddhas of the three times do not see it and equally is not non-existent because sentient beings' experience of it is something which the buddhas cannot stop.

"There is threefold characteristic, nature, and entity. Characteristic refers to rigpa's shining forth in various ways. Nature is the rigpa's stoppageless luminosity. Entity is wisdom which is experiencing those, its facts. One whole explanation of this mind is given primarily from the perspective of method and another whole explanation is given primarily from the perspective of prajna. For those of low mental ability, the foremost instruction of method is mainly used and then, when the mind has improved, foremost instruction of prajna is mainly used. Moreover, it works that, by using method, prajna naturally comes to the fore and becomes primary, and that, without severing appearance and discursive thought, they naturally stop of themselves.

"When the Kadampa approach to the view is put to the fore, it does not mean that talk of 'it is like this tenet view' is given great significance, rather, it means that, by looking at the view, the seeing of emptiness is given the greatest significance. Guru Mila did not give great significance to talk that said 'it is like this tenet view' either; he gave the greatest significance to self-shining forth, saying that a view that did not arise from meditation was problematic." He said,

---

[255] ... that is, to both enlightened knowing and ignorant knowing ...

[256] ... of the entity ...

"The method for determining the view is to give significance to the channels, winds, and chakras."

He said, "Advocacy of a view needs to be done on the basis of internal experience of all dharmas. If views are known on the basis of inner experience, you will never be adversely affected by any tenet system; you will not be adversely affected by what the Mind Only school asserts—self-knowing, self-illumination—nor by the Middle Way's birthlessness, nor even by Mantra's emptiness. If on the other hand, you look at this externally, and express it verbally, it would have to not contradict the seven sections taught by the siddhas or the tantras taught by Vajradhara."

He said, "The three steps of karmic cause and result are generation, propulsion, and completion. They correspond to rigpa enlightenment mind[257], development-completion, and the three kayas, and also to not-rigpa ignorance, the karma of evil deeds, and the three bad migrations.[258]"

He said, "Discursive thought is both subtle and coarse: the coarse one is its grasping in deep solidification at containers and contents[259]; and the subtle one is its production in various ways by the

---

[257] Rigpa enlightenment mind is a term used in Essence Mahamudra to refer to rigpa. It means that rigpa is the ultimate enlightenment of a buddha, not that it is the path enlightenment mind of a bodhisatva.

[258] In other words, karmic cause and effect with its threefold process is something that belongs to both enlightened and un-enlightened processes. In the former case, it corresponds to the development, through three levels of enlightenment, and in the latter case, it corresponds to the development of samsara, which in its worst case results in migrations into the three bad realms.

[259] One aspect of the mind that grasps at a self is that it solidifies empty reality into a very concrete reality. This solidification is what

(continued...)

moment. Its one entity has four characteristics: mentating mind, rigpa, mind, and wind. When it is grasping an object, it is mentation. When it is doing the work of knowing and comprehending that, it is rigpa. When it is un-stopped illumination of that fact, it is mind. When it is based on the channels and winds and includes them, it is wind."

He said, "Generally, for this profound Secret Mantra, the three things: practise of its oral instructions, the experiences involved, and information about the yogin's body are best kept hidden. Secret Mantra is explained to be 'secret'. If it is not kept secret, the attainment associated with it in general will be lost. Also, one's personal experiences are to be discussed with the guru and not even with friends with whom you share your experiences in general and with whom you have pure samaya." Then Rinpoche said to me, "I have not kept it secret in the past nor do I keep it secret now; having this little certainty in it that I do will prevent my showing it to others from turning into loss. My experience of it could not be lost this way, but where has yours gone?!"

He said, "Relying on gurus who talk to you out of their meditational experience and whose blessings have caused a little certainty in you, and compared to whom your qualities are no more than a hundredth part of a hair, you are introduced to the awareness. We talk only about samsara and nirvana and buddhas and sentient beings; we do not talk about recognizing rigpa and not."

He said, "What are the five buddhas, boiled down? They are the front and back of your hand. Therefore, by looking inwards, first a very pure form of rigpa arises and that is the Yoga of One-Pointedness. By intense supplications to the guru and meditation on it, evil deeds are exhausted then rigpa freed from elaborations dawns.

---

[259](...continued)
manufactures the container worlds and contained sentient beings that make up samsaric reality. See deep solidification in the glossary.

That is the joy in which there is no joy to be made. What was not discovered before has been discovered. It is like a poor man discovering treasure. Appearances, without having been rejected mentally, are decided on as mind. Appearances, free of all suppression and furtherance go onto being indeterminate. Thus appearances, having nothing that stays afterwards, become uninterruptedly part of the experience. That happens whether you meditate or do not meditate. There is no equipoise on the fact and post-attainment following that. When just a little finalization has been obtained, appearances shine forth sometimes as empty, sometimes as illusions, and sometimes they stop. After that, thoughts become ornaments to wear. The thought process is allowed to go wherever it wants, in any way it wants."

———— ◆ ◆ ◆ ————

Dusum Khyenpa asked, "For The Man from Mar[260], what was the difference between the Paramita path and the Secret Mantra path?" The reply came, "For Paramita, complete emancipation is Path of Accumulation, exhaustion is the Path of Connection, overwhelming is Path of Seeing. That corresponds in the Secret Mantra path to the three of best, middling, and least.

"A king avoids the full-ripening that belongs to the conduct of the immature. He is tamed into peace. His conduct is made attractive. That and the other parts, what they are and what they do correspond to the Path of Accumulation[261]. Then, having attained a little

───────────────

[260] Marpa the translator.

[261] From "A king ..." to here is an indirect reference to the process of ripening the disciple through empowerment and all other activities that precede the main practice of the Vajra Vehicle, which is development and completion stage practice. Empowerment treats a disciple as though he were a king and that approach sets him apart in every-
(continued...)

finality through development stage, he performs the Secret Mantra
conduct and gains some progress. At that time, the conduct of the
secret is to be done. The things needed for it, isolation, enhance-
ments, appropriate views, and so on are used to do the conduct. At
the time of things needed, name, and so on are given secretly. This
conduct of the secret corresponds to the Path of Connection. With
non-dual self-knowing and other-knowing, rigpa has its worldly-
type discursive thoughts tamed, then, for the purpose of others, the
yogic activities of rigpa—killing and reviving, hooking what has
gone to space, and so on—are done as the conduct, and this corresponds to the first bodhisatva level. The conduct of the great
equipoise corresponds to the Path of Seeing."

He asked, "What would the bodhisatva path be seen to correspond
with?" The reply came, "One offering of the meaning of meditation." He said, "At the start where there is nothing, if there is no
difficulty in regard to one-pointedness of mind, it corresponds to
the Path of Accumulation. Within accumulation, if there is no
difficulty in regard to one-pointedness of mind, it corresponds to
the Path of Connection. If there is no difference between equipoise
and post-attainment, it is close to corresponding with the first
bodhisatva level."

"If you ask what the difference is between Paramita and Secret
Mantra, Paramita is to make the generic image's superfice into the
object[262]; using logic, all dharmas are dissected in order to arrive at

---

[261](...continued)
thing he does from the approach of a person in the Paramita and lower
vehicles.

[262] Tib. don spyi'i rnam pa. The conceptual structure by which objects
are known in rational mind is called a generic image. It is not the
object known in direct perception by the faculty consciousness. The
generic image is not the emptiness which would be the entity of the
(continued...)

their non-existence and then, having emptied them so that they are like a completely purified space, the rational mind is placed on that. A Secret Mantra person takes the actual fact and makes that into the path. By intensively adjusting the winds with the method path, they are inserted into the Dhūti. At that time, using the key point of non-dual wind-mind, no-thought and bliss arise in the luminosity. When that has been done, the guru introduces you with, 'This awareness of yours—your own mind, your own rigpa, emptiness itself—well this is it!' That having been done, it is the disciple's turn to do something, which is that he has to do the meditation for that. By doing so, his initial experience in the introduction is freed from the view of grasping as supreme which brings certainty of his own mind being the innate. Rigpa is luminosity that is bliss and emptiness. Not being distracted from that is samadhi. When the vajra-like samadhi has been finalized, that rigpa is the dharmakaya.

"Furthermore, Paramita is the severing of exaggeration. Separating oneself from the external, grasped objects via a clearness of view, causes them to fall apart which in turn makes them empty. The grasped aspect is removed bringing what is referred to as 'being without grasper' and the object of the grasped factor having been thereby annihilated, there is this, which is referred to as 'the shackle of grasping released of itself'. In that way, there is no examination-analysis done in relation to the internal, grasping mind.

"Secret Mantra cuts exaggeration internally. No examination-analysis is done on the object, instead, it is dealt with by sealing it. The internal grasping mind is looked at and, by looking at it, the certainty occurs that it is has not been born to begin with, does not disintegrate at the end, and is not abiding anywhere in the present,

---

[262](...continued)
item but is the superficial aspect of it, which is called the superfice. This conceptual superfice is the mistake that rational mind trumps up. Finding its absence leads to the emptiness of the object in this system. For more on generic image, see the glossary.

and therefore is not existing by way of any sort of nature. More-over, if it is also not wisdom's object, then how could the discursive-thought-based rational mind see it? The fact of it shines forth very pure from deep in rational mind, which is experience. Not being distracted from it is abiding. Knowing its entity as not having been born from the beginning is realization. If it has not introduced to you by the guru, lengthening the duration of that experience will lead you to a flat emptiness and that kind of blanked-out state being taken as emptiness is a trumped-up wisdom which cannot be used as path, though, given that it frees you from clinging, it has a small amount of overall benefit. So you can see that, to be guided along the path of emancipation, you need a guru who has experience and realization."

"Paramita makes intention into the path and Secret Mantra makes blessings into the path[263]. Secret mantra does not look at the grasped object, rather, it investigates precisely the internal side, the grasping mind. Moreover, the guru introduces you to it. He intro-duces you, in a way that is like being separated from the four objects of illusions, reflections, and so on, to the mindness that exists primordially within you so that you are left free of all doubts about whether it exists or not. After that introduction, you meditate and, through that, confidence is produced. By prolonging the duration of the fact known in meditation, you see mind's emptiness. For this, there is both certainty and uncertainty. If realization is finalized, it is the vajra wisdom of a lord of yogins. That person will be a vajra master and will be non-deceptive. Having found the fact

------

[263] Paramita works by using the dualistic mind of intending to go beyond dualism. Secret mantra on the other hand uses the direct blessings of someone who has already progressed to the state beyond rational mind to show the practitioner that state of mind. In other words, Paramita is about directing yourself towards a future result, while being on the side of rational mind, whereas Secret Mantra is about trying to be the future result by relying on direct connection to it, now.

in the most excellent way, he will have no desire for the dharma of
tenet systems. Having discovered a wish-fulfilling jewel, he will not
desire to be a monk. His root of samsara will have been cut. For
him, not-rigpa ignorance having been liberated in its own place, all
formatives[264], and so on have been stopped.

"In general, there are three paths. Making inference into the path
goes like this: all dharmas are dissected using the method of being
free from one and many, making them into being without nature.
That brings the practitioner to the point of 'no further destination
beyond this' as it is called. That is how the meditation is done.
Making blessings into the path involves reliance on the development stage in which the development of a deity's body cleanses the
channels and winds, and so on. Making direct perception into the
path is innate Mahamudra.[265]

"Moreover, for three paths, the path of discarding the ground is
Paramita: there is that to be discarded and the antidote used to
discard it, seen as separate items. The path of transforming the
ground is Secret Mantra: the basis is transformed and developed
into a deity's body; what is based on it is transformed, the faculties
being made into vajra and padma; and all dharmas are transformed,
afflictions being made into the path and thoughts being made into
wisdom, with stains washed by stains and thought severed by
thought. The path of knowing the ground is Mahamudra: there is
nothing to be discarded and no antidote, no transformation to be
done and no transformer to do it—all of that is mind's trickery;
instead, mindness, the fact which primally is without birth, has

---

[264] Formatives are the contents of the fourth skandha, named for the
fact that they are what cause the formation of future lives.

[265] Inference is the use of logic. It is the approach of the sutra system.
Blessings are the approach of Secret Mantra's development stage.
Direct perception of reality is the approach of Secret Mantra's comple-
tion stage.

dharmakaya inherent in it so, by recognizing, seeing, and habituating oneself to it, one goes to buddhahood.

"Moreover, for the three paths, the person of dull faculty with faith enters the Path of Accumulation, which is Paramita. The one of middling faculty with thoughts and afflictions enters the path of method, which is Secret Mantra. The one of sharp faculty with prajna enters suchness, which is Mahamudra.

"It has been said,

> Shamatha and vipashyana is
> The door to all dharmas.

This pair has five topics associated with it: cause, action, obstructors, obscuration, and total purification of the path. Shamatha's cause is completely pure discipline; vipashyana's cause is the prajna of hearing and contemplating. Shamatha's path is the action of liberating oneself from the fetters of concept tokens; vipashyana's path is the action of liberating oneself from the fetters that take a bad birthplace. Shamatha's obstructors are to hanker after body and possessions. Vipashyana's obstructors are to be not satisfied with stories about the noble ones. Sticking with entertainment and taking it to be all right in even the slightest degree is an obstructor for both. The obscurations: agitation, regret, and doubt obscure shamatha; sleep and dullness obscure vipashyana; and desire, other aims, and harmful mind obscure both. Overcoming dullness and sleep fully is the right approach that goes with shamatha's path. Overcoming agitation and regret fully is the total purification that goes with vipashyana's path. When the two of those fully overcome the two obscurations, the completely pure dharmakaya is obtained.

"The five faults of using emptiness as a pillow are that: the profound dharma activities are discarded; relying on a view of words, karmic cause and effect is reduced to no importance; an empty blankness causes pride and reduction of other's importance; and, divorced from method, the path turns into the shravaka's path. As it says in a doha,

> Engagement in emptiness divorced from compassion
> Causes the supreme path not to be discovered.

"The fault of meditation with emptiness erased from it is that the root of samsara is not cut with the result that the place of escape from it is not found. A doha says,

> Well then, if you meditate only on compassion,
> Remaining in samsara, emancipation will not be
>   obtained …

and,

> You might have made ten thousand offerings to the
>   deity
> But that will only become a fetter for you.
> That sort of thing does not sever this samsara.

"The fault of not knowing the times for meditation is this. Having developed the fictional enlightenment mind, if you do not meditate on superfactual enlightenment mind, dharmakaya wisdom, not having had its seed planted, will not shine forth. Your emptiness meditation will be lost with faults of being sealed with not knowing, and so on. The fault of not knowing the points of deviation from emptiness, are the point of deviation of view, the point of deviation of meditation, and so on.

"Jetsun Mila said, 'Due to becoming acquainted with the view, I have no view.' He said, 'Because of your view, you pursue a practice that leads nowhere. This is to have the point of being mistaken regarding emptiness.'

"There are five points of being mistaken. Going astray in sealing with emptiness is that, having apprehended emptiness as existent to start with, you practise dharma activities then seal them with an

emptiness which is extreme. Going astray in relation to the antidote is that, at the time when affliction has arisen, you have the
antidote of knowing that it is birthless but, instead of applying that,
you make the affliction into something to be discarded and then,
with that as an antidote, meditate on it being empty. Going astray
in relation to the path is that, having decided upon rigpa—the
empty, birthless dharmakaya—as existing inherently within, you
assert that you attain dharmakaya by meditating on all dharmas
being empty. Going astray in relation to the inner disposition of
knowables is as follows. All dharmas are one's own mind. By
having looked at mind but not having looked at what has to be done
to make that sufficient, you allow that all the dharmas of samsara
and nirvana are empty of nature, primordially pure, primordially
liberated, primordial buddhahood and then, having said 'There is
no meditation to be done at all', you rest yourself in an emptiness
trumped up by rational mind. Going astray in a rationally con-
structed emptiness is as follows. It is sufficient to set yourself
without alteration in the state of birthless mind but, not knowing
that, you dissect all dharmas with rigpa then, having created a state
like the centre of space, you place your rational mind on that,
taking that to be empty. In doing so, you are settling rational mind
on an awareness that is a flattened emptiness[266]."

He said, "Well then, what is true, un-mistaken emptiness? It is
mindness, the innate unaltered, without any support at all, its doorway[267] never stopped at all, never falling into extremes, never given
to long-term possibility, having no aim so being without hope and
fear, divorced from anger and desire, not demonstrable by any
example, not arrived at through any verbal expression at all, appearing clearly to buddha. It naturally arises for the yogins due to their

---

[266] A flattened emptiness is one that is merely empty, devoid of all
content. The term conveys the sense of an unlimited stretch devoid of
all features.

[267] ... to appearances shining forth from it ...

reliance on an unthinkable number of methods at which time it is thought severing itself of itself, affliction ceasing of itself, wisdom naturally shining forth, the view realized by its own strength, never impeded by conventions. Being the direct experience of mind, it is impossible to express it in speech—it is like the bliss of a young woman and like the dream of a mute.

"Mindness is co-emergence. Wisdom is had by all sentient beings. When it is like the poor man's treasure[268], it has no benefit. It is easy to realize, it is right in front of you. It is divorced from all the difficulties that come with the process of identification. It is beyond being an object of thought.

"You might ask what are the methods for its realization? They are the accumulation of the accumulations and supplication."

❀   ❀   ❀

[Part seven: a collection of six interviews with Gampopa.]

»[269] Namo Guru.

He asked, "There is both mind and light of mind, isn't there?" The reply came, "That is so. If appearances are then included within mind, there is nothing else than mind alone."

---

[268] This refers to a famous example that illustrates how sentient beings have this but do not realize it. It is like a poor man who has a treasure buried directly under his house but does not know of it so makes no use of it and remains impoverished in the process.

[269] The text from here down to the next closing brace is repeated starting on page 241 of Yogin Choyung's interview.

He asked, "There is both dharmakaya and light of dharmakaya, isn't there? The two do not exist apart from dharmakaya alone, isn't that so?" The reply came, "That is so. When dharmakaya has become the single sufficient solution, there is nothing apart from dharmakaya alone."

He asked, "For a nirmanakaya buddha like Shakyamuni who had the remainder of a full-ripened body, would that count as being the single sufficient solution?" The reply came, "It would. The body having gone to nirvana, its birth was purified, so it was not there in own appearance though there were form kayas that occurred in others' appearance."

He asked, "In regard to the two form kayas not being there in own appearance, would you say that this is an absence in own appearance of discursive thought that operates as the doing of others' purposes or would you say that it is an absolute absence of in own appearances of thought?" The reply came, "There are two different systems regarding that. The Kadampa geshes assert the former. Our guru asserts the latter. They are wholly in agreement on the point of asserting appearances within others' appearance."

He asked, "I am there with the fact, then lose touch with it because of distraction. Later, having regained mindfulness, I return to the fact. After being distracted for that interval, if looking again brings me back to dharmakaya, will that be alright or not? In that interval is there the capacity to become obscured or not? Is it necessary to meditate perpetually undistracted or not?"

The reply came, "If looking again after that makes dharmakaya go to dharmakaya, it is alright. The discursive thought of the interval does not have the capacity to cause obscuration. It is not necessary to be absolutely un-distracted—there is no function of distraction given that in actuality there is no distraction and non-distraction."

He said, "This is the mind of the Jetsun guru and the Buddha. It can't be taken higher or enhanced. «[270] Rinpoche said, "Still, when it is done, it is prajna's eye that sees it. That is how it is done. Co-emergence inexpressible by another initially is identified as rigpa. Having done so, the method for gaining experience in it is to put oneself in freshness, looseness, and no-contrivance and the experience of it is that discursive thought is experienced as one taste in the dharmata. Then the realization is, as has been said, that,

> The pervasive owner, the vajra kaya,
> Is unchanging and is all the time.

The meaning is as follows. 'Pervasive' is like space; being unborn it wholly pervades outer and inner, containers and contents[271]. 'Vajra kaya' means indestructible. 'Unchanging' means that, because it is primally, naturally spontaneously existing, it is without birth and cessation. 'All the time' is not like past, present, and future; it means without interruption. (It has been said,)

> Realization, like space, pervades everything.
> Experience, monkey-like, going all over the place,
>   changes.
> Non-dual awareness is compared to water and milk.
> The real nature is cultivated, elephant like.
> (The essential nature) is without change.

First realization, next familiarization (non-distraction), and last (wisdom itself) that becomes one's own space, then buddhahood."

Rinpoche said, "At the time of relentlessly cutting to the non-duality, you are at One-Pointedness, and the like."

---

[270] End of the first section of repeated text.

[271] For containers and contents, see the glossary.

He said, "It is the side of not-rigpa ignorance and what goes with it[272]. It involves meditation but there is no contradiction[273]. (Everything in one is that[274]) the entity is without interruption. It involves no meditation but there is no contradiction. It has no existence as an entity. Overall, this concerns the need for internal interdependency to cause the external appearances to disintegrate. The six migrator sentient beings' entity and the three types of noble ones' wisdom, and the buddha's enlightened mind are, all three, the same. If sentient beings realize it[275] they shift places to being one of the three types of noble ones. Except for experience of the entity, co-emergence, all experience is transitory. When the three of this life, the next, and the bardo, are known in equality, the oral instructions of Bardo are not necessary; it has been said that,

> Luminosity dwelt in continuously
> Results in the city of the bardo not being seen.

In other words, if you realize that buddha and sentient being are non-dual, that itself has included you in the noble ones. Then, although you generate great compassion, there is no concept of sentient beings.

"If this uninterrupted experience of the entity were the fictional, there would be the fault of its being transitory. If it were the superfactual, there would be the fault of seeing truth. The Jetsun asserted that: it is the superfactual; it is be inseparable with great

---

[272] There are two sides: not-rigpa and rigpa, samsara and nirvana. One-Pointedness is on the side of samsara, and the other three yogas are on the side of nirvana.

[273] It involves dualistic meditation but there is no contradiction with its being part of the non-dual path.

[274] Whereas One-Pointedness is one of many things, the entity when realized is a single thing that includes all.

[275] Here realize does not mean understand but is the special meaning of realize used in this system, which is to see it in direct perception.

bliss; and because of the place where it acts it is the fictional. However, he claimed no superfact separate from such and therefore stayed in accord with fact. Because of the key point of cause and effect being together as one, to assert when there is a cause that there is no effect would be the view of nihilism. It would be no different from the Tirthika's permanence and nihilism.

"Secret Mantra is to go to buddhahood in one life, one body. There is no consideration of whether the support is good or bad, no taking into account evil deeds' magnitude. If the entity does not come forth, evil deeds need to be cleansed. Evil deeds happen in the mind. The entity's coming forth happens in relation to an absence of evil deeds.

"The Mind Only school asserts a rigpa which is beyond the object of philosophers[276] for which there can be grasping in the luminosity. Mantra asserts rigpa that is birthless and luminosity which has no grasping in it. The entity is not observed by the buddhas even and it will not be observed by them either; there is nothing to see. From the aspect of conceived-of things and concept tokens, the entity is free of birth and cessation; it is uninterrupted; it has no thought in the luminosity; and the great bliss, if it had form, would not fit in the entire extent of space. At that point, when the breath ends and the body is cast off, although humans call it "death" we, because of not being separated from the entity, are deathless."

Rinpoche said, "If because of wanting experiences[277] one strays from the entity, liking it if bliss and luminosity arise, and not liking it if they don't, this is 'straying from the entity because of the

[276] Being beyond the object of philosophers means that it is beyond rational mind, that it is not something that can be known by concept.

[277] "Wanting experiences" means being attached to the three experiences of meditation, bliss, and so on, and pursuing them when one should not.

experiences'. If, even when there are bad experiences, the entity remains unstopped, the experiences together with realization are gained. Even when you have fallen asleep, the entity continues without interruption; it is the emission of thought. Experience might be interrupted but the entity has no interruption. All sights and sounds shine forth in one[278] then, meditating undistractedly from that state also is the entity. When distraction and non-distraction have become irrelevant, that is the greatest level of it. It is equality."

Rinpoche said, "From the aspect of the co-emergence's entity being a single ground, it sits as something which is all-pervasive. From the aspect of the entity being beyond both existent and non-existent, it sits as something without pervaded and pervader. It is both of those." And, "Because of being birthless, it sits as something that pervades everything." And, "Because the entity is something which is not seen, it is without pervasion."

Rinpoche, said, "When the full-ripened body has been discarded, this self-illumination without interruption goes on to a vast pure luminosity. Now the yogin's trap of the body has not disintegrated but when it has, that self-illumination without interruption goes on to a vastness of luminosity over one hundred times greater than it is now.

"Now what is the difference between Paramita (which does not assert experience) and Secret Mantra (which does assert experience)? There is a difference of path (a difference is made for all paths). There is Naropa's system with meditation and Maitripa's system without meditation[279]. At the time of the path there is meditation to be done. At the time of fruition meditation to be

---

[278] Meaning, "in the one entity".

[279] For the Kagyu lineage, Naropa is the great source of the practices of the path and Maitripa is the great source of the view.

done or not is irrelevant. All dharmas are one. Experience and realization are asserted as one. It is not an existent sort of thing and not mere non-existence, either. One has confidence in oneself, personally, but because of acquaintance with what has realization, an emptiness comparable to space happens. If the fact of mind's entity is realized, the supreme siddhi is attained regardless of whether the body is cast off or not. There is no going to excellence by casting off the body. A Secret Mantra person does not give relevance to the path. For as long as the thought[280] of the two form kayas is un-interrupted, he creates himself as the yidam deity in each instant. Realization comes indeed from oneself."

Rinpoche said, "There's neither virtue to be deliberately done nor, as a matter of course, is there engagement in evil deeds. The present body is a body of non-realization to start with, so one needs to set about the accumulation of merit. For as long as one needs to press the development of loving kindness and compassion by rational mind, the meditation is done as a path of non-distraction from the state of equality. In the fruition, there is none of the examination and analysis of whether there is distraction or not. For a beginner appearances come as enemies. The middling level meditator has appearances come as assistants. The best meditator gives no relevance to appearing and not appearing. The Middle Way to be established by rigpa[281] asserts appearances and mind as one; in this, mere appearance which is the fictional divorced from the duality of existence and non-existence, a merely nominal appearance, is what is practised. Then, if its continuity is cut, that

---

[280] Thought here does not mean samsaric thought but thought occurring within the entity as part of the entity. From the foregoing it will be understood that, in this system, thought which partakes of the entity is what produces the form bodies.

[281] This is the Middle Way of Secret Mantra, not the Middle Way of sutra—the latter establishes by reasoning and does not assert the union of appearance and mind.

is asserted to be going towards buddhahood. The guru sits even
higher than that."

Rinpoche was asked, "In the context of shared appearances[282], the
appearances are counted as mere illusions, merely nominal appearances, so wouldn't both the bliss present in the upper possibility,
sambhogakaya, and the suffering of the lower possibility, the hells,
be equal?" He answered, "Yes, it would." The question came,
"Well, then, does the upper one require the accumulation of the
two accumulations or not, does the lower one require that the two
obscurations be purified or not?" Rinpoche did not reply to that
but said, "If the two obscurations are to be purified, then there will
be a difference. Now, this equality just mentioned is an un-evaluated one[283]. The sambhogakaya and the hells equally are merely
nominal. The upper one needing the two accumulations to be
accumulated and also the lower one with its two obscurations are
merely nominal. They are merely one's own mind's appearances.
To that extent, they are equal."

He said, "From the standpoint of Mantra, the one thing is realization of Mahamudra. From the standpoint of Paramita, once the
Path of Seeing has been produced, there is no higher meaning to be
produced. If there were something higher to be gone to, what
would one use to go there? If there is no method for the purpose
of going higher, there is no key point concerning it and so it could
not be there. For those of the best of the best faculties, Secret
Mantra is relied on and there is no reliance at all on Paramita. A
yogin who is the best of the best has realization no different than
that of buddha but there is a difference in their qualities. For this

---

[282] Shared appearances are the appearances had in common by groups
of sentient beings whose karmas are similar. For example, human
beings as a whole have a certain level of shared appearance, and so on.

[283] "An un-evaluated one" means that it is known in direct perception
not known through dualistic rational mind.

single sufficient solution, everything starting from the Middle Way and Mahamudra and going through to the Tirthika systems at the other end is without suppression and furtherance. For something which has the entity, nothing at all can get in the way of it. Even though the signs of the path of Paramita are explained, because they are no more than Paramita's own style of grasping, they do not actually happen, therefore that path is provisional meaning."

Rinpoche said, "Development stage is a basis for both supreme and common ones[284]."

Rinpoche said, "Sleep and dreams are method, luminosity is prajna. Appearances are method. Meditation on the entity leads to inconceivable[285] compassion. Because appearances are rigpa enlightenment mind shining forth, recognizing them as own appearances is sufficient. Nothing at all needs to be done to them. If samaya is distilled right down, it condenses to realisation alone. There is no change in the primally present dharmata. The entity is dharmakaya. Becoming buddha does not entail any improvement of it; going to the hells does not entail any worsening of it. The entity having really been produced brings with it luminosity which has nothing standing in its way and so stopping it. There is nothing hindering it. The produced entity has experience with it. The experiencer has been stopped. At the level of a truly complete buddha, it is beyond mental or verbal expression. All vows and samayas are included in mind. Of the paths of abandonment, conduct, transformation, and knowing the ground, it is the latter."

———— ◆◆◆ ————

---

[284] That is, siddhis.

[285] Inconceivable here does not mean "unfathomable amounts of" but means "a type which cannot be conceived of".

Rinpoche said, "Drepa said, 'There is no loss of vows when karma has been sealed but evil deeds need to be purified.' My guru said, 'It is like topping up a Dre measure; in guru Marpa's system, it is one vow.'[286]"

He said, "Having seen the truth of the first bodhisatva level, un-outflowed vows are functioning. You yourself are the one who creates virtue and non-virtue. The entity without thought is self-illuminating, is unstopped. It primally is peaceful and unborn, and struck with the eight aspects of profundity of the *Heart Prajnaparamita*[287]. That entity which has no thought pervades all. At the times even of sleeping, intoxication, fainting, and death it is uninterrupted. Mantra explains sleep as the dharmakaya. It explains dream as nirmanakaya. It explains waking as sambhogakaya. However, in fact, dreams are thought. From the perspective of realization, Fierce Heat, and so on, meditations cause them to be the entity itself. Until the entity has been realized, any meditation done is thought. Losing the entity to experiences is the least fault. When that sort of thing has been purified, the certainty produced brings liberation. Losing realization to experiences is the greatest fault. Committing even the four root downfalls of the vows of personal emancipation, entails no loss of Secret Mantra's samaya;

---

[286] Drepa is one of Gampopa's Kadampa geshes. His guru is Milarepa. Karma is sealed off when the Path of Seeing has been achieved. Vows cannot be broken at the point in the way that vows are broken by ordinary sentient beings because the afflictions have been abandoned. The un-out flowed vows mentioned in the next paragraph are the vows that operate after that point. Those have been sutra explanations. In Marpa's system of tantra, there is still the one vow of completing the entity and becoming a buddha, which is similar to the idea of completing the task of bringing something to full measure.

[287] This is the first three of the several qualities of enlightenment that were put into words by Shakyamuni Buddha when he spoke after becoming enlightened. "Peaceful, profound, luminous, uncompounded (the meaning expressed in the *Heart Sutra*) ..."

if you were to die because of the karma involved, you would still have self-arising wisdom. You do not need to do the meditations of water dissolving into earth, and so on, followed by the smokey appearance of a moon rising, and so on—the appearances will arise clearly, then there will be flaring and attainment, and then the entity itself will shine forth[288]. All thought is wholly included in it. The knower involved in thought process proceeds in an interrupted way."

———— ◆◆◆ ————

Namo Ratna Guru.

He said, "For the bardo, best is to go to buddhahood via luminosity. Middling is to go to buddhahood via illusory body. Least is to go to buddhahood via having stopped the door of the womb. For dealing with obstructors, there are many methods but, if they are completely summed up, it is the pair, development and completion. Alternatively, bardo is identified via illusory body of purity and illusory body of impurity; by meditating on womb-birth, miraculous birth, egg-birth, and moisture-and-warmth birth as the development stage deity, another body will not be taken[289].

---

[288] Appearance, flaring, and attainment are the steps leading up to death after the four elements have dissolved. Death happens then the primordial luminosity occurs. The sutra teachings of the Kadampa say that you need to practise the sequence but he is saying that you don't need to practise it because it is going to happen.

[289] This process of liberation in the bardo through purification of the four types of birth based on deity practice is explained in depth in *A Presentation of Instructions for the Development Stage Deity "A Stairway Leading to Akaniṣṭha" by Jigmey Lingpa*, book by Tony Duff, published by Padma Karpo Translation Committee, 2011, ISBN: 978-9937-8386-3-4.

"Luminosity dharmakaya is something that all sentient beings have also at the time of death. If they do not recognize it, they continue from there according to the samsaric way of origination: in the luminosity there is appearance, which leads to flaring, which leads to the occurrence of a multitude of discursive thoughts and that is called 'samsara'[290]. The method for not continuing on into the six classes of samsaric being is as follows. Death rules you, so meditate for one hundred or one thousand years on luminosity and, when you have recognized luminosity as dharmakaya, you will stop entering samsara. By remaining undistracted from the state of non-duality, you will, through purification of the three bodies in samsara, go on to luminosity alone. By not having craving for samsara, you will not have appropriation[291].

The samsaric way of bardo is as follows. In the bardo of birth and death, desire is samsara, therefore one mixes with bliss. In the becoming bardo, father and mother are in the samsara of conjugation, therefore the guru transforms into male and female in consort. In the all-qualities-complete bardo, mother and son mix so space and mind are mixed; mixing mindness with dharmata here is path. The fruition is beyond a mixture and a mixer of it.[292]"

---

[290] If you look, you will notice that this is the reverse of the death process explained just above.

[291] Craving is the link of the twelve links of interdependency which leads to the link of appropriation. For appropriation, see the glossary.

[292] The bardo of birth and death is the period of a being's life, from birth to death. The bardo of becoming is the last phase of the general bardo in between one life and another in which the bardo being takes another birth in becoming, that is, another birth in samsara. The all-qualities-complete bardo is the first phase of the general bardo when the luminosity dharmata has dawned. In that phase, the path to be followed is that of mixing mindness with the dharmata which has dawned. The fruition is that one has become inseparable with it so

(continued...)

———— ◆◆◆ ————

The holy guru said to me, "Having established a good beginning with difficult to obtain freedom and connection[293], it is very important to find a spiritual friend who really can show you emptiness. After that, you engage in dharma and for that there is nothing other than the two things of accumulation and purification; evil deeds are to be purified and merit is to be accumulated. The accumulation of merit purifies evil deeds. This mindness of co-emergence and luminosity does not arise from causes, though it can be seen and arrived at by using the Stages of the Path to accumulate merit in conjunction with meditating on enlightenment mind, so at the same time there is a way in which it arises from causes. This does not arise from conditions though it can be seen and arrived at by accumulating the two accumulations, so at the same time there is a way in which it arises from conditions. This does not arise from method though this can be seen and arrived at through the two things of accumulation and purification in conjunction with meditating on fictional enlightenment mind, so at the same time there is a way in which this arises from method. It is said that,

> If with the support of method meditation a person
> Meditates on the prajna aspect,
> That will quickly bring enlightenment.
> Meditating on lack of self alone will not do it.[294]

---

[292](...continued)
there is no mixing to be done.

[293] This means that you have made a good start in life because of having obtained a precious human rebirth.

[294] This is very much the style of Kadampa teaching. The Essence Mahamudra teaching says that accumulation of merit is not required, though it can be helpful. This issue is dealt with at length here and in
(continued...)

Therefore, the accumulation of merit is very important. Is any-thing of greater value than accumulating merit? Honouring the guru is of greater value.

"All three of Potowa, Chen-ngawa, and the Jetsun[295] have each said so. The Jetsun has said that the offering of practice is of greater value than merit production. At the beginning, there are the four causes for the production of a shamatha, which is that is is born from: the guru's blessing; interdependency; accumulation of merit; and cleansing of evil deeds."

He said, "Mindness's entity in its real form unaltered and untainted is purity in the luminosity which is there at all times without in-terruption, and that has the two further points of certainty and uncertainty in the appearance. Certainty towards the appearance is to realize the appearance like an autumn sky and non-dual with mindness; certainty towards the appearance involves no hope of going upwards to buddha, no fear of going downwards to samsara, and no change even if something else changes it. In uncertainty, experience comes along as well: shamatha causes the experiences of bliss and no-thought but thoughts about the experiences—'Is this it?' and 'Is this not it?'—mean that the experiences create causes and then there is danger of going back down. There is the danger also of its turning into a cause of the form realm or formless realm or a shravaka's cessation."

He said, "At first, at the time of training, you train in a rigpa where the pure aspect of the luminosity is emphasized[296]. You also train

---

[294](...continued)
other places in the interviews.

[295] Potowa and Chen-ngawa are two of the early lineage holders of the Kadampa. The Jetsun is his guru Milarepa.

[296] This is dualistic training in which discursive thoughts are being
(continued...)

in not being distracted from the rigpa's entity. When you have habituated yourself to that, a confidence in oneself is produced."

He said, "Having done the work of ensuring that mindness's entity is not being lost, discursive thought is then allowed to be emitted as much as it wants. Discursive thought also is the dharmakaya. The situation is comparable to the sky which is completely pure by nature but which has clouds, mist, haze, and so on coming into it however much they do then dissipating into the sky itself and leaving. Discursive thought additionally turns into an assistant.

He said, "If discursive thought is not allowed to be emitted, it regains capability and there is the danger of birth in the formless realm. Sometimes meditate on the completion of the development stage of the deity." And he said, "Develop yourself as the yidam deity using completion the moment it is thought of then that will be meditation only on luminosity."

He said, "Moreover, that luminosity with purity emphasized is experience. The not being distracted from it is abiding. By looking with prajna, its not existing via any entity at all is realization."

He said,

"Samsara's characteristic, nirvana,
Is mindness wholly known[297]—

---

[296](...continued)
removed from the luminosity. Once this has been accomplished, the nature of the luminosity will be readily visible with vipashyana and Freedom From Elaboration is attained. After that, thoughts are re-introduced into the luminosity but this time there is no grasping.

[297] Tib. yong su shes pa. Wholly known is a technical term for one of two ways of knowing. The other way, knowing individual attributes, is a concept-based way of knowing something which never sees the

(continued...)

If it becomes wholly known as samsara,
That is nirvana.

The root of samsara is ignorance, that is, not-rigpa, so if that is recognized for what it is, one transcends it, going to nirvana.

"The truly complete buddha Vajradhara said, 'There is neither meditation nor meditator.' One yogin said, 'I do not listen to buddha—there is a meditator! How is there a meditator? I am rigpa! My entity with no stoppage of the luminosity's status and no interruption of it—this is the meditator. This, my entity, cannot be removed by the buddha! I also am meditation! There also is meditation to be done! I have a little bit of experiencing! Now then, buddha is true! I am a follower of buddha. There is no meditator. How is there no meditator? Being divorced of identification in its entirety, there is no example or wording at all that could demonstrate a meditator. From the aspect of concept tokens, even the buddhas of the three times will never observe one. Thus, in that entity there is no object that would be meditated on. There being in this way no experience to be had, there is also no meditation in the slightest to be done. I do not wish for the three of bliss, luminosity, and no-thought. Wanting that sort of thing is pain. There is no demonstrating it by any example nor is there getting at it with any words. I do not engage in manufacture and alteration, I put myself in what I am.'"

---

[297](...continued)
whole picture because it is knowing things through concepts. Wholly knowing is a wisdom-based way of knowing something which sees the whole picture and sees it as it is because it is seeing in direct perception without concepts.

The inner character of samsara is that it is actually nirvana. This is known when one's own mindness is wholly known. When mindness is wholly known, even the samsara aspect of it is nirvana. That is the great equality.

He said, "Secret Mantra's path is the pair, development and completion. Moreover, the best practitioner of development stage will accomplish the realization of unification. Middling and least both will turn away clinging to the ordinary form. Alternatively, the best actually sees himself as the yidam deity; middling has the certainty of illusoriness, and least has intention. The best practitioner of completion stage sees his own mind as buddha and sees appearances sometimes as illusory and sometimes as empty, but at no time as appearance separate from his own mind—this is referred to as the 'Yoga of One Taste'. Middling realizes the entity as birthless and has appearance glittering brilliantly—this is referred to as 'the Yoga of Freedom from Elaboration'. The least, using elaboration, trains in one-pointedness—the moment of awareness in which there is no stoppage in the luminosity is referred to as 'One-Pointedness'.

"If there is no certainty in regard to rational mind, whatever dharma is explained will not be profound. If there is certainty in regard to rational mind, whatever dharma is explained will be profound. The Kadampas know much Secret Mantra but, because they develop certainty in rational mind over the three beings[298], that is where they hold Buddha's teaching to be. Due to developing certainty in rational mind over the three beings, they understand loving kindness and compassion enlightenment mind as foremost instruction, then it arises for them through their practice of it. Following on from that, for them the fictional enlightenment mind in which they cherish others over themselves is most important. For them, this is requisite initially because, without it, the path of the Great Vehicle has not been entered; this is requisite in the middle because, without it, one falls into the shravaka path; this is requisite at the end because, without it, the two kayas for others' sake do not arise. Similarly, for their impermanence meditation: this is requisite initially because, without it, rational mind is not turned away from being concerned with this life; this is requisite in the middle because, without it, one grasps at permanence and

---

[298] ... of their Stages of the Path dharma ...

because of that deviates into the shravaka path, and the like; this is requisite at the end because, without it, impermanence and emptiness have the same meaning. Similarly, for their karma and result meditation: this also is requisite initially because completely pure discipline is what stops bad migrations; it is requisite in the middle because the illusoriness and dreamlike-ness of it is what completes the two accumulations; and it is requisite at the end because the fictional taken to the end is the two types of form kaya.

"That being so, the Stages of the Path are very relevant. If they are not produced in the mindstream, the innate might be produced in a blurred way, like floaters in the eyes, but attachment to country and close ones and possessions will mean that what has been produced will not help the innate. You will go down, not up. That being the case, do not be attached to this life! You should plant firmly in mind the certainty that these phenomena seen and heard are like illusions, like dreams. Train in the loving kindness and compassion enlightenment mind! If you develop that sort of certainty, even if the innate does not happen for you, you will go up and will not go down.

"For someone who has produced the real innate in his mindstream, then the three things—the innate's entity, the innate's fruition, and the innate's cause—will be as follows. The innate's entity is the fact which is not non-existent, free from all birth and cessation. The innate's fruition is that that very absence of birth and cessation is the dharmakaya. The two form kayas arise from it. Moreover, the three kayas that arise from the threefold bliss, luminosity, and no-thought experiences of the innate are the innate's fruition. Such bliss, luminosity, and no-thought when it arises from Fierce Heat becomes the cause of the innate. Even if the innate has been produced, without Fierce Heat, it is prajna alone. When there is Fierce Heat, method and prajna are not separate items of a pair. I heard Guru Mila say, 'The view which has not come from meditation is difficult', which was to the point that it is very important to exert yourself at Fierce Heat."

———— ◆◆◆ ————

He said, "The three types of wisdom are as follows. By meditating according to this system, a shamatha will come. At that time, an internal sign like of smoke or of fireflies will come indicating that there is now a little control over wisdom. Then, a pairing of sha-matha and vipashyana[299] will come—when shamatha has been taken to the end, the inner sign of a butter lamp will come indicating that there is control over wisdom. Then, a sign like a cloudless sky will come and that, called 'vipashyana's prajna', indicates control over the wisdom of the authentic.

"In the wish-fulfilling tree of the body the Avadhūti channel sits and in it are the four types of chakra. In the one at the navel, the manifestation chakra, are sixty-two[300] wisdom channels. Within its city, the mind's king called 'Tilaka' is seated. To see its face, a being who has faith and an accumulation of merit will use the key of prajna to release the lock of discursive thought and then, having opened the door, will see and its face and arrive at it. When he sees it, both ordinary and supreme siddhis will be there. At the heart is the eight-branched dharma chakra. In it, the mind's king Vasanta is seated. The others above it are the same sort of thing: in the throat sambhoga chakra there are sixteen branch channels and in it, the mental drop is seated; in the crown great bliss chakra there are thirty-two branch channels and in it the wisdom drop is seated. For the four chakras there are four key points: the navel is the key point of Fierce Heat; the heart centre is the key point of sleep; the throat is the key point of dreams; the crown is the key point of conjuga-tion. The vajra jewel and the point between the brows makes six.

---

[299] Note that this is a pairing as occurs in the shamatha of Yoga of One-Pointedness, not the unification needed for the Yoga of Freedom from Elaboration.

[300] Usually it is sixty-four. Sixty-two is probably a scribe's mistake.

What is it that makes them into key points? They are key points because they contain a support for knowledge.

"The visualization method is as follows. The awareness is focussed on the navel fire which, through the key point of non-duality of wind-mind, stirs the wind which opens the channels which in turn causes the wind to be inserted into the Avadhūti. The wind having been inserted into the Dhūti, no-thought wisdom blazes. More-over, visualizing the object involves prajna; wind opening the channel door is prajna opening the discursive thought lock; and no-thought wisdom shining forth is that mind's face is seen.

"The three types of compassion are as follows: referencing sentient beings; referencing dharmas; and without reference. Compassion referencing sentient beings is that, unable to bear individualized beings' sufferings, one has the wish to attain buddhahood for their sake. Compassion referencing dharma is with the bodhisatvas of the first bodhisatva level and up, the ones who have realized the absence of the duality of grasped-grasping. Compassion without reference is with the truly complete buddhas, the ones who have attained dharmakaya.

"That was in relation to its external appearance. In terms of its coming forth in oneself, for the beginner, being unable to with-stand the suffering of sentient beings is the compassion referencing sentient beings. Then, when the correct fictional[301] has been determined as dream-like, the thought, 'Oh how I have compassion for them: phenomena are like this yet sentient beings do not realize them to be so and they grasp at conceived-of things and concept tokens' is compassion referencing dharma. Then, having seen the suchness of one's own mind, the power of prayers already made

---

[301] Fictional truth is of two types: incorrect and correct. The former is what is known by a person whose sense faculties are not functioning correctly. The latter is the opposite.

automatically arising as activity for sentient beings' sake is compassion without reference.

"'Emptiness with a core of compassion' is as follows. Emptiness meditation done first leads on to compassion meditation which might bring the thought, 'Is the emptiness left behind?' No. The meditator of emptiness and the meditator of compassion both are rigpa so the two meditations are not separate. Meditating first on emptiness followed by meditation on compassion results in what is called 'emptiness with a core of compassion'. Compassion meditation done first leads to emptiness meditation, which is compassion with a core of emptiness. As above, the two are not separate.

"The three of thing, entity, characteristic are as follows. Things are everything that comes into existence with form. Entity is that their nature is empty. Characteristic is their shape, colour, and so on.

"Moreover, there is certainty and uncertainty in regard to appearance. Appearance is the bliss, luminosity, and no-thought of mind's entity and when that, called 'appearance', is uninterruptedly known as mind's entity, it is certainty in the appearance. Bliss, luminosity, and emptiness appear but if that is not known as mind, it is uncertainty. That uncertainty is the world's ultimate view; engaging in grasping at supremes in relation to bliss, luminosity, and no-thought causes deviation into the three realms. Shravakas make a basis out of it then concept tokens are involved; with that they are experienced so they are asserted to be empty without the view of grasping at supremes. Bodhisatvas make a basis out of it then training in samadhi is involved; not clinging to it, desire realm realization is roused, then that discursive thought is carried on to rigpa and that rigpa is carried to mind which is training in samadhi.

"'What are the three of common awareness[302], non-alteration, and the innate?' Common awareness is the initial awareness not

---

[302] For common awareness, see the glossary.

changed by other tenets by rational mind. Non-alteration is, while not manufacturing and altering, giving oneself over to exactly what is there. The innate: because what was just mentioned is, in being unborn and unceasing, uninterruptedly there, it is the innate[303].

> "The receiving consciousness[304] is profound and subtle.
> All seeds descend like a flowing river. If it turns into a
> thought of self it is called 'unsuitable'. This is
> something which I do not show to the childish.
> Profound meaning difficult to plumb to its depth; this is
> profound.[305]

In other words, the karma and result of 'from this cause this result arises' is exceedingly subtle. That being so, it is not known by anyone other than the all-knowing one[306], so is 'profound'. Subtle means 'not visible'. 'Seeds descend like a flowing river' is as follows. Where do latency's seeds first come from? They come from consciousness. Where are they planted? They are planted in consciousness. Where do they ripen into a result? They ripen in consciousness. How do they sit there? For example, if letters are written on birch bark in white goat's milk, the birch bark and letters are not two separate things and, when the right conditions are met, the letters appear[307] and, similarly, for a latency's seed which has been planted in consciousness, the consciousness and latency are

---

[303] In other words, it is always there, realized or not, so it is always innate to every being, hence its name.

[304] The receiving consciousness is the consciousness which receives karmic seeds. It is the alaya consciousness according to the Mind Only school and Secret Mantra.

[305] This is the Buddha speaking in a sutra.

[306] The Buddha.

[307] By gently scorching the bark, the milk turns brown and the lettering appears. This was a way of making secret writing in Tibet.

not different and, at the time when the appropriate condition of virtue or evil is met, the latency from before is aroused and the result, pleasant or suffering, comes. That moreover, is confusion.

"'What are the two, expanse and wisdom?' Expanse as something to be known has the character of all samsara and nirvana. Wisdom as something to be known is mindness completely purified, luminosity.

"The three of dharma, dharmin, and dharmata[308] are as follows: dharma is that which has become an object of samsaric rational mind; dharmin is the awareness that grasps it; dharmata is the complete purity which primally does not come into existence.[309]"

————— ◆◆◆ —————

I heard Rinpoche say, "Faith is important".

He said, "Seeking a spiritual friend involves faith. There are three types of faith: the best is to cultivate trusting faith, middling is to cultivate aspiring faith, and least is to cultivate admiring faith." And, "Trusting faith is trust in cause and effect. Aspiring faith is born in relation to the four truths. Admiring faith is born in relation to a special object. Something else that depends on faith is the spiritual friend."

He said, "If you have no spiritual friend, faith could cause you to join up with bad friends, so we have the approach of the spiritual friend being important because of that. The mindstream of a truly

---

[308] For dharmin and dharmata, see the glossary.

[309] The first two belong to samsara and thus are seen in a context where things are believed to exist. The last one is the inner nature of dharmas so is the complete purity that comes with the removal of samsara and all that it entails.

complete buddha is stirred: authentic statement[310] is given; foremost instruction hidden in his mind is exposed; within tantra, the lower things to be expressed first are shown; then development stage is explained; then completion stage is explained; then, the seven branches are explained. That is what it means for the mindstream to be stirred. Expert acharyas teach the treatises containing authoritative statement and the treatises which unravel the authoritative statement; the treatises which unravel authoritative statement commentaries are given as commentaries, such as Ṭīka[311], and so on, and the treatises which contain authoritative statement are given as sadhanas—sadhanas also are foremost instruction of the hidden[312]."

He said, "You might practise according to what the Buddha said but if you have no guru, there are no blessings to be had."

He said,

"I prostrate also to the guru
Whose body is the nature of all buddhas.
Even before prostrating, one has to seek a guru.
Even before making offerings, one has to offer to the
    guru.

---

[310] "Authentic statement" refers to the words of anyone whose statements come from correct knowledge. In this case, it is the words of the Buddha.

[311] Ṭīka is the Sanskrit word for a treatise that comments on something else in order to clarify its meaning. In this case, it will be a commentary on the Buddha Word.

[312] Where "hidden" refers to the fact that the things of Secret Mantra are hidden by nature.

The guru and buddha are not different:

> The guru is the vajra holder.
> No difference at all is considered.

Moreover, if all dharmas are summed up, loving kindness, compassion, and enlightenment mind are very important."

He said, "Moreover, it is produced in three ways: from habituation, from meditation, and from realization." And he went on, "Production from habituation refers to being produced as a result of training done in former lives up till this one. Production from meditation and production from realization are similar things."

He said, "Production from realization refers to a person who has training already; it is sahaja[313] luminosity, un-outflowed emptiness seen in direct perception. It is the dharmin which is mutually reliant on the two types of enlightenment mind. Geshe Gyayon Dag said to me, 'In Tibet, there are many dharmas which have been sweetened for easy digestion like food chewed before giving it to a child. For example, the one called 'Dzogpa Chenpo' says, 'If you realize it in the morning, you are a buddha in the morning, and if you realize it in the evening, you are a buddha in the evening.' And the group called 'Characteristics' says, 'By dissection done using free from one and many, I will be buddha.' And the group called 'Paramita' says, 'By relying on method and prajna, I will be buddha.' And the group called 'Mantra' says, 'By relying on the channels, winds, and drops and on development and completion stages, I will be a buddha.' And the group called 'Kadampa' says, 'By the oral instructions of the three beings greater and smaller[314] I will be a buddha.' I don't like them as a whole; I dare them to tell me what they are doing! I don't like them as a whole, they are not doing anything except for changing the ten non-virtues into the ten

---

[313] Sahaja is the Sanskrit for co-emergent.

[314] The texts omit "and lesser" which should be here.

virtues!' And he said, 'Those with greater intelligence will switch from outflowed virtue to un-outflowed virtue!' And he said, 'There is one group which says, 'The ten non-virtues will not contaminate me!'; they have befriended evil deeds!'"

He said, "The Buddha taught eighty-four thousand dharma doors, but when all of them are summed up, they come down to body, speech, and mind. And even then, body and speech are just the retinue; the principal one is mind."

He said, "Not even one moment of non-virtue should be done. And you also should not lose yourself to one moment of indeterminacy from the perspective of the antidote."

I heard Rinpoche say, "It is necessary to travel the three types of path: inference has to be made into path; blessings have to be made into the path; and direct perception has to be made into the path.

"Characteristic or Paramita is the one that makes inference into the path. Great Vehicle Secret Mantra is the one that makes, based on the pair development and completion, blessings into the path. The one that makes direct perception into the path is co-emergence, luminosity.

"There persons who enter the three paths are two: the gradual and sudden types. The sudden type is said to have trained himself to the point where his latencies of the afflictions are light and his latencies of dharma are massive'; this one's approach is extremely difficult[315]. I heard my guru say, 'I prefer the gradual one.'"

---

[315] "This is extremely difficult" means both that it is very rare to meet this kind of person and also that for the average person who has not developed these qualities to try to follow such a path is exceptionally difficult.

On one occasion many of the best type came before guru Mila, at which time I asked, "What is this Great Completion about?" He replied, "I heard guru Marpa say, 'There is talk that it is not dharma but that is not so. It is a dharma that goes from the sixth and seventh bodhisatva levels on up'. It would be something like pointing to a child of about five years and saying that Great Completion practitioners are like this, then this child saying, 'I have the abilities of a twenty-five year old.' Great Completion practitioners are said to speak of becoming buddha now, but that talk of theirs has no meaning."

He said, "If you want emancipation from samsara, unless you have the superfactual enlightenment mind, there will be no way to be emancipated." He said, "The superfactual enlightenment mind is extremely difficult. It will be easier for us if there are no ties. Geshe Yondag said to me, 'Where is the buddha you are previously acquainted with? Buddha is something like the front and back of your hand'. Well, for people like us who are tied to this and tied to that, where did this superfactual enlightenment mind go? The key point here is that the ties themselves are samsara."

He said, "Generally, when doing real dharma, where is there room to be continually assessing everything in terms of is and isn't, good and bad? Not giving any consideration to those at all, please look at your own awareness in the instant! A worldly person should be seen as a blunderer! Worldly people need be ridiculed! That is the right way to see it. I ask that all of us here do that. We involve ourselves with the eight items in four pairs meant to promote this life[316] but how will doing this, that, and the other cut our ties to samsara?

---

[316] He is referring to the eight worldly dharmas.

"We say[317], 'I will enact the mind of the buddhas and will take across those who have not been taken across', meaning that we will act for individualized beings[318]. We say, 'I will liberate those who have not been liberated' meaning that we will act for 'shravakas and pratyekabuddhas'. We say, 'I will take those who have not gone to total nirvana to total nirvana' meaning that we will act for 'first bodhisatva level up to tenth level beings'. We proclaim that we will but its merely words!"[319]

Spoken by Lord Gampopa. The end.

❀   ❀   ❀

[Part eight: two interviews with Gampopa.]

I prostrate to the precious guru.

He said, "The system of Paramita enlightenment mind causes realization to be born on the mindstream through reliance on threefold enlightenment mind, being illusion-like, and being empty. The system of Mantra causes realization to be born on the mindstream through reliance on threefold body as deity, speech as repetition, and mind as dharmata. If there is no realization, there is no buddhahood. In our Buddhist system, these approaches to dharma

---

[317] He is now going to lay out the four lines of commitment to a bodhisatva's activity which are commonly recited after taking the bodhisatva vows.

[318] Individualized beings are ordinary samsaric beings.

[319] In other words, we should give up on all worldly approaches and get on with what we repeatedly proclaim that we have dedicated our lives to, which is to act to bring every sentient being, low and high, to the state of enlightenment.

only lead upwards, never downwards: the person of best faculties will be a buddha; the one of middling faculties will be born in one of the five places of noble ones; and even the one of least faculties will be born as a god.

"From the standpoint of the two truths, the rigpa of the thought process in all its variety is fictional truth and the mind's entity is superfactual truth. This experience of the entity, the entity which exists in the present, comes from buddha itself. It might shine forth as various awarenesses but these can be turned to use; it is similar to ice being able to give rise to water[320].

"Emptiness and compassion not done in a separated way is asserted to be light which has come off from light. All thought is asserted to be like light which has come off from light. In sleep it is neither greater nor lesser. The entity having been realized as free from birth and disintegration, is viable[321] because it is not transitory. If all phenomena are distilled down, they can be condensed down to being with thought and absence of thought. Thought itself also is dharmakaya. By realization of it all as one thing, everything is brought here on this side then comes as such[322].

"There is nothing at all to explain to you here—not even the guru's words will not take you to that superfact. It is beyond being an object of a philosopher. If it were seen by philosophers, then the

---

[320] The buddha mind which is present as the entity shines forth for samsaric beings as various awarenesses, for example, as the various thoughts and consciousnesses possessed by them. These might be frozen, fixated awarenesses but they are not useless. As with ice being a frozen form of water so ice can be used to get back its essence, so with thoughts.

[321] ... as a solution ...

[322] All phenomena are now included within the one mind of the entity which is an internalized realization, not an externalized projection.

fictional would be seeing superfact and then superfact would also be transitory. If it were seen by superfact, then to make it out solely as this together with thought would mean that, »[323] even if you meditated that that, your own mindness, luminosity, was equal to the limits of space, it would still be born and present in that way[324]. Even if you meditated on it as another place of the noble ones, it would still come and be present. And for as long as you sat there, even if you meditated on it, it would still come and be present. Whose luminosity is it? It is yours. Realized and not realized, it pervades everything. It is present as knowing which itself knows itself, self-illumination in which the luminosity is un-stopped, luminosity without up and down, luminosity without edge and centre, luminosity without the presence and absence of discursive thought. To abide in its state is to function beyond the world. There is no enhancement to be done to it. If you did try to en-hance the realization, whatever you produced would be faulty. If an enhancement or sign[325] or higher state than it were to come from doing so, that would be faulty."

I asked, "For all the old dogs who have produced the entity then meditated on it for a long time, will there be a point at which there is a need for enhancement or some special acquaintance to be made?" The reply came, "There will be neither acquaintance nor enhancement to be made. People have these ideas because of thoughts like, 'There is something higher that can come to me.'"

I asked, "In regard to the entity which has become a single suffi-cient solution, I am not apprehending it in dreams; will it be apprehended in the bardo or not?" The reply came, "All gurus have said that it must be apprehended in dreams. Having looked

---

[323] The text from here down to the next closing brace is repeated starting on page 242 of Yogin Choyung's interview.

[324] That it has thoughts is the key point here.

[325] Meaning sign of practice, sign of progress.

into this myself, I see that even if it is not apprehended in dreams, it will be apprehended in the bardo. In the present context it turns out unclearly in dreams so you do not apprehend it, but in the bardo it turns out more clearly than now, so you will be able to apprehend it then."

I asked, "If the entity is something that has to be deliberately roused now, then after death, in the bardo, will it also be that way or will it turn to a single sufficient solution?" The reply came, "If the entity is there without discontinuity now, it will turn into a single solution in the bardo, too. That deliberate rousing will also happen as deliberate rousing in the bardo; by meditating in that way it will be enhanced over its present status and will turn to a single, sufficient solution." «[326]

»[327] I asked, "If superfactual enlightenment mind is continuously realized and dwelt in, will fictional-enlightenment-mind meditation be necessary or not?" The reply came, "There are three aspects to it: coming from habituation, coming from meditation, and coming from realization. Coming from habituation is that enlightenment mind has been meditated on in former lives, so it comes in this one without needing to meditate on it. Coming from meditation is what has happened already due to meditation in this life. Coming from realization is that, because of realizing its fact, the loving-kindness-and-compassion enlightenment mind automatically comes for those who have not realized it, sentient beings. It is not necessary to do two separate meditations on fictional and superfactual enlightenment minds. If superfact is realized, the arising of loving kindness and compassion for the sake of others is cause and effect. This automatically turns away affliction. If you say that you have realized the entity but engage in non-virtue, you have small loving-

---

[326] End of the second section of repeated text.

[327] The text from here down to the next closing bracket is repeated starting on page 244 of Yogin Choyung's interview.

kindness-compassion enlightenment mind and this effectively is the same as not having produced the entity. The Jetsun guru[328] said this, and it is so."

I asked, "When the Jetsun[329] is sick, does his mind become upset or not?" The reply came, "Even when I am sick, I suffer no upset in mind and no harm comes to me at all. By meditating on luminosity at the location of the sickness, it comes totally into luminosity and there is no harm to me. Compared to doing mantra for a person who is sick because of a malevolent spirit, directing your attention to the location of sickness then meditating on luminosity is more beneficial."

I asked, "What would you say about merging entity and equipoise?" The reply came, "For 'meditation', no matter which of the four types of behaviour you are doing, if, without separating from luminosity, it is always coming as the entity, that is merging.[330]"

I asked, "Sometimes I lose mindfulness and go into discursive thought. Regaining mindfulness then coming into the entity is merging, isn't it?" The reply came, "That is not merging."

"Well then", I asked, "Is it not realizing one portion of the entity? Isn't it meditation for a short time then habituating?" The reply

---

[328] Milarepa.

[329] Gampopa.

[330] His answer is to the point that the entity is realized by merging equipoise with post-attainment. (Having the four types of behaviour means everything possible within post-attainment.) His answer implies that Dusum Khyenpa has misunderstood the meaning of "merging". He says so explicitly in the next paragraph.

came, "That is not realizing the whole entity. It is not habituating. It is meditation for a short time on the fact[331]."

"Well then", I asked, "For as long as I have this body of full-ripening[332], is it that at all costs I should not go into an absence of equipoise and post-attainment?" The reply came, "No, that is not it. You have this body of full-ripening and by meditating for a long time you can go on to meet with the absence of equipoise and post-attainment in this very life."

"Well then", I asked, "This losing mindfulness immediately followed by going into latencies as such[333] is a come-back from what?" The reply came, "It is what you get in return for not having purified grasped-grasping. Meditating for a long time purifies grasped-grasping then, because there is no holding on with mindfulness to be done, it goes on to absence of equipoise and post-attainment."

"Well then", I asked, "If I have produced the entity but die without having merged equipoise and post-attainment, will this purify birth in the bardo or not?" The reply came, "It will purify it, there is no doubt about it!"

"Well then", I asked, "Won't the discursive thought which has not been apprehended by present mindfulness cause obscuration?" The reply came, "It will not cause obscuration. Those discursive thoughts do not have the capacity to accumulate karma. It is like planting a seed in space—there is no place for the fruition to be

---

[331] This is a subtle distinction of the process of Essence Mahamudra meditation.

[332] "Body of full-ripening" means this body produced by karmic ripening.

[333] "As such" means that the afflictions, and so forth arising from the latencies are coming on in their samsaric mind form, not as ones that have been liberated.

produced. This is through the key point of realizing everything as birthless."

"Well then", I asked, "If at the time of a deep sleep or dream I have not apprehended the entity, will the entity be apprehended in the bardo or not?" The reply came, "That is not having apprehended the entity at the times of sleeping and dreaming but you will apprehend it in the bardo. It turns unclear now during sleeping and dreaming compared to that. In the bardo, it turns clearer than now. Compared to now, it is easy to apprehend."

"Well then", I asked, "If, un-apprehended by mindfulness, the entity is not coming and the discursive thought as such is apprehended by mindfulness, will it purify the previous discursive thoughts or not? It is necessary or not to apprehend an absence of their dying and not dying through mindfulness?" The reply came, "Discursive thoughts as such that have not been apprehended by mindfulness immediately they are apprehended by mindfulness are cleared off and so purified. It is not necessary to have apprehended an absence of their dying and not dying through mindfulness. Nonetheless, if you have made yourself undistracted through mindfulness, that will help to speed up the process of merging equipoise and post-attainment. And then, discursive thought, even if it has not been apprehended by mindfulness, absolutely will not harm, cause obscuration, or be a hindrance."

"Well then", I asked, "Is there no practice to do other than to be apprehending with mindfulness and remaining undistracted?" The reply came, "Except for being prodded by mindfulness, there is no other practice to do at all." «[334]

---

[334] End of the third section of repeated text.

»[335] I asked, "Compared to doing only entity meditation, is it necessary or not to development stage and recitation?" The reply came, "If you do a little mantra recitation, it will cause speech to be blessed; other than that, reciting mantra and meditation on the deity is not necessary. Within the state of luminosity there is recitation." «[336]

———— ♦ ♦ ♦ ————

Again, the precious guru said, "Dharma goes to dharma, dharma goes to the path, the path's confusion is dispelled, and confusion dawns as wisdom. 'Dharma' means that, having trust in karma and result, the slightest bad action is avoided. 'Goes to dharma' means that at the time of doing some virtue, one is not contaminated by it. 'Dharma goes to the path' means that, propelled by the loving-kindness-and-compassion enlightenment mind, all virtue and doing of it is dedicated to others' sake. 'The path's confusion is dispelled' means that, by meditating on the two enlightenment minds, all phenomena are realized to be dream-like, illusion-like. 'Confusion dawns as wisdom' means that even though that was done for others' sake, it is still confusion so, if the entity free from thought grasping at I is realized, the confusion will dawn as wisdom. There is no dispeller of the confusion apart from the confusion. It is the entity itself, so it does dispel the path's confusion."[337]

The end.

❀   ❀   ❀

---

[335] The text from here down to the next closing bracket is repeated starting on page 244 of Yogin Choyung's interview.

[336] End of the fourth section of repeated text.

[337] See the comments about this third one in the introduction on page xviii.

[Part nine: a talk given by Gampopa.]

The precious guru said, "There's practice based on going here and there for food and here and there for clothes (he was saying that doing so separates you from the guru in which case dharma does not happen). Then there is practice done with the force of blazing perseverance (it will not happen for the lazy); for this, first (the inner acharya) mindness shines forth as the acharya. Then (when you are not captured by the guru) whatever volumes you look at shine forth as the acharya. Then, all the phenomena of sights and sounds shine forth as the acharya (the outer guru). All phenomena shine forth as non-dual. If that much happens, the person is functioning at the level of a meditator who has no rejecting and accepting or a non-meditation meditator. What is said, 'Being without absorption[338] yet with realization, they become buddha' (via Mahamudra)' will happen. All phenomena will shine forth in one. Freed of all artifice (in being freed of elaborations of the three times), unaltered (which appears naturally and without interruption) in being freed of elaboration in its entirety, freed from identification in its entirety (rigpa itself), freed from grasping in its entirety (lacking dualistic grasped-grasping), not existent via any entity at all, freed from the rational mind of meditating (without conceived efforts and activities), and not not meditating either (freed from the elaborations of the three times) so (in not being freed of everything at all times) pure from the primordial outset (thinking that it is difficult to realize the original situation), originally one is buddha without meeting and parting (thinking that it is easy to capture). That wisdom realized which is changeless, (from the first it has never experienced interruption, therefore it is) all the time, without identification in the luminosity (unified luminosity-emptiness), without outflows in the bliss (un-outflowed mind's emptiness), free from all anxiety, the great birthlessness free of ground shines forth from within.

---

[338] Skt. dhyāna, Tib. bsam gtan.

"A guru with realization (because if you ask a guru with blessings, no house of confusion will occur) gives to a qualified disciple a true blessing, then all good qualities arising all at once in one mass is the dharmata. The blessings of all the gurus of the three times enter. The blessings of all the baskets of the Buddha word enter. The blessings of all the buddhas and bodhisatvas enter. All the dakinis and dharma protectors also gather there.

"In general, the dharma of the Great Vehicle comes from blessings (he was saying that all the authentic dharma of the Great Vehicle comes from a spiritual friend). So, within that, all the dharma of the Secret Vehicle also comes from blessings. In particular, the Nāropa's Dharmas come from the blessings of the Kagyu lineage holders. This, my lineage, is a transmission of blessings that comes from an uninterrupted attainment of siddhi. The banner of the Kagyu has arrived and by it the forefathers perform the acts of ripening and liberating their heirs. The heirs treasure their forefathers, cherishing them as the jewel at their crowns or like their own eyes. These profound oral instructions of the Kagyu lineage are like the heart extracted from the Secret Mantra or the juice of the four sections of tantra. These dharmas are held in the hands of the dakinis so are exceedingly profound and strong."

The Jetsun guru said to me, "Do not give these even to your acharyas and associates!" He said, "Otherwise, they will pursue you and you will provide them with a deceptive offering of something which you do not really have to give." He said, "The alternative approach of keeping hidden the three things of the yogin's body, the Secret Mantra's profound oral instructions, and advice given from your own experience is the right way." He said, "When something has been concealed, there is no source from which it can come." Rinpoche said, "I have broken guru Mila's command". I asked, "How is that?" He said, "Because I explained all of the dharma to other people." Then, after a moment, he said again, "I have done as the guru commanded". I asked, "How is that?" He said, "Because I made this life worthwhile."

That was a talk given by Lord Gampopa.

❋   ❋   ❋

[Part ten: a collection of nine interviews given by Gampopa, which collectively impressed on the audience the need not only to practise but to do the authentic type of practice of a yogin rather than a scholar.]

I heard Rinpoche say, "The treatises on the truly complete buddha's word, the compositions by expert acharyas of treatises which unravel that authoritative statement and treatises which contain the authoritative statement, the treatises not depending on the buddha word in that they have come from within for the yogins who have accomplished siddhi, the actual word of the Buddha, talks of gurus, and experiences that have been produced in your own mindstream are consistent with each other. If you do not find them to be consistent, you have not understood dharma."

He said, "Generally, if you practise dharma genuinely, it has great meaning. If you cannot do it genuinely, you can at least take some part of it and make a basis from that. If you do it genuinely, you will make a life like that of a rabbit. Do not stay in one place only. Do not stick with a single sponsor. Do not stay with a single friend. A very dear friend is a root of affliction. Do not be very close with a guru and do not be far away." He said, "It is like fire. If you stay close you get burned, if you stay far away you do not get warmed. Alternatively, either there are experts who create dissention or those who nicely leave. Those who are expert create dissention, which happens based on desire for something which is not required; it creates difficulty. Those who are not experts leave, which they do in order not to be contaminated by affliction and the like. If you want emancipation from samsara, you also need to avoid worldly people."

He said, "We involve ourselves with the eight items in four pairs meant to promote this life[339]—but how will doing this, that, and the other cut our ties to samsara? Doing what we want and being hungry for everything should cause us to doubt ourselves: "If I hunger, then I am deceiving myself.""

Rinpoche said, "Mahamudra can be connected with the five paths as follows. If you meditate on one seat, doing the preparations by rousing enlightenment mind and doing the main part by meditating on phenomena being dream-like, illusory-like, that is the Path of Accumulation. Meditation on emptiness in the style of intending[340] is the Path of Connection. Having produced Mahamudra on the mindstream is the Path of Seeing. Engaging in habituating onself to it is the Path of Meditation, which has also been explained in these words:

> Because of seeing the not seen, the Path of Seeing.
> Because of habituation to seeing, the Path of
> Meditation.

---

[339] He is referring to the eight worldly dharmas which come as four pairs.

[340] Tib. mos pa. "Intending' is a function of dualistic mind. The Prajnaparamita teachings in which the five paths were originally taught teaches emptiness meditation done with intention; the emptiness is not directly perceived but the causes for later directly perceiving it are set. Intentional meditation on emptiness always implies Path of Connection

When that has been manifested, the freedom in its entirety from hope and fear, vacillatory foci, and grasped-grasping is the Path of Graduation[341].

"You might think, "Even at the level of having achieved the Path of Seeing, it is explained that there are one hundred emanations listening to the dharma, and so on. Here, are limitless qualities also explained for each of them?' The answer is that there are two explanations, one concerning superfice in the superfactual and one concerning superfice in the fictional. For the first, even though there are none of those kinds of signs, it is not contradictory; those signs would be explained in the fictional. Buddha is talked of as being ornamented with the marks and signs. There is nothing produced autonomously[342]. This mindness which does not exist via any entity at all itself is buddha."

He said, "Moreover, the sutra *Petitioned by Kashyapa* says,

> Mind is something which even the buddhas of the past did not observe, do not observe, and ... (the sutra, *Gathering the Intent* says that that mind is something that even buddhas have not seen, do not see, and will not see).

This is explaining its being 'changeless'.

---

[341] For vacillatory foci, see the glossary. "Path of Graduation" is another name for Path of No More Learning.

[342] This means that these qualities are only produced in interdependency with sentient beings needs; they are not there in and of themselves.

"If mind's actuality like that is realized, then of all protections that there are, it is the supreme one. As for emptiness meditation, it has been said,

> The Lord of Death does not see it but
> He does wholly see the pure nature[343].

"Within all of the offerings given in worship that there are, it is the supreme one; it has been said,

> Offerings made with something to be offered and an
>   offerer
> At that time the yogin does not see.
> That is the supreme of offerings thus
> The wise will meditate on enlightenment mind[344].

"It is the supreme laying aside[345] for corruptions, obscurations, and so on; it has been said,

> Laying aside done with something to be laid aside and
>   layer aside
> Is something that the yogin does not ever see.
> The pure nature is wholly seen;
> That is the supreme laying aside.

"That fact of Mahamudra is freed of the four maras. In this mind: there is no birth and death, therefore it is free from the mara of the Lord of Death; there is no affliction, therefore it is free from the mara of the afflictions; there is no existence of form, therefore it is

---

[343] Emptiness meditation is not ultimate because, as is the case during the death process, emptiness as such is not seen but the pure nature, luminosity is seen.

[344] Enlightenment mind is sometimes used, as it is here, to mean the entity.

[345] For laying aside, see the glossary.

free from the mara of the aggregates; there is no clinging, therefore it is free from the mara of the son of gods.[346]

"If Mahamudra's actuality is realized, then of all methods that there are, it is the supreme one. It has been said,

> There is no interruption in the luminosity.
> The city of the bardo by that is not seen.

And the same is so for transference, too.[347]"

———— ◆◆◆ ————

Also, Rinpoche said, "A meditator needs the four assurances. To have assurance of the view is to have all dharmas shine forth as facts of their actuality, therefore one needs the sort of awareness where all that appears as an object of rational mind shines forth within that state. To have assurance of Secret Mantra's ability is that one needs to have the thought that, having done the approach practice of one's yidam deity, any obstacles of pretas, and so on that arise can be dealt with by exclaiming PHAṬ. To have assurance of the guru's foremost instructions one needs to have the knowledge of what the pacifying, enriching, magnetizing, destroying, and so on activities are and how they should be performed."

———— ◆◆◆ ————

---

[346] The four maras are explained in the glossary under mara.

[347] The quotation is saying that the Mahamudra fulfils all practices designed to lead a being to enlightenment and so ends the bardo. For example, it fulfills the Bardo dharma of the Six Teachings of Naropa according to the verse and likewise it fulfils the Transference dharma, too.

Namo Guru.

He said, "A person who has turned his mind away from this life goes to an isolated place then does the three tunings according to the guru's oral instructions. By tuning the channels, the elements are brought into balance. By tuning the winds, the ability to meditate on tree-tops arises. By tuning the mind, affliction does not create a sheath and it shines forth within experience.

"The recognition of rigpa and experiencing of the resulting realization are important", he said. "Recognition involves no identification of rigpa. It is realization of it free of every extreme of elaboration and without interruption. It is also the ignorance of not-rigpa being recognized as rigpa and being realized without any doubt", he said.

He said, "The assistants of not-rigpa, ignorance, are the five poisons and their shining forth as the five wisdoms is something that cannot be prevented by anyone at all; for the mind to shine forth like that is what is meaningful. Such shining forth in the mindstream does not result in everything being heaped into one.[348]"

———— ◆◆◆ ————

He said, "The great guru Naropa said the following:

> The king of Secret Mantra of seven letters
> Was recited one hundred thousand times.
> The earth quaked and the prophecy was gained.
> In the east, from Tailopa in person,
> The instructions were received.
> The actuality of conceived-of things has the stages

---

[348] The afflictions and wisdoms will not all become jumbled in together. If the afflictions are allowed to shine forth as wisdom, which is good, you do not need to worry that samsara will be retained with it.

Of being produced of path and fruition.
Conceived-of things' actuality is twofold:
It is to be known as that of body and mind.

There, the actuality of conceived-of body things is present in the personage of the channels and chakras and the actuality of conceived-of mind things is present as inseparable rigpa and emptiness. The path is twofold: the path of empowerment for ripening the unripened and the pair development and completion as the method for liberating the ripened. Empowerment is fourfold: vase empowerment, secret empowerment, prajna-wisdom empowerment, and precious word empowerment.

"The development stage also has the kusulu's system in which recollection of it is complete in one moment. Furthermore, there is the superfice of the deity, its nature emptiness, and its entity inseparable luminosity-emptiness.

"Completion stage has paths of meditating with concept tokens and without them. There are the four key points of body, channels, object, and time from which wisdom is asserted to shine forth. The key points of body are two: the actual key points of body and the ones connected with that through the winds based in the body. The actual key points of body are seven: the legs crossed lattice-like; the spine straightened similar to a plantain; the squeeze of the equipoise mudra; hooked like an iron hook; expanded as though to full-grown size; tightened like copper; eyes directed down the nose-tip. There are seven purposes belonging to those: being crossed lattice-like produces heat; being straightened like a plantain inserts the winds into their own places; equipoise mudra creates ease; being hooked like an iron hook stops thought; being expanded to full-grown size adjusts the key point of wind; tightened like copper quickly develops heat; eyes directed down the tip of the nose brings clarity of mind."

———— ◆◆◆ ————

Namo guru.

Rinpoche said this: "Wandering in samsara is payback for what? It is the payback for having not-rigpa, ignorance. What is not-rigpa or ignorance like? It is present as emptiness. It is present as indeterminacy; if it meets a virtuous condition, it becomes associated with virtue, and if it meets non-virtue, it changes to being non-virtuous. A formative[349] has arisen so the not-rigpa, ignorance, has come forth as a formative which shifts to being either virtuous or non-virtuous. A perception[350] arises in relation to that and, because of apprehending it as either virtuous or non-virtuous, the not-rigpa, the ignorance, enters affliction. A consciousness[351] arises in relation to that, causing a latency seed to be planted in the consciousness, which in turn causes cycling in samsara. Well then, what is the method for emancipation from samsara? Using the oral instructions of a holy guru, the ignorance of not-rigpa is introduced as rigpa, through which consciousness shines forth as luminosity, through which the latency's seed has no place to be planted. Formatives also shine forth as luminosity whereby there is liberation from cause and effect. There is realization at the time of the cause of the fruition, whereby cause and effect are simultaneous."

———— ◆◆◆ ————

Namo guru.

Rinpoche said this. "Generally, everyone has to have a yoga of eating. That being so, the Secret Mantra yogin must know both the eating yoga and conduct yoga. Blessing all food and edibles

---

[349] Fourth skandha.

[350] Third skandha.

[351] Fifth skandha.

with OM ĀH HŪM then thinking of one's yidam deity and making an offering of them is the eating yoga. Doing all activities in the state of dharmata is the conduct yoga. By that Mantra yoga, there is no 'this type of food is not to be eaten, this type of activity is not to be done, this kind of clothing is not to be worn'. All are to be used without intimidation as though one were a brave lion.

"Once the mantra path has been entered, it is necessary to remain within samaya and in relation to that there are both the samaya to be protected and the samaya of utilization. Of the two, the samaya of utilization is like this: body not being separated from the pride of the deity is the enlightened body samaya; speech not being separated from the recitation is the enlightened speech samaya; and mind not being separated from birthlessness is the enlightened mind samaya. That is the utilization samaya. The samaya to be protected consists of abandoning the fourteen root downfalls and ten non-virtues." And he continued, "The three of body are body samayas. The four of speech are speech samayas. The three of mind are mind samayas.[352]"

Also, on one occasion of apprehending rigpa, he said this: "Oneself is the deity and others also are the deity so how could there be killing of one deity by another, or hitting or being angry, or lying to another? Please develop that kind of mind, too!"

He said, "Generally, mantra is explained as secret; if not kept secret, the door of siddhi becomes lost."

——— ◆ ◆ ◆ ———

---

[352] He has equated the ten non-virtues with body, speech, and mind samayas.

Namo guru.

The precious guru said, "If a qualified guru and a worthy disciple
meet, then, when the student's mind is led along, the path will be
accomplished without difficulty (because of relying on the spiritual
friend). Otherwise, there is no opportunity for development along
the path."

He said, "The guru has both the prajna eye and the dharma eye.
Having the prajna eye (the one that determines knowables), he is
expert in phenomena both in terms of both their general and
specific characteristics, thus he shows the meaning of phenomena
without mistake and without mixup (not confusing one generic
image[353] for another). Having the dharma eye, he has plainly
realized the fact of dharma without error. He has experience of the
fact's own entity. It shines forth for him within an awareness which
is true (so he has not lost the inner disposition[354]) and, having shone
forth, his own personal connection to it (gives him the ability to
liberate disciples) means that he can make it appear in others.

"Alternatively, there are four qualification for a guru. He must:
have faith in the Three Jewels (the uncommon ones that exist); have
compassion for sentient beings (he should have, through compassion, brought every sentient being into his thoughts); have certainty
in regard to the profound dharma (have realization of the actuality
of all dharmas and given birth to confidence in it); have the ability,
without going all over the place (without personal ties and for
others benefit), to teach dharma (which is saying that if he has that

---

[353] A generic image is the concept by which a particular thing is known
to intellect. Not confusing generic images means to have an intellect
which properly discriminates between one item of knowledge and
another, in other words, a finely tuned intellect.

[354] The inner disposition is one's innate situation, which is the entity.

dharma already himself, he will have the ability to lead others through it).

"Mainstream teachers assert severing exaggerations externally in order to realize the dharma. They assert hearing much dharma. They would not consider not hearing much dharma. Not meditating is the system of teachers (my guru said to me, 'If you determine the grasper[355] it will lead to the shackles of the grasped aspect opening of themselves and that is how it happens' and I have had this happen to me, too. On the other hand, acharya Sherab Zangpo said to me, 'If you set about determining the grasped aspect, then the shackles of the grasper will release of themselves.') but if discursive thought does not end, there will be no end to the words of conventions and the person will be tied to words that never get to their intended point.[356]

---

[355] To do so is the inwardly-directed possibility used in the tantras. The first possibility mentioned would have determined and eliminated the grasped aspect first, which is the outwardly-directed approach of the sutras.

[356] This paragraph lays out the way that most teachers teach dharma, which is that they say that all excesses of understanding must be eliminated through hearing dharma then meditating on it, something which only goes as far as realizing the conceptual meaning. This is to look outwards. It has the problem that it promotes concept rather than defeating it at the root. The note in the paragraph could be confusing. It is pointing out that not meditating conceptually is another approach and one that did work for Gampopa when his guru Milarepa taught it to him, though his Kadampa teachers taught him the opposite approach, the approach of cutting exaggeration externally. The next paragraph lays out the approach of the Mahamudra yogin, someone who cuts exaggerations internally using the approach of not meditating, and who in doing so realizes the non-conceptual meaning directly.

"Practitioners assert severing exaggerations internally in order to to realize dharmata; they proceed by 'knowing one and becoming expert in all'. My guru Mila said to me (basing himself on the oral instructions of the practice lineage), 'Forget all dharmas belonging to the training where everything is sized up and decided on! All dharmas without having been trained-in do shine forth and become present. I have given some hundred thousand explanations of dharma but it still hasn't ended!' Gurus Marpa and Ngog both, if they were here today, would still be giving dharma explanations! In regard to dharmas not trained in, they still can be understood! There can be understanding which is meaningful."

He said, "Gonpawa said to me, 'Sing a fresh little song. What value there in just hooting like an owl? Give oral instruction that is based on your experience. What value is there in something said without experience?' It's like that, I do have some experience in meditation. Kadampa (meaning only what is made by rational mind) geshes, and teachers of characteristics, and mantra practitioners, and so on—I have what you meditate on but you don't have what I meditate on (experience freed of rational mind). Potowa said, 'If you want to know dharma, meditate!' Drepa said, 'If, compared to listening for three years, all of you were to meditate for one year, you would have a very great samadhi; it is so true that it can't be discussed even! Individually-discriminating prajna even greater again would happen.' Having heard that, the geshes went to places like the mountains and got on with meaningful accomplishment.'"[357]

---

[357] With this paragraph, he is saying that, of the two approaches mentioned above, the only one worthwhile is the one in which one gains direct and personal experience. Even amongst his Kadampa gurus, the one's who really knew dharma, understood. They criticized their mainstream followers who were famous for embracing the first approach and never even getting to meditation because of it. On one case, the followers listened and, having gone off to meditate, gained some actual experience because of it.

"We also till now have made no effort not to do this[358]. Because we apprehend using conceived-of things and concept tokens, it is not possible for us to get above samsara. The expert scholars, preceptors for others, acharyas, first order thousand-fold wheel-wielding kings, and so on also have made no effort not to do this. From the peak of becoming on down, sentient beings just do not gravitate to the cause of emancipation. There are those experts who can recite the entire Tripitaka (those who have not given themselves over to realization in the mindstream—experiences of abiding are experienced from the peak of becoming on down), and the ordained ones who do not stray into breaking their vows, and those who have not recognized meditation that is continuous day and night, and so on, but if you (who, if you would realize mindness, co-emergence, as the dharmakaya would have the fruit) do not realize your own mind, you will not reach buddhahood. I—and even though I have an excellent meditation[359]—do attach great significance to realization of mind."

He said, "A seasoned meditator who leaves aside meditation and is satisfied with just basic abiding, who explains dharma to others to increase the mind of benefiting others, who defends and protects, and so on, has left aside the main part of dharma and is acting out a mere reflection of it. A seasoned meditator should never accept positions as an elder, a principal, an advisor, a minister, and so on. Why? Because he has committed himself to meditation. Now for us, we must, like a deer being hunted down, flee from all of this. We must rouse a mind that is determined never to get involved

---

[358] We, up to this point in our long history of samsaric lives, have made no effort to give up on the outer approach of externally cutting exaggeration and turn to the inner approach which produces real experience.

[359] Because of his training with the Kadampa, he developed excellent abiding meditation. Even though he has tasted this, he still says that realization of the mind is paramount.

with it. It is so true for harming others that it doesn't need to be discussed but we need to flee even from situations where we could be providing benefit. If we don't flee from these things, then it means that we will have to fend for ourselves. If we do that, (this means needing to get the basics) then our spiritual practice will not happen.

"For the person who does practise, there are two things: understanding tenets and being able to stand on his own. To understand tenets is to be expert in the general meaning of dharma, the main presentations, and the meaning of the view, and to understand the way that all dharmas are and where they lead. The ability to stand on his own is that, without looking about at anything else and having put everything aside, he puts these profound oral instructions of the practice lineage into his heart and, for the benefit of all sentient beings, practises them. Not looking outside but looking within, he cuts off every tie that he has. He needs no harmony with worldly beings (because it would mix his mind with hopes for this and that). Worldly ones have awareness that runs the wrong way. We want to turn away from that. The Indian word for worldly people, 'puruṣha', has the force of that[360]. Similarly, when we have the strength of youth we must practise. If we do not, we will not go to buddhahood. Guru Mila said, 'If you have not practised yet still call yourself a yogin, (this is referring to a yogin who does not see the dharmata) then where did that name come from?'

"Also, the guru said, 'I stayed in an isolated rock cave for a long time. Looking meant that I looked at my own mind. You disciples too, must look at mind!'

---

[360] "Puruṣha" of both Sanskrit and Hindi languages means "individualized being" which points exactly to the problem that the being's mind has cut itself off from the all-pervading reality of its own enlightenment and reduced it to a crystalized, separated, insular form of being.

"Gonpawa said to me, 'If you ask me about meditation, then I would tell you that those dharmas you previously trained in to be beneficial are like a wiped conch; drop them. Then, set about the work of going to emancipation. You need to part from the mistaken mode of awareness. Relying on the guru's foremost instruction, you need to not mix yourself in with tenets and rational mind.' After he had given that advice on meditation, he said to acharya Yondag, 'Setting yourself in holding the mind in place by focussing it on a bindu[361] does not capture primordial mind! Various geshes have been helped by hearing this, so please do pay some attention to it. If you would listen to an old man like me, then meditate!'

"Then, nine months later on, a meditation having occurred for me, I asked the guru about it and he said, 'Your meditation is one of putting a lance into a mouse-hole. Now the one of flourishing a lance in space has to come[362]. Now, for each session, whatever you hear is beneficial. For each session, whatever you see is beneficial. Meditate without mixing my dharma with that of others!' I continued to meditate and found that I had no strong desire to listen, no strong desire to look; my mind had turned to meditation alone. Because of it, later, my meditation became a personally experienced expanse. I asked the guru about it. He said that it was flourishing a lance in space.

"Then acharya Yondag asked Gonpawa, 'Acharya, I practise your dharma. Do you have other trainings that you explain to the geshes?' Gonpawa said, 'If one valley has two streams, one pure river and one impure one, they will mix and go on. Listen or not, explain or not, do meditation alone!' After that, he did nothing but

---

[361] This is a meditation commonly done for developing concentration of mind.

[362] See also the explanation of these two approaches with a lance in part five of Dusum Khyenpa's interviews.

meditate and later became a person who, like Gonpawa, possessed many good qualities.

"What is needed is an expert guru who will lead the disciple according to the disciple's mental capacity. When the disciple asks about whatever comes to mind and the guru answers with whatever comes to mind, it is a careless approach and by it dharma will not go to the path."

———— ◆◆◆ ————

Namo guru.

The precious guru said this. "Generally, persons are divided into three—best of faculty, middling, and least. The person of best faculty presents a difficulty; mostly this kind doesn't appear." Dusum Khyenpa asked, "What is difficult about that type of person?" He replied, "For a person of best faculty, at the time of distinctly realizing birthless dharmata's fact, the outer container world with its earth, rocks, and mountains, its steep ravines and impassable canyons, rocky ledges, walls, wickerwork fencing, and so on, all of it, is taken into dharmakaya. And the inner contents, sentient beings with their men, women, horses, oxen, and so on, all are known to be impermanent, known to be mere dreams, illusions. All of this appearance becomes mist-like. When that has happened, at the time of an awareness that thinks, 'There is no worthwhile way to take all dharmas except for their being birthless in superfact', there is no good or bad for any of them, no big and small, no is and isn't—gold and a clod of earth, enemies and sugar are the same, clinging to this samsara is left behind, all dharmas have been freed from elaboration's extremes. Someone like that is referred to as 'a person of best faculty' and is difficult in that such a person does not happen."

He said, "In comparison, a person of middling faculty also is difficult to find." Dusum Khyenpa asked, "Why is that?" The reply came, "For a person of middling faculty, the bardo awareness happens so he must train in apprehending dreams and bardo." Dusum Khyenpa asked, "What exactly is needed for identifying dreams and bardo?" The reply came, "Something like sleep and death, something like dreams and bardo!" Dusum Khyenpa asked, "How does it work?" The reply came, "At the time of sleep, this material body with its flesh and blood is like a corpse on a bed and then where does mind's discursive thought go? What does it do? That example is also applied to the bardo awareness. Thus it is necessary to train in an identification of dream and bardo."

He said, "Overall, the person of middling faculty will not meditate solely on the fact of birthless dharmata, so for him, moreover, it will not come. That person accumulates the causes, the accumulation of merit, and then having done so, must bring the fruition, the accumulation of wisdom, to the path." Dusum Khyenpa asked, "How is the accumulation of the cause, merit, done?" The reply came, "It does not happen in relation to either a greater or smaller amount of virtue. It must be accumulated without any of these biassed extremes of degree of accumulation getting in the way." Dusum Khyenpa asked, "How is the fruition, the accumulation of wisdom, brought to the path?" The reply came, "Both development state and completion stage have to be brought to the path." He said, "One is indeed sufficient so what need for both? The reply came, "For a person of middling faculty, the two will be done alternately then he will meditate on the unification of development and completion stages so, when he dies, he will not attain the first bardo enlightenment mind yet, because of development stage mind could be apprehended and because of completion stage mind not apprehended. Or, even if both of them do not apprehend it, because of his causes, his accumulation of merit, he will not fall into the bad migrations. He will gain a precious human rebirth, then the previous meditation's karmic propensities will awaken, and then he will attain the fruition, the dharmakaya, that is, he will become a buddha."

Dusum Khyenpa asked, "Of those two which is difficult, which is easy?" The reply came, "The approach of a person of least faculty is easiest. His approach is to practise." Dusum Khyenpa asked, "How would he do that?" The reply came, "Hold the vows of personal emancipation nicely and without corruption. Discard the ten non-virtues. Take up the ten virtues. Accumulate the cause, the accumulation of merit, in its entirety. Dedicate all roots of virtue to unsurpassable enlightenment. Make prayers of aspiration for the Great Vehicle dharma. Rouse the loving kindness and compassion enlightenment mind. Finally, for the sake of sentient beings he will attain unsurpassable enlightenment."

———— ◆◆◆ ————

Guru namo!

The precious acharya said, "If one is genuinely going to do dharma itself and practise it from the heart, then first, in this life, one has to turn one's thinking around. If one intends to go that way but strives for gain, respect, fame, reputation, and so on—the eight worldly dharmas—one's thinking has not been turned around. Being an expert does not help with this and monks and the like have good qualities but that also does not help with this. However, if you meditate on death and impermanence, there is no way that your ideas will not be turned away from this life. You will not escape the depths of death and will take another birth due to karma, therefore you must by whatever means gain trust in karma and result. Great non-virtues do not need to be discussed, their situation is so obvious, given that it has been taught that even subtle non-virtues can result in birth in the bad migrations, therefore, even the subtlest of subtle evil deeds must be abandoned via the appropriated antidote—and that, by the way, is exactly the function of the vows of personal emancipation. Also, you might not want to get a god's birth, but by conducting yourself virtuously, you will get a birth in the higher levels; if you do not gain unsurpassable en-lightenment, there will be nothing to assist you to be born human, either. It is the same right now. You are not emancipated from samsara's suffering and everything is impermanent, so you are not comfortable; a characteristic of the truth of suffering is impermanence. That being so, it is important to be revolted by samsara. When that kind of mind that renounces the suffering of samsara has arisen, if you then realize selflessness of the person because of considering peace and happiness for yourself alone, that is taught to be the nirvana of a noble shravaka. In that partial, one-sided emptiness, there is none of the enlightened activity of a buddha done for the sake of sentient beings, therefore, the Great Vehicle itself is supreme. From the standpoint of worldly persons, the Tibetan race might be bad but, mind training done only for the sake of others makes them the Tibetans of the Great Vehicle line. One says 'Great Vehicle', but if you have meditated on the loving kindness, compassion, and enlightenment mind as a connected whole, whatever you do will be done for the sake of sentient beings, and that is Great Vehicle."

He said, "Secret Mantra teaches that fictional enlightenment mind via the four immeasurables, and so on. Jowo Je himself has said that if those three things mentioned just above are meditated on such that they are a connected whole, the four limitless ones will be included. Moreover, of all sentient beings there are none whom have not been our father and mother. They have been so an unfathomable number of times." He said, "This is so because of the point that samsara is without beginning or end."

He said, "At the times of being our parent, every one of them has been kind, so we have to think, 'I should help them'. Thinking, 'I will give them happiness' is loving kindness. We are equal in that just as I do not want suffering so all sentient beings do not want to suffer, and we are equal in that just as I want happiness for myself so all sentient beings want happiness. Therefore, we think, "I will free sentient beings from suffering', which is compassion. This idea of oneself and others is mind, so it is an equalization merely of idea. In fact, the idea of self is mind. Mind looks at itself. That frees it from the identification of conceived-of things because of which the selfish approach of doing something for oneself does not occur. Because of that, one has the thought, "Well then, for the sake of all sentient beings, I will attain complete enlightenment', which is the enlightenment mind. That rational mind is then trained in the two stages of aspiring and entering."

That was the final understanding.

❀   ❀   ❀

[Part eleven, a single interview or teaching given by Gampopa.]

He said, "This superfactual enlightenment mind pervades all of samsara and nirvana; this is called 'dharmata'. It is a theoretical understanding of the dharmata but, with it, Paramita proceeds, based on the dharmata's total natural pervasion of external objects, by tearing them apart with reasoning then meditating on the objects known through intention to be empty[363] and so manifests the dharmata.

"That is one path. It helps to free a person from his manifest clinging to conceived-of things. Our path involves both view and meditation. The view moreover is not a dharmata which is sought externally. One's own mind, this rigpa luminosity without identification in it, itself is dharmata. It is called 'un-compounded'. A rigpa knower is not something we have as a nature so it is called,

---

[363] Objects known through intention to be empty has the meaning explained some pages back for intention and emptiness. This paragraph is slightly pejorative, saying that those who insist on the Paramita approach are taking a very conceptual approach. The next paragraph lays out the other possibility.

'dharmadhatu'[364]. Suchness, the limit of the authentic[365], which is called 'superfactual truth'—that is our view. Our meditation is a practice which brings that view into experience as Mahamudra and this is the way we do it. It is taught that to begin, we free ourselves of concept-based striving then relax the body-mind complex, and so on. Then, in an isolated place on a comfortable seat, the tathagata's way of sitting (eyes not moving, looking straight ahead) and looking are taken up. Enlightenment mind is meditated on. Your own body evident as the deity, then the guru on top of your crown as the deity, are meditated on. Then, you put yourself directly into exactly what you are, however that is, without alteration and left to be itself. If you alter it, it is thought, so not altering is important. If, within that state, thoughts arise, do not reject them; they come forth of themselves, so put yourself directly in that with the thoughts un-altered, left wholly to be themselves. Do not make a duality of them. Mahamudra is non-duality. All dualistic appearance comes from the ignorance of not-rigpa as its cause so it is confusion arising in various ways. In short, it has been taught that Mahamudra is to meditate free of the stains of rational mind.

"A beginner will do short sessions many times. Through meditating undistractedly, continuously according to that, the experience of the Four Yogas gradually comes forth. By appearance and mind being made non-dual, no condition can harm you and all the good qualities of samsara and nirvana will be complete within you."

---

[364] Here nature indicates a nature known as dualistic mind would know it, with a fixated, solidified entity. Because the luminosity aspect is a rigpa knower but without a fixated entity, it can be and is the all-pervasive source of every phenomenon. Therefore, it is the dharmadhatu, meaning the range which is the birthplace of all phenomena.

[365] Suchness is a final thing that one comes to both intellectually when determining tenets and when practising for enlightenment. Therefore, it called a 'limit' of accomplishment.

He said, "For those who have entered the door of Secret Mantra working the winds' key points also is important; the tantras teach that if the wind is held, mind will also be held, for mind's mount is wind. Wind and mind are not two."

Due to writing down this talk of the guru
May those who practise it accordingly
Accomplish the aims of self and others.
May they complete the guru's mind.

❀ ❀ ❀

[Part twelve: seven interviews or teaching sessions with the last being given to Gomchung.]

The precious guru said, "You might ask, 'What is the difference between the innate and Co-emergent Unification?' Co-emergent Unification means to take thought onto the path. There are two types of thought, good and bad. Whichever one arises, by regarding it as kind, thought is made into the path; compared to that, wandering in samsara is to wander because of not recognizing discursive thinking for what it is; when that is dealt with by making thought into the path, intimidation by samsara is removed.

"You mentioned the innate. Your way of taking thought onto the path has the duality of that to be severed and that which severs. Now there is no end to thought and in regard to that you might be recognizing the occurrence of one thought then also recognizing the next occurrence, but unless you are seeing the entity at the same time, doing that is not up to what is needed. If something to be seen arises, just that is it! There is nothing else to see. If you do not see 'I', because there actually is no end to discursive thought, you have the fault of no connection with to it. 'I' initially is without birth, in the interim without dwelling, and at the end without cessation. The entity is free of identification; the nature is without interruption; the characteristic is beyond rational mind.

"In regard to 'I', from the standpoint of Secret Mantra, when this is looked at from the aspect of concept tokens, it is something that even the buddhas of the three times never observe. When it is looked at from the aspect of absence of concept tokens, it is there at all times without interruption. From the standpoint of Paramita,

> For I there is neither anything to be cleared
> Nor the slightest thing to be added.
> Look authentically at the authentic.
> If the authentic is seen, that is complete liberation.
> The authentic in that is what I am!

"Then, for Mantra there are the three of entity, etymology, and divisions. Its entity is birthless, so it is buddha's enlightened mind. To understand what that is, the *Saṃpuṭa* says,

> The birthless nature is mantra.
> The certainty of mantra is nothing whatsoever.

Its etymological definition is "to protect the mind"; as *Guhyasamaja* says,

> Ma na is yid, trāya is protection.

Its divisions are: thought mantra; self-knowing rigpa mantra; and communication signs' mantra. First, thought mantra is 'the imagined' which is the wind complex and 'the dependent'[366] which occurs when it is said verbally. Second, the self-knowing rigpa mantra is ayatanas' luminosity. Third, communication signs' mantra is the entirety of dharani and the entirety of development stage. In it there are letters having a beginning, having an ending, like snakes, and abbreviated letters; the *Guhyasamaja* says,

---

[366] The imagined and the dependent are the first two of the three characteristics of the Mind Only system.

An OM̐ shown at the start and no SVĀHĀ at the end is
explained to be 'letters having a beginning'. No OM̐ at
the beginning and having SVĀHĀ at the end is explained
to be 'letters having an ending'. No OM̐ at the
beginning and no SVĀHĀ at the end is explained to be
'abbreviated letters'. An OM̐ at the beginning and a
SVĀHĀ at the end is explained to be 'snake, the peaceful
worker'.

———— ◆◆◆ ————

And Rinpoche said, "A practitioner by practising causes good
qualities to appear in his mindstream. Due to that, when he meets
a disciple with faith, he explains the dharma to him. The practitioner tells him that he is to become a buddha in this life and to do so
has to proceed by making that part stronger. He tells him that this
is the doorway to siddhi. Now, the Kadampas, or you could say one
group, says about this, 'If you merely say, 'It's done by making the
hidden part come out' and the person though not sensing it has
meaningful accomplishment or if, having the capacity within
himself, is a fortunate disciple, that sort of person should be told
that it is necessary to preserve it even at the cost of his life.' Otherwise, to say such things is just to waste one's breath on the practitioner; the practitioner, having produced a single good quality in
himself will turn to external entertainments that become an obstacle to accomplishment. Generally, this entertainment which some
want to call 'merit' is also explained as the work of mara."[367]

———————————————————

[367] The meaning here is that a qualified Mahamudra guru will tell a
worthy student to practise the highest dharma. The Kadampas—and
here Gampopa catches himself and says well, a group who follow the
Kadampa at least—were well known for their attitude that this kind of
dharma was too dangerous for nearly anyone to practise. A disciple
with a qualified guru might perhaps get one good quality because of
having been given the introduction to the nature of mind but having

(continued...)

And Rinpoche said, "Generally speaking, there are many points at which one could deviate in meditation. However, there are the six realms, four absorptions, and four sets of ayatanas[368] explained for the points of deviation—where there is even a little grasping, these become deviations. The deviation into being a shravaka is that, by abiding in the cut-off emptiness that goes with it, it is deviation. If there is certainty of abiding in the entity without grasping, there will be no point of deviation at all."

He said, "Also, there are two places of becoming lost: in relation to experiences and in relation to realization. For experience it will be to become lost through having gone into grasping the supreme in relation to bliss and luminosity and for realization it will be to become mistaken due to grasping at the experiences which are discontinuous; those are the two places of becoming lost."

——— ◆◆◆ ———

---

[367](...continued)
done so, he could easily fall into drinking and having sex, and so on when he did not have the capacity to use those types of behaviour properly on the path. Although the Mahamudra system would explain such behaviour to its followers as meritorious, the Kadampas reject that outright, saying it is the opposite. Of course, Gampopa does not quite agree with that.

In the next paragraph he lays out the places at which a Mahamudra practitioner could deviate, which is to cling to the experiences of bliss, luminosity, and no-thought, with the result of being born in the desire, form and formless realms respectively. The third one can also lead to taking up a shravaka's cessation.

[368] The six realms here is equivalent to the desire realm; absorption refers to the four levels of the form realm; and four sets of ayatanas are the levels of the formless realm.

He said, "There are the three of no-thought, wisdom, and being empty. No-thought is to be freed from thought. Wisdom is mindness co-emergence luminosity recognized as primordially present within. Being empty is that free from identification.

"Then there are the three of awareness, knowables, and prajna. Awareness is self-knowing's entity[369]. Knowable refers to all dharmas which have become an object of rational mind and prajna is what comprehends that.

"There are the three of not referencing, being empty, and concept tokens. Emptiness being experienced or concept tokens not being referenced at all, is not referencing. The external grasped object, does not come into existence via a ground or root, and the internal grasping mind also does not come into existence via a ground and root; this is being empty. To be together with grasped and grasping means to have concept tokens.

"There are the three of profound dharma and not profound dharma and in-between. Not profound is this: having trust in cause and effect because of knowing that, having involved oneself in causes that exist—virtue and non-virtue—results that exist—good and bad—will be experienced. Middling is this: all the dharmas of samsara and nirvana never having known existence, each one is known to be like a dream, like an illusion. The profound one is that the innate, being like an ocean whose depth cannot be found, is deep.

"There are the three of mind, sentient being, and mindness. Mind is the rigpa that grasps onto I. Sentient being, that which has a mind, is all beings who have a mind. Mindness is the uninterrupted dharmakaya.

---

[369] As I have said before, awareness does not correspond to rigpa. Here it means that minds knows, is aware, no more and no less.

"There are the three of cause, path, and result. There is what creates so there is the cause. There is what develops it so there is the path. There is what completes it so there is the result. Moreover, if that is taken from a standpoint of going down, the cause, the ignorance of not-rigpa, gives rise to evil deeds; small evil deeds develop into great evil deeds whereby there is the result, a bad migration. That makes three. Then, from the standpoint of going up, Paramita has causal rigpa which is enlightenment mind, the path of the six paramitas or else the three paths of training, and the result of the three kayas. Secret Mantra has causal rigpa which is enlightenment mind, the path of the pair development and completion, and the result of the three kayas."

———— ◆◆◆ ————

He said, "By meditation on death, one does not involve oneself in the purposes of this life. By meditation on the disadvantages of cyclic existence, one is not born in samsara. By meditation on cause and result, one is not born in bad migrations. By meditation on loving kindness, compassion, and enlightenment mind, one is not born as a shravaka or pratyekabuddha. By meditation on the profound dharma, emptiness, one is not born in the formless realm.

"There are three benefits and five good qualities associated with death meditation. Disenchantment is born. Faith is restored. It becomes a goad of perseverance. It stops attachment to being a worldly person. It puts one on the side of nirvana. There are three levels of death meditation: best, middling and least. The best does not grasp at conceived-of things for more than a day. Middling does not grasp at them for more than a month. Least does not grasped at them for more than a year."

———— ◆◆◆ ————

I prostrate to the holy gurus.

He said, "There is mindness's co-emergence, dharmakaya. There is appearance's co-emergence, the dharmakaya's light. Mindness's co-emergence is mind's nature or its entity. Appearances' co-emergence is the discursive thinking that arises from that. Moreover, this is like the sun and the sun's light or sandalwood and sandalwood's scent.

"There are three dharmas in connection with the realization of that and three dharmas in connection with practising to gain experience of it. For the first, there is the realization that appearance co-emergence is nothing whatsoever shining forth in various appearances; there is the realization that although various appearances shine forth, they are in fact nothing whatsoever; and there is the knowledge that it is not possible to explain the non-duality. The three dharmas of practising to experience that are: first, in the mindness co-emergence, body and mind are relaxed by freeing oneself from conceived-of striving; next, doubt-free, one puts oneself into mind unaltered, fresh; and finally, all sensed occurences[370] are known to be birthless."

———— ◆◆◆ ————

He said, "The three of view, meditation, and conduct are as follows. View is the unaltered innate's awareness. Meditation is no-thought common awareness[371]. Conduct is, with no clinging, the sixfold group left loose and unrestrained. The technique is to be undistracted with the thinking process allowed to continue.

"Moreover, the one cause of buddhas and sentient beings is appearance and mindness not different. The innate's nature, suchness, is

---

[370] Sensed occurrences are thoughts that pop up and are known.

[371] For common awareness, see the glossary.

not known by the childish, they are confused about the garbha's fact[372]."

That was a talk of the precious guru. It was advice to acharya Gomchung.

❀ ❀ ❀

[Part thirteen: a single interview or teaching session given by Gampopa.]

He said, "Among the methods for alleviating sickness there two methods for curing it with rational mind: going along with it and eliminating it. There are two methods for going along with it: taking the sickness itself as a method and knowing it by prajna so leading it elsewhere.

"Taking the sickness as a method is that the sickness which is a sickness of being involved with the imaginary[373] is to have become sick due to dharma or meditation not going well—you have taken a place where there is no sickness and apprehended it as sickness— so, based on that, it becomes a method for meeting with an un-mistaken dharma. It is also a method for producing un-mistaken dharma on the mindstream. It is also a method for quickly attain-ing the fruition." Having been taught that way, he stopped viewing sickness as a fault then, thinking of it as a source of good qualities, his faith in the sickness caused it to alleviate itself.

"The root of not curing sickness is hope and fear; hope prevents the cure and fear brings on the sickness. He, by knowing the sickness itself as a method, let go of the clinging involved in his fears about the sickness and his hopes that it would end, which caused the

---

[372] Garbha means tathagatagarba or sugatagarbha.

[373] The imaginary is the first of the three characteristics of Mind Only.

sickness to end of itself. Harm created by demonic ghosts should also be dealt with like that.

"Next, there is the method of curing it by going along with it. In going along with it, one way is to invoke the deity's blessings. The mind training of using prajna as a way of leading it to another type of mind is as follows. Without mind dwelling on the sickness, if you look into what the sickness's awareness is doing, that will lead it elsewhere. When it wanders to something else, the awareness itself that grasps at being sick is identified as prajna then this mind being allowed to change and change as it wants becomes the dharmata.

"Alternatively, via elimination of the rational mind, the sickness will be alleviated; right on top of the sickness itself, by contemplating where the mind which is being counted as the sickness is going, the earlier sickness will be alleviated, it being the dharmata. Alternatively, by coming to a definite decision about where this sickness arose from, and an examination of its colour and shape, the sickness will be understood to be not there and will be alleviated; it is the dharmata.

"First, one does not engage with referencing and conceived effort. In the interim, one does not abide. Finally, one does not grasp.

"There are four types of person connected with this path in the family of bodhisatva mahasatvas[374]: in the bodhisatva at the time of a shravaka, in the family of needing to ask the guru when he does not realize it at the time of a pratyekabuddha, in the family of needing to realize himself as others have also done at the time of a bodhisatva; and, if the sakes of both self and other arise (if he can mix his mind with self and others) the times of the great bodhisatva and of the bodhisatva.

---

[374] These are the bodhisatvas on the seventh bodhisatva level and up, the ones on the pure levels.

Pleasant feeling (if attachment to, form realm), unpleasant feeling (if attachment to, desire realm), neutral feeling (if attachment to, formless realm. A small connection to each type of birth).

❀ ❀ ❀

[Part fourteen.]

A talk given by the precious guru when Lord Gomtshul was staying in Lhasa. Yola Chitam also listened. Acharya Tsultrim Yeshe was given the advice. He gave it to me.

"Guru namo.

"This supplication of the guru buddha is the best of methods, so I make intense devotion from the depths of my heart, blood, and bones then, I need to supplicate for the desired meaning just as it is. Doing so requires me to do a clearing of samaya and an amendment.

"All of the desired meaning (which is the root of all siddhi) is to be accomplished. For compounded virtue, there is no dharma of greater value than supplication done while seeing the guru (he explained that, especially, practising according to the advice given is the best way to honour the guru) as buddha—the precious guru has said so. By cherishing only oneself, even the smallest circumstance (bad and so on) will not be tolerable (like touching an open wound) and with great fanfare all the afflictions will arrive with great intensity. This is a great obstruction to qualities being produced in the mindstream (for maras, there has never been anything greater than this, this actually is a bull-headed rakasha in person! This is just my thought about it, he said). Within oneself, a violent wind is a great hammer that defeats all happiness. It is necessary to consider whether you will be emancipated from samsara by thinking only of yourself when putting the guru on high (having carried myself up till now with only that conduct, I have held myself down and not let myself have the chance for liberation) and yourself down low as a tiny ant. The needs for cleansing the mind and training in meditation is that the aims of myself and others will be perfected. Outer and inner wishes afflicting you like a thirsty man wanting water is the work of mara. Not turning to having respect for the guru is the work of mara. Having no trust in the advice given and taking no account of it is the work of mara. Not working at staying in samadhi and always having a distracted mind is the work of mara. Thinking 'I' and holding to cherishing yourself is the work of mara. Cling to this life and being parted from the guru is the work of mara (this is you seeing some negativity in yourself and then not liking it, he said). There is a great need to understand that until now due to this alone I have been bound in samsara."

"To exert yourself at the means for turning that away, the very essence of what you desire internally is that you need to meditate like you need to climb the iron Shalmali trees[375] (a fruition little desired) or like you need the aconite poison mentioned in the sutras. For what you desire externally, you need to meditate like has been said by the Buddha and Ananda. As an antidote to not respecting the guru (as appears in the *Fifty Verses of the Guru*), do not look at the faults of his ways, look at his good qualities, consider his enlightened being and at all times, supplicate him from your very marrow. As an antidote to not trusting the oral instructions, think of the oral instructions as nectar and yourself as a sick man and then you will understand the good qualities of the oral instructions. As an antidote to boasting over how you are better (you need to understand dispelling the sickness of samsara), look to see for yourself what good qualities you have. Ask yourself whether everyone says how wonderful they think you are or the other way

---

[375] One hell is made of these kind of trees. They are made of razors. The hell-beings there have no choice but to climb them.

around? As an antidote to not abiding in concentration and being distracted, samadhi is the guru. Concentration is the wish-fulfilling jewel so (not being distracted, the path of all buddhas) there is no way to be distracted night and day, so meditate in a continuous stream. As the antidote to mind turning away (he made this mind turning away and not into a major point) look into what happiness sentient beings of samsara have (saying the three bad migrations are a definite place and just not seeking at all for going to the higher realms is how he was talking). Think about what happiness and sorrow you have had up till now. Please contemplate what Rinpoche has said.

"Generally, if there is not a bit of compassion, at the time of dharma (everyone has self-cherishing) you will think that all dharma is produced like stones or salt[376]. Thus one puts effort into having enlightenment mind with emptiness."

❀   ❀   ❀

[Part fifteen: Acharya Gomchung instructs Acharya Tolungpa in the foremost instructions of Mahamudra according to the lineage gurus Marpa, Milarepa, and Gampopa. Dusum Khyenpa gets it from him.]

He said, "I prostrate to the holy gurus. A person who wants to realize Mahamudra will meditate like this:

Mindness co-emergence is the dharmakaya;
Appearance co-emergence is the dharmakaya's light;
The phenomena of samsara and nirvana have the same
    nature—meditate on that.
If this dharma which is like space is realized, it's that.

---

[376] In other words, you won't know the right way to produce it, thinking that it is purely mechanical and heartless.

Put yourself in that, mindness's entity, not chasing after the past, not going out to greet the future, and staying in the present without referencing anything. By putting yourself like that, mind's entity, without thought in the luminosity, like being in the centre of a completely pure space, will happen.

"Moreover, do not look at its quality for long periods. With shorter periods, you will not see in a faulty way. At all times put yourself undistractedly in its state.

"If you are able to meditate that way on the birthless fact, all phenomena will shine forth within the state of the innate. Phenomena will be continuously realized as same taste in the three times. Put yourself continuously into not being distracted from that sort of fact.

"The foremost instruction that truly demonstrates Mahamudra's fact, suchness, this understanding of the buddhas of all three times, has been realized by the guru siddhas; may the migrator sentient beings be liberated from the mire of samsara! May I too have enlightened activity equal to that of the guru."

A lamp of precious foremost instruction on Mahamudra, which is the talk of the three uncles[377]*, was given as advice by Acharya Gomchung to acharya Tolungpa. He gave it to me. May there be auspiciousness.*

---

[377] The three uncles are Marpa, Milarepa, and Gampopa.

Plate 3. Lord Phagmo Drupa from an ancient thangka

Text 5

Lord Phagmo Drupa's Interviews

Lord Phagmo Drupa's Interviews

[Interview one: the beginning.]

I bow to the realized Precious One,
The buddhas of the three times in person[378].

The precious guru from Kham rounded up all of his issues and
asked precious Lord Gampopa about them. "Precious guru, sir,
what is most important in regard to the cause, accumulating the
accumulation of merit?" The guru replied, "In glorious
Guhyasamaja it says,

> Compared to making offerings throughout the three
> times to all of the tathagatas of the ten directions,
> making an offering to one hair pore of the guru is
> superior.

---

[378] Phagmo Drupa has come from far away in East Tibet. He is
already renowned as a master who is both learned and accomplished
in meditation. He already has many disciples so is known as "guru
Phagmo Drupa". This early interview records the time of his getting
to know Gampopa, which includes the necessary phase of testing him,
to see whether he has the qualities needed so that he could be accepted
as a guru.

and in *Manjushri*[379], it says,

> It is appropriate to make continual ritual
> At those places worthy of offering and worthy of praise.
> Better is to make offerings to those worthy of esteem.
> Best is make them to the guru who is worthy of
>   prostration.

and also, in guru Mila's words,

> Carrying out the command of the guru, just as he has
> spoken it, then supplicating the guru with devotion and
> doing the practice as it should be done, this alone is the
> most meritorious."

Well then, he asked, "In terms of practising to gain experience, which is the most profound oral instruction?" The reply came, "The tradition of Jowo Je's lineage[380] says,

> For the thinking mind to become certain of
> Death and impermanence then karmic cause and effect
>   and
> Loving kindness and compassion is profound.

I have heard one group say, 'If the view, emptiness, is not realized, there is no benefit.' I have heard some say, 'Meditation on the yidam deity is the profound practice.' I heard guru Mila say, 'The meditation on the pranayama of Fierce Heat is the profound meditation.'

"The dharma for which any given person develops certainty is the profound one for that person. Still[381], to take this further, if you

---

[379] ... the Manjushri tantras ...

[380] Atisha and his Kadampa lineage.

[381] Now he is giving what he personally regards to be profound, that is,
(continued...)

devote yourself to the guru, meditate by pairing Fierce Heat with Mahamudra, and train your mind in enlightenment mind, because both your own and others' aims will be fulfilled at the same time, this is the profound one."

"Well then", Phagmo Drupa asked, "Do you prefer to lead people through Fierce Heat to start with or through Mahamudra?" The reply came, "Which one will depend on the person's type. Younger people with good physical elements and channels who are instructed in and meditate on Fierce Heat itself will quickly prodduce the signs of progress. If I then give them Mahamudra, experience and realization will quickly dawn. For older people who are in the category of not being able to adjust the winds, I prefer to give Mahamudra or Co-emergent Unification, though there is the possibility that, if Mahamudra is given to them first but then not aroused within their mindstreams, they might fall into bad activities and develop a very jaded and problematic character."

"Well then", Phagmo Drupa asked, "What difference is there between the sudden and gradual types of person?" The reply came, "The difference lies in the degree of training that each one has. The sudden type, through the force of greater previous training, just on being given the oral instruction has a stable realization dawn at the same time. This type will stay in the entity uninterruptedly, have greater devotion to the guru, have greater compassion for sentient beings, and have an absence of fixation on grasping at a self come on because of which this type does not need the mere techniques of enhancement. For this type, there is nothing else to do except to preserve that which has already been produced in the mindstream. The gradual type, due to a smaller amount of training, sometimes does not even give birth to experience, not even when he goes step by step, so supplicating the guru and practising a meditation of remaining undistracted from devotion is very

---

[381](...continued)
the way that he prefers to teach his disciples.

important for this type. The best of this type will have wisdom that realizes the entity shine forth in this life and the middling one will have it happen at the point of death or sometime afterwards in the bardo." Then the guru said, "To go further with this, it comes from having a full-fledged shamatha abiding; within that, it will shine forth in a moment of vipashyana in which it becomes evident."

"Well then", Phagmo Drupa asked, "If realization has been produced, does meditation have to be pursued or not?" The reply came, "If the realization that has been produced is non-meditation, then meditation done with the feature of restraining the mind with mindfulness is not needed. After all, it is not possible to revert from being a buddha to a sentient being! So there is no meditation to be done in that case but there does have to be habituation to the realization's dharmata itself and there also has to be training of the rational aspect because it is necessary to manifest a fruition of the realization that includes, as part of it, the six extra perceptions, five eyes, five wisdoms, the arrangement of the physical body, miracles—that is, the qualities of the knowledge of things in their extent[382]. Furthermore, by training up the dharmata's liveliness[383], the awareness will gain independence[384]. That shining forth of all knowables in crystal clearness and immediacy is called 'the qualities of the all-knowing aspect[385]'. If you say that this means 'there is

---

[382] This is one of the two knowledges of a buddha, the other is knowledge of things in their depth.

[383] For liveliness, see the glossary.

[384] Independence means that it will be in control of itself, unlike samsaric sense consciousnesses which, not being control of themselves, always follow the objects of consciousness.

[385] The all-knowing aspect is the all-knowing of a buddha's mind. It is summed up as having the two knowledges of knowing things in their

(continued...)

nothing to be done', then just let thought do as it will—the result will be that you will not be able to produce a fruition which will actually function and the all-knowing aspect will not come about."

"Well then", Phagmo Drupa asked, "Through what is the entity discovered?" The reply came, "It is discovered through the forces of the guru's blessings, one's own devotion, and perseverance in meditation and not through anything else. As *Hevajra* says,

> Co-emergence inexpressible by other
> Is not obtained anywhere;
> It will be known in dependence on the guru's method of
>   time
> And through one's own merit.[386]

This is not known by master scholars. It is not known by prajna. It is not the domain of philosophers. When there is the lineage of ultimate realization, a guru who has realization because of it, and a disciple who has devoted himself to that guru, then, because of the force of the blessings, that which is divorced from words, that

---

[385](...continued)
depth and in their extent.

[386] In the Kagyu instructions on Mahamudra, this verse, which comes from the "Two Parts"—the portions of the *Hevajra Tantra* remaining with us—is very often quoted. The first two lines state that co-emergent wisdom is not something that another person can tell you about and also not something you can go and get from somewhere, leaving the question how do you get it? The next two lines are the answer: you can only get it by the specific method of utilizing the guru's method of time and for that to happen that depends on your own merit. The "guru's method of time" has largely been mis-translated up till now. It often appears as "timely method" or any of several other mistaken wordings. It refers specifically to the method of introducing a disciple to his own mind using a method that is connected with time.

which is beyond the domain of rational mind[387], shines forth from the disciple's own mindstream. The entity cannot be stated in words—even experts like the noble one Nagarjuna could not do it—so *Hevajra* says,

> Absence of meditator, absence of that to be meditated
>   on,
> Absence of deity, and absence of mantra, too,
> Absence of even the slightest thing to be meditated on.
> In the nature which is absent of elaborations,
> The true deity and mantra are present.

And in *Manjushri*[388] also, it says,

> The realizer of absence of time of the three times
> Knows all about all sentient beings.

At the time when that is produced, the single universal solution[389] has gone to being "knowing one, liberating all" and because of that, buddha has been discovered in oneself. By that, the shackles that were holding the person in cyclic existence release themselves and through that the person's mind now operates on the level of great bliss."

"Well then", Phagmo Drupa asked, "What difference is there, if any, between Mahamudra and Co-emergence Unification?" The reply came, "Mahamudra is as follows: all of the phenomena of samsara and nirvana are, primordially, spontaneously existent; the dharmata, like space, is the wisdom on at all times; and the two are a non-duality that goes on without discontinuity. Co-emergence Unification is as follows: any thought produced is to be unified with

---

[387] For rational mind, see the glossary.

[388] ... the Manjushri tantras ...

[389] "The single, universal solution" is a name for Mahamudra.

the four kayas, so it is not asserted as 'on at all times' and 'has discontinuity'."[390]

"Well then", Phagmo Drupa asked, "How different are experience and realization?" The reply came, "Experience is something that does not go beyond being part of rational mind. As with the sun shining through gaps in clouds, the three experiences of bliss, luminosity, and no-thought will come to be present sometimes more prominently and sometimes less so. If you preserve this presence without clinging to it, the dirt of conceptual mind will be cleared, then realization of the primal state will shine forth.

"Realization is as follows. First one develops the rational-minded understanding that appearance and mind are not two different things. On that basis, by staying un-interruptedly in the state of luminosity, realization is gained when there is separation from something to meditate on and a meditation to be done; it is said 'to shine forth at that same time'."[391]

"Well then", Phagmo Drupa asked, "How is this seen as different from the Path of Seeing?" The reply came, "No attempt is made to make this fit with the Path of Seeing[392]. Still, this could be said.

---

[390] Note that the words behind the English "co-emergent unification" are actually "co-emergence yoga". When seen in that light, it is easy to understand that Mahamudra is a name for the fundamental reality as it is, where co-emergent yoga is a name for the practice of joining with that reality. Mahamudra is not a path term per se, Co-emergence Unification is.

[391] See also realization in the glossary.

[392] The development of realization taught in the sutra vehicle is the system of progression through five paths. In it, the point at which one gains direct insight into reality is the third path, the Path of Seeing. The teachings on the development of realization here are Vajra

(continued...)

The seeing, a little, of mind's entity could be said to be the shrava-ka's Path of Seeing. Therefore, seeing Mahamudra a little would be the noble arhat's[393] Path of Seeing. Seeing the dharmata like the centre of a complete pure space would be the bodhisatva's Path of Seeing. Seeing the non-dual nature of all samsara and nirvana as great equality would be the Path of Seeing of a truly complete buddha. Further to that, it says in *The Heart Prajnaparamita*, 'Form is empty, emptiness also is form'. Then, from the standpoint of a yogin, 'Seeing mind's entity a little is the Path of Seeing of the lowest-level yogin. Seeing the entity just free from elaboration is the Path of Seeing of the medium-level yogin. Seeing mind's entity divorced from birth, cessation, and dwelling then staying uninter-ruptedly in that is the Path of Seeing of the highest level of yogin.'"

"Well then", Phagmo Drupa asked, "In terms of this appearance we have, what is the difference between sentient beings, noble ones, yogins, and buddhas?" The reply came, "At the time of being a sentient being, appearances operate as something that is coming from grasping at things. For noble ones, they operate as illusory appearances. For yogins, they operate as the appearances of experiences. For buddhas, they operate as appearances of luminos-ity or you can say appearances of unification."

---

[392](...continued)
Vehicle and do not belong to or even fit with the five-path system of the sutras. Phagmo Drupa asks his question because the realization that Gampopa is talking about is one in which a person gains direct insight of reality. Phagmo Drupa is asking whether that realization is the same as the realization that occurs on the Path of Seeing. Gampo-pa says to him that the comparison cannot really be made because the two systems are different and do not fit together, but continues to give advice on it, nonetheless.

[393] See noble one in the glossary for the meaning of noble.

"Well then", he asked, "What is the difference between illusory body, luminosity, unification, and Mahamudra?" The reply came, "In terms of illusory body, the impure illusory body is grasping at the ordinary and the pure illusory body is the appearances of a buddha's body. In luminosity, there is the training luminosity which is a feature of samadhi and belongs to the time of the yogin and there is also the non-training luminosity which is referred to as belonging to the time of a buddha. Unification also has two aspects, development and completion. The training unification is present on the yogin's path of unification. The no-more training unification is the indivisibility of both dharma- and form-kayas which is referred to as belonging to the time of a buddha. Mahamudra also has the phase of being on the path which is called "path Mahamudra" and the phase of being divorced from acceptance and rejection due to realizing the great wisdom of the nonduality of samsara and nirvana which is ultimate Mahamudra in operation. That is the un-mistaken mind of the buddhas of the three times so you will not find it if you look somewhere apart from buddha. To stay in the earlier one of each of those two cases is to stay in the yogas of the path. To stay in the later ones are to have seized buddhahood, to have seized enlightenment. If we want to go further or higher than that, given that there is not just buddhahood, we also speak of 'sugata', meaning the one gone to bliss[394]."

"Well then sir, is there a timing for the performance of other's benefit?", Phagmo Drupa politely asked. The reply came, "When

---

[394] Of course, one cannot go higher than being a buddha; that is a central truth to Buddhism. He is saying, "Look, if you don't like this dry buddhahood of unification, we can go further and say sugata instead; the term sugata is very practical, not theoretical at all. Detailed explanations of unification in relation to Mahamudra are in *Drukchen Padma Karpo's Collected Works on Mahamudra*, 2011, ISBN: 978-9973-572-01-9.

the realization of great One-Taste[395] has been produced in the mindstream, it is possible to guide disciples. Nevertheless, the extra perceptions do not come until a genuine realization of non-meditation has been produced and without the ability to know in these extra-sensory ways it is not possible to know the capacity of another person's mind, high or low, and whether it is time to guide them or not. When the realization of Non-Meditation has been produced, because of great compassion the mind does turn towards the aims of others and does turn away from one's concerns of this life. Then, when one has totally severed concerns for this life and uninterrupted great compassion has shone forth, the aims of others arises in a perfect way."

"Well sir, has all of this which has been born in the precious guru's mind happened because of Fierce Heat meditation? Or has it happened because of Mahamudra meditation?" The reply came, "These qualities of mind that have been produced in my mindstream are also there because of meditation informed by oral instructions. To go further with that, they are there because of practising just as guru Mila commanded and because of the blessings that came through devotion to him. Guru Naropa also did just as his guru commanded and so obtained the supreme and ordinary siddhis all at once."

"Well then", Phagmo Drupa asked, "What is the cause of this entity being easier to produce in the mindstream now compared to before?" The reply came, "Compared to the Nawa[396] which is born earlier, the goat which is born later is taller; the guru's blessings and realization have gone to the end. For the disciple, the force of

---

[395] The Mahamudra system divides the levels of the Four Yogas of Mahamudra into sub-levels. The great One Taste is the top of three levels of One Taste. Drukchen Padma Karpo distinguishes all of the levels and their features in the book cited just above.

[396] A Nawa is type of mountain goat. It is smaller than a domestic goat.

increased devotion is what makes it easily born in the mindstream."
Gampopa said, "Jowo Khampa[397], the teacher—for someone like
you these are not very expert dharma questions!" He went on
further, saying, "It does mean though that there is higher realization and a much greater amount of excellent virtue here."

Phagmo Drupa finished with the prayer,

> In this very remote hermitage of Gampo Zang Valley,
> In front of the very soft Lord Rinpoche,
> I asked this string of jewels of essential issues.
> By it may non-dual wisdom blossom
> For every single one of the migrators.

Gampopa, finished with the advice, "In order to attain the rainbow-
body dharmakaya in this life, you should totally discard the tethers
of looking at the material things of this life and, in an isolated place,
by relying on the guru and yidam, join the wind-mind to non-dual
Mahamudra. Many examples and lots of conventions are not
required for this[398]."

❀   ❀   ❀

---

[397] Gampopa is being very respectful towards Phagmo Drupa by calling
him "Lord from East Tibet" but teases him following that. Gampopa
does this several times in the interviews following.

[398] This means that Phagmo Drupa is very learned and can easily
engage in discussion using all the conventions, meaning agreed upon
terminology, of dharma language, doing so is not necessary now.

[Interview two: Phagmo Drupa asks for the introduction to reality.
Gampopa gives him the introduction followed by the practical instructions
for progressing on the path. The instructions explain Mahamudra
through the path of the Four Yogas of Mahamudra. All of this is given
based on Gampopa's own personal experience.]

Phagmo Drupa started by saying, "Guru Rinpoche Namo! Guru
Jewel, I have fully settled the two things, samsara and nirvana, and
now request an introduction to dharmata[399]." The guru answered
his request as follows.

"We speak of 'the two, samsara and nirvana', and of 'the two,
buddhas and sentient beings', so what does this mean? In mind,
there are both rigpa and not-rigpa which are present as the two,
recognizing rigpa and not recognizing it. If rigpa is recognized,
that is what is called 'buddha' so, rigpa is what has to be introduced
for you to have an introduction to the dharmata.

"You go to congenial places—mountainous areas, and so on—
where disenchantment can be produced and experience can develop. There, you arouse the mind, thinking, 'For the sake of
sentient beings, I will attain buddhahood.' You meditate on your
body as the deity. You meditate on the guru over your crown. Not
letting any thought spoil your mind, not altering mind in any way
because it is nothing whatsoever, put yourself in a cleared-out
purity, vividly present, cleaned-out, wide-awake state!

"After setting themselves in that state, some people have the
thought, 'When meditating, there is a cleared-out kind of purity; is
that the meditation or not?' Just that much is the function of the

---

[399] This means that he has, in accordance with the teachings of Buddhism, conceptually nailed down what samsara and nirvana are. Now
he is asking for the introduction to the nature of mind so that he can
know them in direct perception through practice of the non-conceptual path of Mahamudra.

Yoga of One-Pointedness. You decide to persevere. You continue with the meditation and because of that find that mind starts out with a style of emission of thought but that the latencies behind the thoughts decrease. Thoughts having decreased, mindness becomes increasingly clear and, correspondingly, all its obscurations become spent.

"At that time, you drop all other activities, supplicate the guru, the personal deity, and so on, and intensify devotion. Having dropped all other activities, you persevere at the meditation and for this, you need to take the kind of approach that you will only take time to drink water when thirsty.

"At the time, despite any thoughts you might have that, 'The meditation is not coming', by doing it assiduously it will come along. Thoughts like those will prevent a cleared-out purity kind of evenness of meditation coming right at the beginning. However, by continuing to meditate on that kind of cleared-out purity of the knowing, bad actions will be exhausted and a genuine Yoga of One-Pointedness will be born within your mindstream.

"Following that, if you set your awareness without support, not contacting anything at all, then, rigpa's entity freed from all elaborations—as though with its husk removed or as though you have entered into the core of the entity—will come. When that much has happened, it is called discovering the un-discovered, recognizing the un-recognized. Like a poor man finding a treasure in his hand, an undefiled, vast joy will blossom in you. There will be pure delight, pure joy.

"You increase your assiduousness then continue to meditate, which causes confused thoughts to be cleared out. Separated from practice done with conceived efforts, rigpa has gone onto being without elaborations, therefore, this is called 'the yoga of freedom from elaboration'.

"Now, for appearances, you do not cast them off mentally nor decide not to be involved with them, with the result that they are separated from the process of suppression and furtherance; all appearances now turn to being indeterminate.

"By continuing to meditate on that, you can abide in it for long periods and, because of that, what is called "the Yoga of many in One Taste" shines forth from within. Without needing to cut off the exaggerations in discursive thought's appearances using rigpa, a definite decision comes that everything is mind.

"When that much has happened, the ability for the knower to stand on its own[400] arrives. Then, in addition to that, having rational mind as part of it comes; an awareness that this appearance[401] is mind manifesting is produced and, without needing to meditate, this appearance each time will be seen as illusion, each time will be seen as empty, and each time will be the cause of thought emitted. Through the point of having been introduced to rigpa and emptiness, rational mind is put in together with the entity and, following that, all thoughts turn to being indivisibly part of the dance. By staying purely in that for a long period, what is called 'the yoga in which there is no meditation[402]' is produced; all appearances now shine forth as dharmata luminosity. Afflictions of desire, and so forth, and discursive thought arise and shine forth distinctly as dharmata luminosity. And both shine forth in plain view at the same time. Why does that happen? It is because appearances and

---

[400] As mentioned in an earlier footnote, the knower is not a dualistic consciousness any longer so can stand on its own even in the face of appearances—which includes thoughts—without being seduced by them.

[401] ... of a thought which has been allowed to come as part of the practice ...

[402] This longer phrase clearly explains the meaning of Yoga of Non-Meditation.

thoughts are the dharmata itself. By this point of rigpa and dharmakaya, the meeting of rock and bone[403], the dharmakaya shines forth in plain view without needing to meditate. When that much has happened, there is no such thing as equipoise and post-attainment; when you are meditating there also will not be any meditation. No matter what you do—whether you are going, moving about, lying down, or staying put—you remain uninter-ruptedly within dharmata luminosity.

"Then, since you have certainty in the rigpa-empty entity, when you look internally, nothing affects that fact of the entity. The 'inexpressibility by word or thought' of the Paramita system will not affect it. Engaging in the 'never been born by way of entity' of the Middle Way followers also will not affect it. Engaging in 'due to Mahamudra it is beyond rational mind' also will not affect it. Engagement in the view of the Mind-Only system, 'it is self-knowing, self-illumination', also will not affect it. The words that I have used to express it also will not, right from the beginning, affect it.[404]

"When that awareness with certainty looks outwardly, even if that fact is shown with mere words, it will not be contradicted by them in any way. Why is that? Any attempt to stop rigpa and appear-ances will not stop them. Any attempt to produce their very fact, emptiness, will not produce it. When that much has happened, it is not in the domain of the words and conventions of thought. Even if you tried to show it from all possible conceptual angles, whatever you came up with would not correspond to it. At that time, it is also called 'the yoga of great equipoise'."

---

[403] Meeting of rock and bone is a Tibetan phrase meaning the same as the English one "down to the crunch".

[404] In other words, because you are now fully immersed in what actually is, no matter what other approaches to reality you might think about, they will not affect your actually being in reality.

Phagmo Drupa said, "This is dharma born from the experience of the precious guru. It gives the introduction to those who have produced experience, then it sets the facts straight for those who have developed doubts and dispels obstructors. It elicits the experience of those who have genuinely given birth to the entity so that it can be combined with our own."

❋   ❋   ❋

[Interview three: Phagmo Drupa asks for follow-up dharma. It was given by Gampopa in the form of a detailed and extensive view of the Four Yogas from the knowledge that had been born in his own mind.]

Homage to the holy gurus.

I requested the precious guru for follow-up dharma. He replied as follows.

"Through the approach of coming to know rigpa, the general and specific characteristics of dharmas have been determined[405]; this might have produced a good type of thought but the chain of thoughts is still present. You meditate on the profound method path but discursive thought is still imposing itself as such so, even though good experiences of bliss, emptiness, and no-thought might have been produced and even though you have the guru's blessing and the special, profound method path of secret mantra, and your own devotion, and an auspicious time for undertaking hardships, as a yogin who does not have the means yet to deal with the forces of powerful passion, aggression, and so on when they arise together with experiences divorced from thought and expression at the time of intoxication with liquor or inexpressible by word or thought at

---

[405] The fictional and superfactual aspects of dharma have been understood conceptually.

the time your young lady experiences bliss or you come to orgasm, frequenting towns will, when the sensory attractions muddle you, cause all of those good experiences to turn into something like coming out of a drunken haze. If that is all such activity comes to, then it will not further your penetration of the meaning of dharma and so will not help at all.[406]

"So, let me ask you: at the time when, of the four yogas, a genuine yoga of one-pointedness has been produced, which particular certainty rises with it? Then, when an un-mistaken yoga of freedom from elaboration has been produced, which particular ce tainty rises with that? Then, when an un-mistaken yoga of o. taste in many has been produced, which particular certainty rises with that? Then, when an un-mistaken yoga of no meditation has been produced, which particular certainty rises with that?" He smiled and said, "Oh, a virtuous friend does understand the dharma here."[407]

Then he said, "For myself, I could do with a hundredth part of a hair of my guru's qualities. Compared to my holy kind guru, I have only a minute amount of certainty. However, thinking that it might help migrators, I have openly discussed the entity then introduced rigpa and emptiness. Many people are coming here, talking all sorts of fancy words and asking for instruction in the method path, yet all the teachers and many of the meditators who do come here

---

[406] In other words, having had the introduction and necessary instructions, you must have developed some significant accomplishment before you can attempt the special yogic practices of utilising liquor, sex, and so on as part of the path.

[407] Gampopa is saying, "Do you have that level of accomplishment yet? If you do, please explain to me through direct experience what it means to have accomplished each of the Four Yogas! You can't do that, can you?! There is someone sitting right in front of you who can!"

have not produced certainty in it[408]. The virtuous friend, understanding it, bestows it by saying, 'It is like this, now unify your mind
with it!' Regarding that, first, when an un-mistaken yoga of one-
pointedness has been produced, this self-knowing rigpa stays put,
not being pushed around by discursive thought, with no alteration
to it at all, not thinking about anything at all; this is the king of
samadhis, so certainty of it must be produced. One person says
that, even though such is produced, not knowing that it is so, the
meditation turns to being with referential focus or with experience,
or alternatively, that discursive thoughts having stopped and
appearances subsided, turns to being a corpse-like state. That is not
it."

He said, "Then, when an un-mistaken yoga of freedom from elaboration has been produced, training rational mind in luminosity-
appearance has caused all dharmas of samsara and nirvana to be
manifestations of one's own mind, so it requires the distinct production of the certainty that, mindness having been definitely
known to be birthless, all of the dharmas of samsara and nirvana are
pure in their own place. This sort of thing is mentioned in one of
the Dakini dohas:

> Mind meditation results in buddha;
> From the precious mind what comes
> Is absence of buddha, absence of sentient beings.

"Then, when an un-mistaken yoga of many in one taste has been
produced, mind's appearance, the liveliness of the rigpa, moves out
as various discursive thoughts but, without needing to rely on
antidote which is other than them to deal with them, those very
discursive thoughts of mind, given that they do not exist truly and
permanently, do not come into being via an essential entity. Thus

---

[408] They ask for it, get it, but then do not practise it or practise it
sufficiently to have some accomplishment in it.

it requires the distinct production of certainty of them as being dharmata.

"Then, finally, when an un-mistaken yoga of nothing to meditate on has been produced, discursive thoughts of mind, experiences of meditation, and prajna of realization are, by the power of seeing their entity, dissolved into the expanse. Thus it requires the distinct production of the certainty that identifies unaltered common awareness[409] as the dharmata.

"Further to that, first, at the time of meditating on the yoga of one-pointedness, all activities having been mentally left aside, the body-mind complex is relaxed and mind is elevated high as the sky, broadened vast as the earth, settled like a mountain, made brilliant as a lamp, and has its stains removed to be like a crystal ball; it is put into luminosity-emptiness in vividness and purity free of thoughts. At that time, various experiences will arise as effects of the constituents and physical elements[410]: sometimes a pure type of luminosity will arise; sometimes a pure type of emptiness will arise; sometimes thoughts will be emitted; sometimes there will be intellectualization and sometimes darkness of thinking 'I have no meditation.' No matter how it changes, you assiduously cultivate just the purity of experience of mindness as uncontrived luminosity-emptiness. If that occurs in full, then a genuine yoga of one-pointedness has been produced in a full-blown way. When you experience it, your awareness will have a pure delight, pure joy. Even if you deliberately try to elaborate over appearances, it will not work and there will be a resting in pure luminosity. At that time a certainty is produced; a crystal clearness occurs which is like water left un-muddied or like a flower. Not altering the rigpa, recognizing it as dharmata, you are separated from hope and fear. That is the yoga of freedom from elaboration.

---

[409] For common awareness, see the glossary.

[410] The makeup of the person practising.

"Cultivating that further, there will be the experience that all of elaboration's extremes are rigpa's own magic show and because of that, the rigpa which has now been purified into luminosity-emptiness, will be up, right there, naked, and being stared at directly. At that time, a certainty is produced; like a fresh Myrobalan put into your hand[411] or a wiped-clean crystal ball put into a large bowl, all the extremes of elaboration are the manifestations of rigpa, and, the rigpa having been recognized, the luminosity is purified into its pure portion and at that point, the pure portion of rigpa-emptiness arises in plain view.

Cultivating that for a long time, the yoga of one taste in many dawn: nd when an experience of it does dawn, without needing to use rational mind for the meditation, the entity is present in wide-awake self-illumination. Without needing to rely on an antidote, thoughts do not arise. Without needing to cut exaggeration, because mind has been purified into luminosity-emptiness, the examining and analysing of rational mind no longer shines forth. At that time, a certainty is produced: like the dawning of the sun causes the darkness to be purified in its own place, rigpa having been purified into luminosity-emptiness means that discursive thought has gone on to purity and has been purified such that even if you look for it, you will not find it. At that time, the awareness looking inward sees the entity, a purified luminosity, the pure luminosity of the bliss of dharmata, and that is equipoise. When the awareness looks outward, it sees indeterminate appearances, and that is post-attainment. Some say there is no equipoise, no post-attainment. That time, which is the meditation of no meditation, the absorption of no absorption, is called 'the yoga of a flowing river'.

---

[411] This fruit is rare, brightly coloured, very useful medicinally, and of unusual shape. If you know what a Myrobalan is then have one in come to hand you will be very sure of what it is in your hand.

"If that too is cultivated for a long time, what is called 'the yoga of non-meditation' is produced. The experience of that is, like the autumn sun in the middle of the sky at noon, one of being purely present with nothing whatsoever produced, not going on to cessation anywhere, not dwelling as anything at all that is in harmony with all, absent of gathering-separation. At that time, a certainty is produced: this uncontrived common awareness[412] is not degraded by compartmentalization or pigeon-holing[413], is un-delimited, is just peace, stays only in bliss, is not spoiled by alteration, is not improved or degraded, but distinctly arises as the dharmata.

"At that time, appearances and rigpa cannot be stopped even if you attempt to stop them; this is due to the key point of self-appearance self-shining-forth as the liveliness of mindness. Even if you try to find thought or confusion you will not; that is due to the key point of its entity being self-emptying, self-purifying. The dharmata, should you try to produce it, will not be produced; that is the key point of non-meditation and the nature[414] not having experienced birth. There is no way to set yourself in an abiding due to the key point that meditation, all of it, is confusion. Alternatively, it is the key point that emptiness, the entity, cannot be met with through meditation. That absence of equipoise and post-attainment is that

---

[412] For common awareness, see the glossary.

[413] Compartmentalizing and pigeon-holing are conceptual minds way of dealing with what is known. Those approaches come with dualistic grasping so they corrupt the realization. Delimitation is the same sort of thing.

[414] For the nature, see the glossary.

dharmata because it is freed from discarding and gaining[415]. This
sort of thing is also mentioned in *Hevajra*,

> There is neither a viewer of absence of form
> Nor a hearer of absence of sound,
> Nor a smeller of absence of smell,
> Nor a taster of the absence of taste,
> Nor a toucher of the absence of touch,
> There is no mind, there are no events of mind.

Also, *Hevajra* says,

> Sentient beings are indeed buddhas but
> Nonetheless are obscured by adventitious stains.
> Those stains dispelled is buddha itself.

And,

> What it is which is not meditated on with mentation
> Is what all migrators have to meditate on.

"Some say this: 'At first, at the time of the Yoga of One-Pointedness, it is important to give up entertainments and develop perseverance. Then, at the time of the Yoga of Freedom from Elaboration, it is important to have an awareness that includes everything
within equality and that has intensity. At the time of the Yoga of
One Taste in many, it is important that the objects being compre-
hended, the general superficies, should be experienced internally
and without mix-up. At the time of the Yoga of Non-Meditation,
it is important not to become stuck with the glue of experience. It
is necessary not to cling to experience.'"

At my request, this interchange came in the form of the precious
guru offering a detailed and extensive view of the dharmas of the

---

[415] Discarding what is seen as an un-needed fault in it and gaining what
is seen as a short-coming in it that needs to be fulfilled.

four yogas from the knowledge that had been born in his own mind.

❋   ❋   ❋

[Interview four: Gampopa teaches how the innate core is brought into manifestation.]

Namo Ratna Guru. I bow to the Precious Incomparable One.

Gampopa taught the following.

> "First, for shamatha, the four causes that produce it
> Are production though the guru's blessing,
> Production from interdependent relationship,
> Production from accumulating the accumulations, and
> Production from the purification of bad actions.

"Shamatha is the entity of mind unaltered, unspoiled, purified into clearness of what is real[416], at all times uninterruptedly present. There are two aspects to it: certainty of its appearance and uncertainty of its appearance. Certainty of its appearance is when there is realization of it being like the autumn sky and non-dual with mind. Uncertainty of its appearance involves change and no change in relation to something else; do not entertain hopes of a buddhahood up above and do not entertain fears of a samsara down below. There are four aspects to uncertainty of its appearance: 1)

---

[416] What is real here means fictional reality without any added overlays. In a more ordinary way of talking, what is real refers to what is seen by a person who is very grounded. It does not mean superfactual reality; that is not seen until the second yoga of freedom from elaboration.

shamatha's bliss, luminosity, and no-thought; 2) for the experiences, sometimes thinking, 'I have it', and sometimes thinking, 'I don't have it?'; 3) through no-thought and making a cause for it, there is the danger of falling back; and 4) there is also the danger of it becoming the cause of going into three-realmed samsara.

"At the time of training, first you are to train in the rigpa coming to mind purely, and in non-distraction of the awareness, and in non-distraction from the entity of rigpa. When you have completed the familiarization with that, a certainty is produced in yourself.

"Due to having worked at not straying from the entity of mindness, discursive thoughts do simply rise within it, for example, like the sky is naturally completely pure but clouds, fog, mistiness, and so on do just come into it yet the sky continues assured of being what it is; it is similar to that. Moreover, discursive thoughts are to be taken as assistants. If you can't go with discursive thought being allowed to be emitted, you just end up in a cocoon again and there is the danger of birth in the formless places.

"It is necessary to meditate on the yidam using completion in an instant. In the instant of it being complete just by recalling it, it is meditation on luminosity alone. Moreover, because of that pure part of luminosity coming to mind, it is experience; because of being undistracted from it, it is abiding; and because, having looked at it with prajna there is no entity by which it exists, it is realization.

"If a realized guru meets a fortunate disciple who can mentally cast off this life, then that guru will bestow the four empowerments which do the ripening of the unripened one, and then the ripened one will train himself in the two paths—development and completion—that do the liberation. Development stage is meditation on the illusion-like body of the deity and completion stage with elaboration of the channels and winds and is that, too. Completion stage without elaboration is the seeing of luminosity-emptiness in direct perception.

"Meditating on those two stages of development and completion brings forth the good qualities, and meditating in isolation does, too. Ease of body and mind will come; five signs will shine forth internally and eight good qualities will occur externally. Internally, the signs and qualities such as smoke occur following which the wind appearances stop because of the winds having been inserted into the Dhūti[417].

"Starting from the shining forth of the second sign, all appearances occur as the following kinds of experience. The dharmas seen and heard, which are to be overcome, occur as very close friends who cheat you. For skilful ones who are no longer thinking of worldly happiness, they occur like rainbows seen. All that appears, whatever it is, appears as the dharmata and, because of this, experience like an island of gold where you cannot find brass even if you search for it occurs. All that is seen and heard has dissolved into experience and because of that, experience like salt dissolved in water occurs. Deep longing for profound dharma, like a son who has not met his father for a long time, occurs. You become in awe of awareness, so experience like a poor man finding a treasure occurs. Knowing every single profound dharma just as it is, experience like a Kalika child[418], occurs. A special, great compassion for sentient beings who have not realized this is born and experience like a lusty man seeing a beautiful woman occurs. The person who has gained the experience of those good qualities and has meditated is called 'a supreme yogin', one who has manifested the dharmakaya of great

---

[417] Avadhūti, the central channel.

[418] The child of Kalika, who is a goddess in the Indian religious system. The child knows all of the dharma, the same as her mother. The child is not yet full-grown, as the yogin has not become a buddha yet, but still knows all of the dharma teaching.

bliss. Then, the two form kayas which are for the purpose of sentient beings will occur."

That completes the "process of the occurrence of the innate entity".

❊   ❊   ❊

[Interview five: Gampopa teaches mindness.]

"Namo guru.

"We refer to mindness as 'changeless, uninterrupted, all the time'. Changeless means that, not existing as colour or shape, it is change-less. Uninterrupted means it is rigpa uninterrupted. All the time means that it does not function as something that exists from this time and does not exist from this time so, because it does not get produced and does not end up ceasing, it is all the time.

"For sentient beings who have not changed themselves using the limits of accomplishment[419] there is thought. For sentient beings who have transformed their rational minds using the limits of accomplishment there is, at the time of realization by rigpa, wisdom.

"There is both self-knowing and other-knowing rigpa and they are as follows. Self-knowing is that itself recognizes itself. Other-knowing is that various appearances—all the appearances of the red

---

[419] Limits of accomplishment has two meanings: the tenets of a philosophical system and the actual experience of the states pointed to by those tenets. Here, it means the latter.

and white[420]—do not arise from other, they are known in one's own mind.

"If there is realization, there is wisdom; if not, delusion[421]. If understood, it is one's own mind; if not, the surface appearance is obtained. If something is done, conceived effort is involved; if not, there is arising of its own accord. If you want it, you have to practise; if not, it is the supreme fruit, divorced from hope and fear."

❀   ❀   ❀

[Interview six: Questions whose answers reveal that meditation on the entity is the one antidote for all which Phagmo Drupa himself called, "the interview of the foremost instruction of the key points".]

Guru Namo.

Phagmo Drupa politely enquired of the precious guru, "How do the main texts of Mahamudra determine dharmata and mindness?" The guru replied, "The central texts that show Mahamudra—the dohas, the New Translation's trilogy[422], and so on—and the persons who give the explanations of the dharma explained in them, too,

---

[420] Red and white thoughts are the thoughts produced in relation to the main channels of the subtle body, roughly speaking. The point is that they include all types of thought and appearance that occur to a being.

[421] Skt. moha, Tib. gti mug. Delusion is one of the five primary afflictions. Here it is a synonym the basic ignorance, not-rigpa, that creates and perpetuates samsara.

[422] The trilogy here is a set of text of the Kagyu hearing lineage coming from Tilopa which are a key part of the textual transmission of the Kagyu system.

explain right on the entity through realization of the entity, explain right on the ground through realization of the ground, understand right on the entity through realization of the entity, and understand right on the ground through realization of the ground. In actual fact, the entity of mindness is empty, though from the perspective of the rational mind of a person, it is understood in a process of item by item understanding."

Phagmo Drupa asked, "Are the two, appearances and mind, one or separate?" The reply came, "The two, appearances and mind, are one. Appearances as anything other than mind do not exist. Appearances are the light of mind or the dharmata of mind, therefore when mind is realized, the shackles of appearances release themselves."

Phagmo Drupa asked, "Are mindness and dharmata one or separate?" The reply came, "The two, mindness and dharmata, are one; the light of mind is dharmata, so by realizing mindness the shackles of dharmata release themselves. For example, once the sun has come up, going back on daylight is not possible and the reverse process is certain too, that when the sun goes down, the light will leave. Similarly, realization of mindness as one[423] causes realization of dharmata automatically, so it will come, and purification of mind causes purification of appearances automatically. Therefore, appearances and mindness, and so on are positioned in their ability to stand on their own, and meditation done only on mind's entity is sufficient."

He asked, "Is it that appearances and dharmata as object and subject are discarded and that one meditates right on the entity of mindness?" The reply came, "At the time of meditation, dharmas and dharmata are predicated with rational mind, then one meditates right on the entity of mind like holding it up and having the old woman pointing her finger at it. Alternatively, outer and inner,

_____

[423] Mindness is one thing that includes all.

containers and contents in their entirety are determined in vividness as mindness, then from that you meditate on the entity. It's
like those two. Through meditating on the ground, dharmata, you
might meditate but unless you discover the entity there can be no
going to buddhahood."

He asked, "Are wind and mind one or separate?" The reply came,
"Wind and mind are one. Moved by the wind, mind's discursive
thoughts shine forth in various ways. There is no other way to talk
about it; at the time of realization of mind, the winds are purified in
their own places and continue on. Non-dual rigpa-emptiness is co-
emergence."

He asked, "Does samsara have beginning and end, or not?" The
reply came, "It has no beginning and end and has no depth and
breadth. For both the general ruling condition of the three realms
and the meaning that rules persons in it, there is nothing within
samsara that can be pointed to and claimed as something that
operates as non-confusion. Nonetheless, the meaning ruling a
person can be identified as co-emergent wisdom which can be
realized and then, when it is, the person is a buddha and there is an
end. While co-emergent wisdom has not been identified, samsara
has no beginning and end. To stay in that co-emergence is to stay
in both samsara and nirvana without difference, therefore there is
nothing except the difference between identifying it and not.
There is no difference at all between buddhas and sentient beings."

"Well", he asked, "At the time of meditation, how should the
conduct of the body be?" The reply came, "There is no way to say
this is the way the conduct should be done; whatever works is the
meditation. Whichever of the four types of conduct are done,
meditate in the yoga of continuous flow that is without equipoise
and meditation."

"Well", he asked, "Do we follow the yoga of continuity during
sleep?" The reply came, "Sleep does not become an obstacle to the

continuous flow. It is indeed as *Hevajra* says, 'Sleep is not to be excluded'. Sleep is luminosity dharmakaya without thought. At the time of deep sleep, due to just an absence of the luminosity factor, you have the other possibility, sleep with absence of discursive thought dharmakaya. It is not an absence of co-emergence; that very no-thought state is dharmakaya. When there is a light sleep, the various dreams that are dreamt are the two types of illusion-like form kayas. No difference between the luminosity when meditating when you have not fallen asleep and when you are sleeping can happen. If that does happen, what difference is there with having and not having fallen asleep? Thus, sleep does not become an obstacle."

He asked, "Should one work at meditation on the four limitless ones beforehand?" The reply came, "Staying uninterruptedly in the experience already produced, there is no need to meditate on the four limitless ones; emptiness is the great equanimity functioning so it has the good qualities as part of it."

He asked, "When the entity has been realized, is it necessary to be involved with the outflowed vows or not?" The reply came, "It is not necessary to go off into the three trainings or three vows as something separate. They are complete within the un-outflowed innate character, being a part of it."

He asked, "Is it necessary to work at meditation on emptiness having compassion or not?" The reply came, "Non-referential compassion is present as part of it so it is not necessary to meditate separately on the two compassions, one referencing dharma and one referencing sentient beings. Their meanings are complete within it and their objects of meditation are non-referenced, so there is no meditation to be done."

He asked, "Is it necessary to work at meditation on the two types of enlightenment mind?" The reply came, "It is not necessary to meditate separately on the two types of enlightenment mind.

Superfactual enlightenment mind automatically is co-emergence, hence fictional enlightenment mind is not necessary. In regard to this, Jowo[424], spokesman for all of the Kadampas, stated, 'If meditation on emptiness is done first, then, because of not training in fictional enlightenment mind, meditation on emptiness will stray into that of the shravakas and will not be the path to omniscience.' However, the shravakas do not have the unassessed emptiness[425] of the superfactual, so it could not stray into the shravaka path. He also spoke of the vast emptiness of the Buddha's shravakas, but that belongs to the bodhisatvas who dwell above the shravakas so he would have to have been talking about manifested shravakas and not shravakas in fact, for whom there is no discussion of vast emptiness. Assessed emptiness is not realized from superfact. Therefore, when staying over superfact, loving kindness, compassion, enlightenment mind, and so on are merely fictionally made dharmas so it is not all right to make them out as thought-of, referenced objects[426]. If you have done so, you have bound yourself up again, therefore, you should not get involved in mentation[427]."

He asked, "Is it necessary to get involved with perpetual accumulation of the two types of accumulation?" The reply came, "At the time of staying in the yoga of continuity of the discovered entity, it

---

[424] Atisha.

[425] Assessed emptiness is emptiness known with concept still involved. Unassessed emptiness is emptiness known without concept still involved.

[426] This refers specifically to objects known within the context of dualistic mind. He is saying that this would be what you would expect with assessed emptiness but with unassessed emptiness, which is the emptiness known in direct perception of superfactual truth; fictional truths are mere fictions on the surface of the superfactual mind so should not be solidified into the dualistic entities known by a rational-type mind.

[427] Mentation is dualistic mind at work.

is not necessary to produce roots of merit through accumulating virtues of body and speech and doing merit accumulation. Jowo said, 'Generally, if equipoise depends on mind, virtue of body and speech should not be made primary', which is it, exactly! Once the elephant has been found, there is no need to search after it; though when you have not sought it out, the fields are not protected."

"But sir", he asked, "Isn't the accumulation of merit the cause of the two form kayas? It is defined that way—so what exactly should be done?" The reply came, "For gaining the two form bodies, your accumulations made up till now will suffice. If there had been no accumulation made previously, then it would not have been possible to arouse enlightenment mind. It is very obvious that, prior to your production of superfact, you had merit, so that indicates that it certainly has to be done."

He asked, "Is it necessary to work at improving the two, development and completion?" The reply came, "Meditation which is a samadhi of interrupted flow of the entity done with the graded practice of development and completion stages is, indeed, not necessary. Still, for as long as the full-ripened flesh and blood body[428] has not ended, you should indeed meditate on development stage using the deity yoga of instantaneous, illusion-like mere vividness."

"Well then", he asked, "Should one work separately at the meditations of the bardo dharma?" The reply came, "Meditation done right on the entity makes it un-necessary to do meditation on the bardo separately. There is no difference between the luminosities of the entity and the bardo therefore it is not necessary to meditate separately on the bardos both of the present and death."

---

[428] "Full-ripened" here means that the body is a result of karmic ripening.

"Well then", he asked, "Whether there is buddhahood in the present or it is still primordial buddhahood for a person, the situation that we have created for ourselves is that hunger, thirst, and sickness will come. Mind might be buddha, but sickness, heat and cold, hunger and thirst, and so on will cause us to suffer. It happens because one's own mind has put itself into this gaol of a full-ripened body so buddhahood becomes a case of being put into the gaol of this body, for example, like a garuda being put into an egg or a lion in the trap of a womb. If one attains buddhahood in this one life, shouldn't it be that one will not have the signs of the path at that time?" The reply came, "Becoming buddha in the bardo is a rapidly-induced buddhahood! If you do not travel the path, there will be no signs of the path!"

He asked, "Is wisdom interrupted or not?" The reply came, "Wisdom is un-interrupted. The two types of form kaya have the two knowledges, the five wisdoms, and so on and, with that, originate for others' sake. The meaning of form kayas shining forth from the dharmakaya is indeed explained a great deal in the main texts of dharma, still, if I explain it from the perspective of mind, the mind of the present's luminosity without thought, the dharmakaya, shines forth as various minds and that is the form kayas."

Phagmo Drupa asked, "Well then, does it come solely through meditation on the entity?" The reply came, "If you condense the meaning right down, it is this: the person who has produced the entity and has realized it stays within the state of uncontrived mind, meditating in the yoga of a continuously flowing river, and will not engage in anything else at all."

This, which neither subtracts from nor adds to what Rinpoche said, is called "The Interview of Foremost Instructions of the Key Points".

❀   ❀   ❀

[Interview seven: Yogin Choyung, another of Gampopa's main yogin disciples, has an interview included here that makes important points about livelihood and what is needed for practice.]

I prostrate to the holy gurus.

This is taken from an interview in which Yogin Choyung asked the Dharma Lord Gampopa for help with honing in on the entity. »[429] He asked, "For purifying evil deeds done in the past which of the two, laying aside via the four powers or meditation on the entity for a short while, is more effective?" The reply came, "Meditation on the entity for a short while is more effective." «[430]

»[431] He asked, "Having mentally cast aside the world, one wanders mountain tracts, but to do so requires food and clothes, so should one take care of oneself by maintaining a simple level of possessions, or should one do Essence Extraction[432], or should one do some simple work to earn a little money? Perhaps all of these are wrong and one should meditate with the approach, 'If I die, I die'?" The reply came, "Guru Milarepa said about this, 'If you have no possessions and be a beggar or put your hopes in others, meditation will not happen'. It has been said, 'You should keep a small livelihood for yourself'. If you do that, leaving everything else aside and meditating will be something you can manage. The dakinis as a whole will help to provide a livelihood. Do not even start on the practice of Essence Extraction—you don't have any accomplishment in it! Chongzhi is for the purpose of curing sickness; except

---

[429] The text from here down to the next closing brace is also found in Lord Gomtshul's Interviews, starting on page 26.

[430] End of the first section of repeated text.

[431] The text from here down to the next closing brace is also found in Lord Gomtshul's Interviews, starting on page 28.

[432] For Essence Extraction, see the glossary.

for using it a little for that, don't use it for anything else. Doing some simple work as needed to earn what you need will not be contrary to your aims."

He said, "May I ask, should I meditate in a place where someone has attained siddhi, or in deserted rocky mountains, or in a valley?" The reply came, "Meditate where you find it comfortable. If it suits you, then there's no difference between mountain and valley. If you become unhappy there, meditate for shorter periods."

He asked, "If one really does not want to engage in virtue-producing activities of body and speech, how would it be to do entity meditation alone?" The reply came, "Guru Milarepa said, 'If you think, 'I do not need to involve myself in virtue-producing activities of body and speech', then that gets a need started! When you are free of the thoughts 'I need to' and 'I do not need to' that is not to be needing!'"

He asked, "What about if I cut the mindstream that concerns itself with others' purposes then meditate?" The reply came, "By thinking about it, sentient beings are not abandoned and, through that, the two types of form kaya in others' appearance are accomplished. It is alright to prepare it with thought then abandon it."

Rinpoche said, "If you take refuge while in the entity, it is a refuge that gains the dharmata. If it is vows, then they become un-outflowed ones. If it is compassion, it becomes the non-referential one. If it is arousing the mind, it becomes the superfactual one. If it is samaya, it becomes part of the entity, the great primordial keeping of it. This sums up all oral instructions into one, and this is the way to meditate."

He asked, "What is the difference between the alaya consciousness and the entity? Are the others un-necessary?" The reply came, "To involve yourself with the others is to be producing falsity. The nature of the alaya consciousness is the entity. The pair, ignorance and co-emergent wisdom, are like the front and back of the hand. For as long as the entity is not realized, it is not-rigpa ignorance, the root of samsara. It is the root of realization and wisdom and buddhahood."

He asked, "Which one of these two is it: the entity sticking out clearly in one-pointedness or rigpa moving and moving?" The reply came, "It is both. There is no saying 'It is this, it is not this' that could be done for the entity for any of all the sentient beings. All appearance is mind. All mind is rigpa. All rigpa is the entity."

He asked, "What kind of behaviour goes with entity meditation? Should the eyes be closed or not?" The reply came, "Any of the four types of conduct are fine with this meditation. There is no certified conduct for it. As for the eyes open and closed, at first not closing them is easier. After you have completed training, closing them is more comfortable." «[433]

»[434] He said, "I have mentally rejected grasping at a self. In this current life, wandering mountain tracts and meditating on the entity is for me. If there is some oral instruction needed for this, please give it. If I meditate in terrifying places or meet wild demonic ghosts in empty valleys and empty mountains, or if maras and spirits make obstacles, what should I do?" The reply came, "For mountain tracts, you must have the three assurances of view, meditation, and the yidam deity's essence mantra. Nothing else is needed. If, in a terrifying place, wild, demonic ghosts start to create obstacles, offer torma to the harmful ones living there and they will not do any harm. Offer torma to the dharma protectors. Supplicate the guru, the Jewels, and the dakinis. Recite many of the yidam's essence mantra then obstacles will not come. There are

---

[433] End of the second section of repeated text.

[434] The text from here down to the next closing brace is also found in Lord Gomtshul's Interviews, starting on page 32.

only four siddhas between us and buddha. That means that all of their dakinis are right behind the meditator, following along like dogs, so no obstacles occur for the disciples who do meditate." «[435]

He asked, "If there is harm from gods and demonic ghosts, which is preferable—to meditate on the entity or to meditate on a real experience of their being empty?" The reply came, »[436] "On the basis of entity meditation alone, gods will not be able to harm you nor will demonic ghosts and negative influences[437] be able to affect you. Emptiness meditation is something that gods and demonic ghosts do know in that they know how to send off various emanations, but they have never realized the entity; they do not know the entity so do not know its meditation and the entity has never become an object of theirs. It is preferable for you to meditate only on the entity." «[438]

»[439] He asked, "For entity meditation, does experience come or not?" The reply came, "It comes and experience could make you proud and attached! What could come is totally casting off worldly clinging. It could turn into dropping all other dharmas as just the outer husk. It could turn into a happy mind of trust in yourself. Those experiences and realizations connected with the entity that has been produced will come." «[440]

---

[435] End of the third section of repeated text.

[436] The text from here down to the next closing brace is also found in Lord Gomtshul's Interviews, starting on page 33.

[437] Tib. gdon. For don, see the glossary.

[438] End of the fourth section of repeated text.

[439] The text from here down to the next closing brace is also found in Lord Gomtshul's Interviews, starting on page 34.

[440] End of the fifth section of repeated text.

»[441] He asked, "How are the two knowledges and five wisdoms possessed at the time of buddhahood?" The reply came, "All such explanations are the property of rational mind! If we too look into the terms using rational mind, we can connect them with dharma-kaya and the two form kayas. In fact, the operation of buddhahood is beyond rational mind; the two form kayas appear as qualities in others' spaces on the surface of their rational minds as what is made up by their rational minds." «[442]

»[443] He asked, "If you do wind meditation with consort, and do it primarily sitting up, will it work or not?" The reply came, "It will work, yes. All medical texts explain that, if you always stay sitting up, it can lead to your intestines going bad. It is explained that there are many good qualities associated with sitting cross-legged so that is preferred." «[444]

Gampopa continued, "Now if you talk about 'realizing the entity' but engage in non-virtue and have only a small degree of loving kindness, compassion, and enlightenment mind, it is, because guru Mila said so, the same as not having produced the entity."

❈   ❈   ❈

---

[441] The text from here down to the next closing brace is also found in Lord Gomtshul's Interviews, starting on page 38.

[442] End of the sixth section of repeated text.

[443] The text from here down to the next closing brace is also found in Lord Gomtshul's Interviews, starting on page 39.

[444] End of the seventh section of repeated text.

[Interview eight: Phagmo Drupa tries to find out why he is not under-
standing and gets further instruction on actual Mahamudra.]

Guru Namo.

Phagmo Drupa said, "After meeting with many gurus, I practised
all the dharmas involved then, later on, conferred with you, Lord
Gampopa. In these conversations, you replied many times with
words like, 'What you said is just more concept', and, 'That too is
conceptual!' Well, exactly what is Mahamudra?"

The reply came, "Teacher from Kham! You said, 'In accordance
with the authentic, the dharma of Mahamudra is like so'. Then you
said, 'No proliferation to external objects of discursive thought, the
awareness not sinking or becoming dull internally, rigpa's status
not-stopped, this, the rigpa-emptiness of the very entity, realized to
be free of root, in a crystal clearness ...' But guru Phagmo Drupa,
you cannot rouse it that way through your comprehension of it as
something divorced from all symbols of communication that would
make it out as being 'this dharma, not this dharma'. Rather, it
comes from the guru's oral instruction given in person. Whatever
it was that those earlier gurus of yours said, it was in replies to you
that you prefer so much—it is also exactly Mahamudra beyond
rational mind that comes from the Lord's oral instruction given in
person. 'Prajnaparamita inexpressible by speech or thought'[445]; that
way of making it out is it! 'Common awareness[446] wakened in the
heart'[447]; that way of making it out is it! 'The ultimate meaning

---

[445] This is a line from Rahula's famous four line praise of
Prajnaparamita which he is using to indicate that, if you understand
the actual meaning of Prajnaparamita, well, that's it!

[446] For common awareness, see the glossary.

[447] This is a famous quotation from a verse by the Indian Mahasiddha
Kotali, commonly used in the Kagyu tradition. This time it uses the
(continued...)

without referenced foci[448]; that way of making it out also is it!
When you have meditated on rigpa's entity, you have no need of
rational-minded foci of mindfulness. You have no need to meditate
using foci made by rational mind which are something to be
meditated on, over there. Meditation itself directs you towards this
side here. That is how it should be talked about."

"Guru Phagmo Drupa! I heard you say, 'Space has no centre or
fringe. A staff has no top and bottom ends. A shoe-string having
been fastened, the nomad encampment is set up. I am that sort of
yogin beyond rational mind. I have, in mind, that root of virtue
which has nothing superior to it, called 'the realization of Mahamudra'. I am someone for whom mindness has been taken and turned
it into something that can be used so other's purpose comes. Now,
I have no reason for going to Kham.'"

❁   ❁   ❁

[Interview nine: an overview of the entire path.]

I prostrate to the holy Jetsun gurus.

The Jetsun gave this reply to Phagmo Drupa.

"Life has no defined length so you will soon die and, because of it,
you need to have no attachment to the dharmas of the world.
Wherever you are born amongst the six classes of migrators, there
will be no happiness and it will only be experienced as a mass of

---

[447](...continued)
words of the Vajra Vehicle to make the same point as the immediately
preceding quotation.

[448] For foci, see the glossary.

suffering, therefore you need to have no attachment to the entirety of samsara. The root of all dharma is compassion, therefore you need a mind that never dismisses any sentient being. All dharmas are known to be unborn and birthless, therefore you need no grasping at conceived-of things and concept tokens at all.[449]

"To produce those ideas in mind, it has been said that you need to make continuous offerings and supplications with faith and devotion to the guru and the noble Three Jewels. Then, you need to experience yourself what you have yourself and need to realize yourself what you have yourself and need to attain yourself what you have yourself. What that is is mind uncontrived, the innate meaning. You obtain certainty in that self-arising uncontrivedness. Then, you put yourself into freshness, put yourself into not being based on a support, put yourself into self-delight, put yourself into looseness, put yourself into lack of acceptance and rejection, put yourself into not basing yourself on referenced foci, put yourself into cleared-out-ness, put yourself in vividness yet stillness, and allow yourself to automatically be in no modifying of it.

"For the method: take up the cross-legged posture nicely; let the eyes run down the tip of the nose nicely; join the tongue to the palate; and hook the chin into the throat just a little. Then, the previous conscious awareness has passed and the next has not been created. Stay, without identification[450], in the present one. Furthermore, the two, mind and mental events, have both coarse and subtle forms. The subtle one is virtuous, non-virtuous, and undetermined in type. Mind which is rigpa—well it is the uncontrived rigpa. For that, please look to see where it comes from to start with, what exactly it abides as, and finally where it goes to when it ceases? First, there is nowhere that it comes from. Next, there is

---

[449] This much sets out the main steps taught in the Kadampa Stages of the Path.

[450] For identification, see under conceived-of thing in the glossary.

nothing existing with shape and colour. Finally, there is nowhere that it goes to when it ceases. You meditate again and again like that. By meditating like that, appearances shine forth as mind and mindness will shine forth as buddha.

"By knowing appearances as mind, you do not go into dualistic appearance. By knowing mindness as rigpa, you do not go into matter. By knowing rigpa as empty, you do not go into concept tokens. By knowing emptiness as bliss, you do not go into suffering. Bliss is your own mind so you do not go into others' appearances. There is none of the process of identification that goes with mind therefore there is neither referencing nor non-referencing, and that is Mahamudra."

That completes the interviews with Phagmo Drupa.

Text 6

Yogin Choyung's Interview

Yogin Choyung's Interview

»[451] Namo Guru.

He asked, "There is both mind and light of mind, isn't there?" The reply came, "That is so. If appearances are then included within mind, there is nothing else than mind alone."

He asked, "There is both dharmakaya and light of dharmakaya, isn't there? The two do not exist apart from dharmakaya alone, isn't that so?" The reply came, "That is so. When dharmakaya has become the single sufficient solution, there is nothing apart from dharmakaya alone."

He asked, "For a nirmanakaya buddha like Shakyamuni who had the remainder of a full-ripened body, would that count as being the single sufficient solution?" The reply came, "It would. The body having gone to nirvana, its birth was purified, so it was not there in own appearance though there were form kayas that occurred in others' appearance."

He asked, "In regard to the two form kayas not being there in own appearance, would you say that this is an absence in own appear-

---

[451] The text from here down to the next ending brace is also found in Dusum Khyenpa's interviews, starting on page 121.

ance of discursive thought that operates as the doing of others'
purposes or would you say that it is an absolute absence of in own
appearances of thought?" The reply came, "There are two different systems regarding that. The Kadampa geshes assert the former.
Our guru asserts the latter. They are wholly in agreement on the
point of asserting appearances within others' appearance."

He asked, "I am there with the fact, then lose touch with it because
of distraction. Later, having regained mindfulness, I return to the
fact. After being distracted for that interval, if looking again brings
me back to dharmakaya, will that be alright or not? In that interval
is there the capacity to become obscured or not? Is it necessary to
meditate perpetually undistracted or not?"

The reply came, "If looking again after that makes dharmakaya go
to dharmakaya, it is alright. The discursive thought of the interval
does not have the capacity to cause obscuration. It is not necessary
to be absolutely un-distracted—there is no function of distraction
given that in actuality there is no distraction and non-distraction."

He said, "This is the mind of the Jetsun guru and the Buddha. It
can't be taken higher or enhanced. «[452] Please say something about
how this level functions." The reply came, »[453] "Even if you
meditated that that, your own mindness, luminosity, was equal to
the limits of space, it would still be born and present in that way[454].
Even if you meditated on it as another place of the noble ones, it
would still come and be present. And for as long as you sat there,
even if you meditated on it, it would still come and be present.
Whose luminosity is it? It is yours. Realized and not realized, it
pervades everything. It is present as knowing which itself knows

---

[452] End of the first section of repeated text.

[453] The text from here down to the next ending brace is also found in
Dusum Khyenpa's interviews, starting on page 149.

[454] That it has thoughts is the key point here.

itself, self-illumination in which the luminosity is un-stopped, luminosity without up and down, luminosity without edge and centre, luminosity without the presence and absence of discursive thought. To abide in its state is to function beyond the world. There is no enhancement to be done to it. If you did try to enhance the realization, whatever you produced would be faulty. If an enhancement or sign[455] or higher state than it were to come from doing so, that would be faulty."

I asked, "For all the old dogs who have produced the entity then meditated on it for a long time, will there be a point at which there is a need for enhancement or some special acquaintance to be made?" The reply came, "There will be neither acquaintance nor enhancement to be made. People have these ideas because of thoughts like, 'There is something higher that can come to me.'"

I asked, "In regard to the entity which has become a single sufficient solution, I am not apprehending it in dreams; will it be apprehended in the bardo or not?" The reply came, "All gurus have said that it must be apprehended in dreams. Having looked into this myself, I see that even if it is not apprehended in dreams, it will be apprehended in the bardo. In the present context it turns out unclearly in dreams so you do not apprehend it, but in the bardo it turns out more clearly than now, so you will be able to apprehend it then."

I asked, "If the entity is something that has to be deliberately roused now, then after death, in the bardo, will it also be that way or will it turn to a single sufficient solution?" The reply came, "If the entity is there without discontinuity now, it will turn into a single solution in the bardo, too. That deliberate rousing will also happen as deliberate rousing in the bardo; by meditating in that way

---

[455] Meaning sign of practice, sign of progress.

it will be enhanced over its present status and will turn to a single, sufficient solution." «⁴⁵⁶

»⁴⁵⁷ I asked, "Compared to doing only entity meditation, is it necessary or not to development stage and recitation?" The reply came, "If you do a little mantra recitation, it will cause speech to be blessed; other than that, reciting mantra and meditation on the deity is not necessary. Within the state of luminosity there is recitation." «⁴⁵⁸

»⁴⁵⁹ I asked, "If superfactual enlightenment mind is continuously realized and dwelt in, will fictional-enlightenment-mind meditation be necessary or not?" The reply came, "There are three aspects to it: coming from habituation, coming from meditation, and coming from realization. Coming from habituation is that enlightenment mind has been meditated on in former lives, so it comes in this one without needing to meditate on it. Coming from meditation is what has happened already due to meditation in this life. Coming from realization is that, because of realizing its fact, the loving-kindness-and-compassion enlightenment mind automatically comes for those who have not realized it, sentient beings. It is not necessary to do two separate meditations on fictional and superfactual enlightenment minds. If superfact is realized, the arising of loving kindness and compassion for the sake of others is cause and effect. This automatically turns away affliction. If you say that you have realized the entity but engage in non-virtue, you have small loving-kindness-compassion enlightenment mind and this effectively is the

---

⁴⁵⁶ End of the second section of repeated text.

⁴⁵⁷ The text from here down to the next ending brace is also found in Dusum Khyenpa's interviews, starting on page 155.

⁴⁵⁸ End of the third section of repeated text.

⁴⁵⁹ The text from here down to the next ending brace is also found in Dusum Khyenpa's interviews, starting on page 151.

same as not having produced the entity. The Jetsun guru[460] said this, and it is so."

I asked, "When the Jetsun[461] is sick, does his mind become upset or not?" The reply came, "Even when I am sick, I suffer no upset in mind and no harm comes to me at all. By meditating on luminosity at the location of the sickness, it comes totally into luminosity and there is no harm to me. Compared to doing mantra for a person who is sick because of a malevolent spirit, directing your attention to the location of sickness then meditating on luminosity is more beneficial."

I asked, "What would you say about merging entity and equipoise?" The reply came, "For 'meditation', no matter which of the four types of behaviour you are doing, if, without separating from luminosity, it is always coming as the entity, that is merging."

I asked, "Sometimes I lose mindfulness and go into discursive thought. Regaining mindfulness then coming into the entity is merging, isn't it?" The reply came, "That is not merging."

"Well then", I asked, "Is it not realizing one portion of the entity? Isn't it meditation for a short time then habituating?" The reply came, "That is not realizing the whole entity. It is not habituating. It is meditation for a short time on the fact[462]."

---

[460] Milarepa.

[461] Gampopa.

[462] This is a subtle distinction of the process of Essence Mahamudra meditation.

"Well then", I asked, "For as long as I have this body of full-ripening[463], is it that at all costs I should not go into an absence of equipoise and post-attainment?" The reply came, "No, that is not it. You have this body of full-ripening and by meditating for a long time you can go on to meet with the absence of equipoise and post-attainment in this very life."

"Well then", I asked, "This losing mindfulness immediately followed by going into latencies as such[464] is a come-back from what?" The reply came, "It is what you get in return for not having purified grasped-grasping. Meditating for a long time purifies grasped-grasping then, because there is no holding on with mindfulness to be done, it goes on to absence of equipoise and post-attainment."

"Well then", I asked, "If I have produced the entity but die without having merged equipoise and post-attainment, will this purify birth in the bardo or not?" The reply came, "It will purify it, there is no doubt about it!"

"Well then", I asked, "Won't the discursive thought which has not been apprehended by present mindfulness cause obscuration?" The reply came, "It will not cause obscuration. Those discursive thoughts do not have the capacity to accumulate karma. It is like planting a seed in space—there is no place for the fruition to be produced. This is through the key point of realizing everything as birthless."

"Well then", I asked, "If at the time of a deep sleep or dream I have not apprehended the entity, will the entity be apprehended in the

---

[463] "Body of full-ripening" means this body produced by karmic ripening.

[464] "As such" means that the afflictions, and so forth arising from the latencies are coming on in their samsaric mind form, not as ones that have been liberated.

bardo or not?" The reply came, "That is not having apprehended the entity at the times of sleeping and dreaming but you will apprehend it in the bardo. It turns unclear now during sleeping and dreaming compared to that. In the bardo, it turns clearer than now. Compared to now, it is easy to apprehend."

"Well then", I asked, "If, un-apprehended by mindfulness, the entity is not coming and the discursive thought as such is apprehended by mindfulness, will it purify the previous discursive thoughts or not? It is necessary or not to apprehend an absence of their dying and not dying through mindfulness?" The reply came, "Discursive thoughts as such that have not been apprehended by mindfulness immediately they are apprehended by mindfulness are cleared off and so purified. It is not necessary to have apprehended an absence of their dying and not dying through mindfulness. Nonetheless, if you have made yourself undistracted through mindfulness, that will help to speed up the process of merging equipoise and post-attainment. And then, discursive thought, even if it has not been apprehended by mindfulness, absolutely will not harm, cause obscuration, or be a hindrance."

"Well then", I asked, "Is there no practice to do other than to be apprehending with mindfulness and remaining undistracted?" The reply came, "Except for being prodded by mindfulness, there is no other practice to do at all." «[465]

At that point his questions were answered and he had no more to ask. The precious guru doctor had an inconceivable number of son disciples who had gained siddhi but of them there were: "four heart sons" or "four siddhas" who were Shorma Phagpa, Zimshi Yeshe Nyingpo, Sergom Yeshe Nyingpo, and Ramnyi Chokyi Yungdrung; "four sons who held the lineage" who were Dvagpo Gomtshul, Je Phagmo Drupa, Barompa Chenpo, Dusum Khyenpa; "four close sons" who were Khanpo Dulwa Dzinpa, Gargom Zhigpo,

---

[465] End of the fourth section of repeated text.

Layag Josay, Kyebu Yeshe Dorje; "four who stayed close" who were Jodan Legdzay, Gompa Sherzhon, Nyenay Saljang, and Salyay. There were two special siddhas: Saltong Shogom and Yogin Choyung. Those are the "eighteen siddhas".

> By the roots of virtue of writing this
> May I and other migrators without exception
> Be totally separated from the faults of bad action
> Then through Protector Chandrakumara[466]
> And becoming one of his principal sons
> Quickly attain unsurpassable complete enlightenment.
>
> The one friend of all migrators in the good kalpa,
> The one taste of all nectar of foremost instruction,
> The one eye of all holy dharma, sutra and tantra,
> Please hold myself and others with your compassionate
>   activity.

---

[466] Gampopa's name when he was a bodhisatva in the Buddha's time.

GLOSSARY

Actuality, Tib. gnas lugs: A key term in both sūtra and tantra and one of a pair of terms, the other being "apparent reality" (Tib. snang lugs). The two terms are used when determining the reality of a situation. The actuality of any given situation is how (lugs) the situation actuality sits or is present (gnas); the apparent reality is how (lugs) any given situation appears (snang) to an observer. Something could appear in many different ways, depending on the circumstances at the time and on the being perceiving it but, regardless of those circumstances, it will always have its own actuality of how it really is. The term actuality is frequently used in Mahāmudrā teaching to mean the fundamental reality of any given phenomenon or situation before any deluded mind alters it and makes it appear differently.

Adventitious, Tib. glo bur: This term has the connotations of popping up on the surface of something and of not being part of that thing. Therefore, even though it is often translated as "sudden", that only conveys half of the meaning. In Buddhist literature, something adventitious pops up as a surface event and vanishes again precisely because it is not actually part of the thing on whose surface it appeared. It is frequently used in relation to the afflictions because they pop up on the surface of the mind of buddha-nature but are not part of the buddha-nature itself.

Affliction, Skt. kleśha, Tib. nyon mongs: This term is usually translated as emotion or disturbing emotion, etcetera, but the Buddha was very specific about the meaning of this word. When the Buddha referred to the emotions, meaning a movement of mind, he did not refer to them as such but called them "kleśha" in Sanskrit, meaning exactly "affliction". It is a basic part of the Buddhist teaching that emotions afflict beings, giving them problems at the time and causing more problems in the future.

Alaya, Skt. ālaya, Tib. kun gzhi: This term, if translated, is usually translated as all-base or something similar. It is a Sanskrit term that means a range that underlies and forms a basis for something else. In Buddhist teaching, it means a particular level of mind that sits beneath all other levels of mind. However, it is used in several different ways in the Buddhist teaching and changes to a different meaning in each case. An important distinction is made between alaya alone and alaya consciousness.

Alteration, altered: Same as contrivance *q.v.*

Appropriation, Skt. upādāna, Tib. nye bar len pa: This is the name of the ninth of the twelve links of interdependent origination. Tsongkhapa gives a good treatment of all twelve links in his interdependent origination section of the *Great Stages of the Path to Enlightenment*, a translation of which is available for free download from the PKTC web-site. It is the crucial point in the process at which a karma that has been previously planted is selected and activated as the karma that will propel the being into its next existence. In other words, it is the key point in a being's existence when the next type of existence is selected. There is the further point that, at the time of death, the particular place that the wind-mind settles in the subtle body, a place related to the seed syllables mentioned in the tantras, also determines the next birth. The two points are not different. The selection of the karma that will propel the next life then affects how the wind-mind will operate at the time of death.

Arousing the mind, Tib. sems bskyed: This is a technical term nearly always used to mean "arousing the enlightenment mind", though it is occasionally used to refer to the deliberate production of other types of mind, for example renunciation. There are two types of arousing the mind—fictional and superfactual; see under fictional enlightenment mind and superfactual enlightenment mind.

Assurance, Tib. gdeng: Although often translated as confidence, this term means assurance with all of the extra meaning conveyed by that term. A bird might be confident of its ability to fly but, more than that, it has the assurance that it will not fall to the ground because it knows that it has wings and it has the training to use them.

Awareness, Skt. jñā, Tib. shes pa: "Awareness" is always used in our translations to mean the basic knower of mind or, as Buddhist teaching itself defines it, "a general term for any registering mind", whether dualistic or non-dualistic. Hence, it is used for both samsaric and nirvanic situations; for example, consciousness (Tib. rnam par shes pa) is a dualistic form of awareness, whereas rigpa, wisdom (Tib. ye shes), and so on are non-dualistic forms of awareness. See under rigpa.

It is noteworthy that the key term "rigpa" is often mistakenly translated as "awareness", even though it is not merely an awareness; this creates considerable confusion amongst practitioners of the higher tantras who are misled by it.

Bardo, Tib. bar do: Literally, "interval" or "in-between place". The general teachings of Buddhism explain this as the interval between one life and the next. However, Mahāmudrā has its own specific teachings on the bardo in which all phases of existence are one bardo or another.

Becoming, Skt. bhāvanā, Tib. srid pa: This is another name for samsaric existence. Beings in saṃsāra have a samsaric existence but, more than that, they are constantly in a state of becoming—becoming this type of being or that type of being in this abode or that, as they are driven along without choice by the karmic process that drives samsaric existence.

Bliss: Skt. sukha, Tib. bde: The Sanskrit term and its Tibetan translation are usually translated as "bliss" but refer to the whole range of possibilities of everything on the side of good as opposed to bad. Thus, the term will mean pleasant, happy, good, nice, easy, comfortable, blissful, and so on, depending on context.

Bliss, luminosity, and no-thought, Tib. bde gsal mi rtog pa: A person who practises meditation will have signs of that practice appear as various types of temporary experience. Most commonly, three types of experience are met with: bliss, luminosity, and no-thought. Bliss is an ease of body or mind or both, luminosity is heightened knowing of mind, and no-thought is an absence of thought that happens in the mind. The three are usually mentioned when discussing the passing experiences that arise because of practising meditation but there is also a way of describing them as final experiences of realization.

Note that this has often been called "bliss, clarity, and no-thought" but that makes the mistake that the word for luminosity has been abbreviated in this phrase and mistaken by translators to mean clarity, which it does not.

Bodhicitta: See under enlightenment mind.

Bodhisatva: A bodhisatva is a person who has engendered the bodhicitta, enlightenment mind, and, with that as a basis, has undertaken the path to the enlightenment of a truly complete buddha specifically for the welfare of other beings. Note that, despite the common appearance of "bodhisattva" in Western books on Buddhism, the Tibetan tradition has steadfastly maintained since the time of the earliest translations that the correct spelling is bodhisatva; see under satva and sattva.

Capable One, Skt. muni, Tib. thub pa: The term "muni" as for example in "Śhākyamuni" has long been thought to mean "sage" because of an entry in Monier-Williams excellent Sanskrit-English dictionary. In fact, it has been used by many Indian religions since the times of ancient India to mean in general, a religious practitioner "one who could do it", one who has made progress on a spiritual path and thereby become able to restrain his three doors away from non-virtue and affliction.

Clinging, Tib. zhen pa: In Buddhism, this term refers specifically to the twofold process of dualistic mind mis-taking things that are not true, not pure, as true, pure, etcetera and then, because of seeing them as highly desirable even though they are not, attaching itself to or clinging to those things. This type of clinging acts as a kind of glue that keeps a person joined to the unsatisfactory things of cyclic existence because of mistakenly seeing them as desirable.

Common awareness, Tib. tha mal gyi shes pa: One of several path terms used to indicate mind's essence. It is equivalent to "mindness" and "rigpa". These terms are used by practitioners as a code word for their own, personal experience of the essence of mind. These words are secret because of the power they are connected with and should be kept that way.

This term is often referred to as "ordinary mind", a term that was established by Chogyam Trungpa Rinpoche for his students. However, there are two problems with that word. Firstly, "tha mal" does not mean "ordinary". It means the awareness which is common to all parts of samsaric mind and also which is common to all beings. It is glossed in writings on Mahāmudrā to mean "nature". In other words, it refers to that part of mind which, being common to all events of mind, is its nature. This is well attested to in the writings of the Kagyu forefathers. Secondly, this is not "mind", given that mind is used to mean the dualistic mind of beings in cyclic existence. Rather this is "shes pa", the most general term for all kinds of awareness.

Complete purity, rnam dag: This term refers to the quality of a buddha's mind, which is completely pure compared to a sentient being's mind. The mind of a being in saṃsāra has its primordially pure nature covered over by the muck of dualistic mind. If the being practises correctly, the impurity can be removed and mind can be returned to its original state of complete purity.

Conceived effort, Tib. rtsol ba: In Buddhism, this term usually does not merely mean effort but has the specific connotation of effort of dualistic mind. In that case, it is effort that is produced by and functions specifically within the context of dualistic concept. For example, the term "mindfulness with effort" specifically means "a type of mindfulness that is occurring within the context of dualistic mind and its various operations". The term "effortless" is often used in Mahāmudrā to mean a way of being in which dualistic mind has been abandoned and, therefore, in which there is none of the striving of ordinary people.

Conceived-of thing, Tib. dngos po: In Buddhist texts, "thing" refers specifically to a conceived-of thing. Dualistic mind creates things as concepts and then relates to the concepts whereas non-dualistic wisdom does not create them to begin with because it does not have dualistic mind's conceptual process. What does wisdom know then, if it does not know things? Wisdom knows all phenomena in direct perception; these phenomena are not called things because if they were, that would immediately imply the presence of dualistic mind in wisdom, something which by definition is impossible. Wisdom knows phenomena in direct perception whereas dualistic mind knows "things" in a specific conceptual process called "identification". Identification is a dualistic process and therefore that process does not exist in wisdom.

Concept tokens, Tib. mtshan ma: This is the technical name for the structures or concepts which function as the words of conceptual mind's language. They are the very basis of operation of the third skandha and hence of the way that dualistic mind communicates with its world. For example, a table seen in direct visual perception will have no concept tokens involved with knowing it. However, when thought becomes involved and there is the thought "table" in an inferential or conceptual perception of the table, the name-tag "table" will be used to reference the table and that name-tag is the concept token.

Although we usually reference phenomena via these concepts, the phenomena are not the dualistically referenced things we think of them as being. The actual fact of the phenomena is quite different from the concept tokens used to discursively think about them and is known by wisdom rather than concept-based mind. Therefore, this term is often used in Buddhist literature to signify that dualistic samsaric mind is involved rather than non-dualistic wisdom.

Confusion, Tib. 'khrul pa: In Buddhism, this term mostly refers to the fundamental confusion of taking things the wrong way that happens because of fundamental ignorance, although it can also have the more general meaning of having lots of thoughts and being confused about it. In the first case, it is defined like this "Confusion is the appearance to rational mind of something being present when it is not" and refers, for example, to seeing an object, such as a table, as being truly present, when in fact it is present only as mere, interdependent appearance.

Containers and contents, Tib. snod bcud: Containers are the outer worlds and environment and their contents are the beings living in them. This phrase is sometimes extended to "outer and inner, containers and contents" with the same meaning. It usually means "the entirety of saṃsāra", though sometimes means "the entirety of saṃsāra and nirvāṇa".

Contrivance, contrived, Tib. bcos pa: A term meaning that something has been altered from its native state.

Cyclic existence: See under samsara.

Dharmadhatu, Skt. dharmadhātu, Tib. chos kyi dbyings: This is the name for the range or basic space in which all dharmas, meaning all phenomena, come into being. If a flower bed is the place where flowers grow and are found, the dharmadhatu is the dharma or phenomena bed in which all phenomena come into being and are found. The term is used in all levels of Buddhist teaching with that base meaning but the explanation of it becomes more profound as the teaching becomes more profound. In Mahāmudrā, it is the all-pervading sphere of luminosity-wisdom, given that luminosity is where phenomena arise and that the luminosity is none other than wisdom.

Dharmakaya, Skt. dharmakāya, Tib. chos sku: In the general teachings of Buddhism, this refers to the mind of a buddha, with "dharma" meaning reality and "kāya" meaning body.

Dharmata, Skt. dharmatā, Tib. chos nyid: This is a general term meaning the way that something is, and can be applied to anything at all; it is similar in meaning to "actuality" *q.v.* For example, the dharmatā of water is wetness and the dharmatā of the becoming bardo is a place where beings are in a samsaric, or becoming mode, prior to entering a nature bardo. It is used frequently in Tibetan Buddhism to mean "the dharmatā of reality" but that is a specific case of the much larger meaning of the term. To read texts which use this term successfully, one has to understand that the term has a general meaning and then see how that applies in context.

Dharmin, Tib. chos can: A dharmin is a dharma, meaning phenomenon, belonging to the world of saṃsāra. It is not only a dharma, a phenomenon in general, but has become a solidified dharma, a conceptualized thing, because of the samsaric context.

Dhyana, Skt. dhyāna, Tib. bsam gtan: A Sanskrit term technically meaning all types of mental absorption. Mental absorptions cultivated in the human realm generally result in births in the form realms which are deep forms of concentration in themselves. The practices of mental absorption done in the human realm and the godly existences of the form realm that result from them both are named "dhyāna". The Buddha repeatedly pointed out that the dhyānas were a side-track to emancipation from cyclic existence.

In a more general way, the term also means meditation in general where one is concentrating on something as a way of developing oneself spiritually. Texts on Mahāmudrā sometimes use the word in this sense when making the point that attempts to meditate on anything are the very opposite of Mahāmudrā practice and will inevitably keep the practitioner within samsāra.

Discursive thought, Skt. vikalpa, Tib. rnam rtog: This means more than just the superficial thought that is heard as a voice in the head. It includes the entirety of conceptual process that arises due to mind contacting any object of any of the senses. The Sanskrit and Tibetan literally mean "(dualistic) thought (that arises from the mind wandering among the) various (superficies *q.v.* perceived in the doors of the senses)".

Doha, Skt. dohā, Tib. mgur: A dohā is a song sung spontaneously from spiritual realization. Dohās are popular in the tantric traditions because they are enjoyable to listen to and go right to the heart of the matter.

Don(s), Tib. gdon: A general term for any kind of negative force that hits a person and brings trouble. It could be any external or internal thing that causes trouble. A good way to think of it is "negative influence" or "negative force".

Effort, conceived effort, Tib. rtsol ba: In Buddhism, this term usually does not merely mean effort but has the specific connotation of effort of dualistic mind. In that case, it is effort that is produced by and functions specifically within the context of dualistic concept. For example, the term "mindfulness with effort" specifically means "a type of mindfulness that is occurring within the context of dualistic mind and its various operations". The term "effortless" is often used in Mahāmudrā to mean a way of being in which dualistic mind has been abandoned and, therefore, has with it none of the effort of dualistic mind.

Elaboration, Tib. spro ba: This is a general name for what is given off by dualistic mind as it goes about its conceptual process. In general, elaborations prevent a person from seeing emptiness directly. Freedom from elaborations implies direct sight of emptiness.

Enhancement, enhancer, Tib. bog 'don: Enhancement is the technical name for a type of practice done to enhance a main practice by bringing out the realization of the main practice. Enhancers are the specific practices used to do enhancement. Enhancers are also used to make the meaning of the main practice come into plain view in cases where the practitioner is not "getting" the main meaning even though he has been doing the main practice.

In most practices the main practice will bring a partial realization and enhancers are used to improve that realization. For example, viewing a dead body could cause the level of realization of impermanence and death meditation to increase. However, Mahāmudrā practice is different from other practices in that once the entity, Mahāmudrā, has been recognized, that realization of it, as it is called, cannot be enhanced because, in the moment of realization, the fullness of Mahāmudrā is seen. In the texts in this book, the issue of whether enhancement practice is applicable to Mahāmudrā practice or not is another issue that comes up repeatedly.

Enlightenment mind, Skt. bodhicitta, Tib. byang chub sems: This is a key term of the Great Vehicle. It is the type of mind that is connected not with the lesser enlightenment of an arhat but the enlightenment of a truly complete buddha. As such, it is a mind which is connected with the aim of bringing all sentient beings to that same level of buddhahood. A person who has this mind has entered the Great Vehicle and is either a bodhisatva or a buddha.

It is important to understand that "enlightenment mind" is used to refer equally to the minds of all levels of bodhisatva on the path to buddhahood and to the mind of a buddha who has completed the path. Therefore, it is not "mind striving for enlightenment" as is so often translated but "enlightenment mind", meaning that kind of mind which is connected with the full enlightenment of a truly complete buddha and which is present in all those who belong to the Great Vehicle. The term is used in the conventional Great Vehicle and also in the Vajra Vehicle. In the Vajra Vehicle, there are some special uses of the term where substances of the pure aspect of the subtle physical body are understood to be manifestations of enlightenment mind.

Entity, Tib. ngo bo: The entity of something is just exactly what that thing is. In English we would often simply say "thing" rather than entity. However, in Buddhism, "thing" has a very specific meaning rather than the general meaning that it has in English. It has become common to translate this term as "essence" *q.v.* However, in most cases "entity", meaning what a thing is rather than an essence of that thing, is the correct translation for this term.

Equipoise and post-attainment, Tib. mnyam bzhag and rjes thob: Although often called "meditation and post-meditation", the actual term is "equipoise and post-attainment". There is great meaning in the actual wording which is lost by the looser translation.

Essence, Tib. ngo bo: This is a key term used throughout Buddhist theory. The original in Sanskrit and the term in Tibetan, too, has both meanings of "essence" and "entity". In some situations the term has more the first meaning and in others, the second. For example, when speaking of mind and mind's essence, it is referring to the core or essential part within mind. On the other hand, when speaking of something such as fire, one can speak of the entity, fire, and its characteristics, such as heat, and so on; in this case, the term does not mean essence but means that thing, what it actually is. See also under entity.

Essence Extraction, Tib. bcud len; Essence Extraction is a practice in which one uses certain substances to relieve the body of its need for food. Chongzhi is a mineral substance used as a basis for certain types of medicine and is also one of the prime ingredients for the substances of Essence Extraction; when Gampopa mentions it, he is telling Gomtshul not to get involved with Essence Extraction.

Exaggeration, Tib. skur 'debs pa: In Buddhism, this term is used in two ways. Firstly, it is used in general to mean misunderstanding from the perspective that one has added more to one's understanding of something than needs to be there. Secondly, it is used specifically to indicate that dualistic mind always overstates or exaggerates whatever object it is examining. Dualistic mind always adds the ideas of solidity, permanence, singularity, and so on to everything it references via the concepts that it uses. Severing of exaggeration either means removal of these un-necessary understandings when trying to properly comprehend something or removal of the dualistic process altogether when trying to get to the non-dualistic reality of a phenomenon.

Expressions, Tib. brjod pa: According to Sanskrit and Tibetan grammar following it, expressions refers to mental and verbal expressions. Thus, for example, the phrase seen in translation of "word, thought, and expression" is mistaken. The phrase is actually "expressions mental and verbal".

Expanse, Skt. dhātu, Tib. dbyings: The Sanskrit term has over twenty meanings. Many of those meanings are also present in the Tibetan equivalent. In the Vajra Vehicle teachings it is used as a replacement for the term emptiness that conveys a non-theoretical sense of the experience of emptiness. When used this way, it has the sense "expanse" because emptiness is experienced as an expanse in which all phenomena appear.

Fact, Skt. artha, Tib. don: "Fact" is that knowledge of an object that occurs to the surface of mind. It is not the object but what the mind understands as the object.

Fictional, Skt. saṃvṛtti, Tib. kun rdzob: This term is paired with the term "superfactual" q.v. In the past, the terms have been translated as "relative" and "absolute" respectively, but those translations are nothing like the original terms. These terms are extremely important in the Buddhist teaching so it is very important that they be corrected, but more than that, if the actual meaning of these terms is not presented, then the teaching connected with them cannot be understood.

The Sanskrit term saṃvṛtti means a deliberate invention, a fiction, a hoax. It refers to the mind of ignorance which, because of being obscured and so not seeing suchness, is not true but a fiction. The things that appear to that ignorance are therefore fictional. Nonetheless, the beings who live in this ignorance believe that the things that appear to them through the filter of ignorance are true, are real. Therefore, these beings live in fictional truth.

Fictional truth, Skt. saṃvṛtisatya, Tib. kun rdzob bden pa: See under fictional.

Fictional enlightenment mind, Tib. kun rdzob bden pa'i byang chub sems: One of a pair of terms explained in the Great Vehicle; the other is Superfactual Truth Enlightenment Mind. See under fictional truth and superfactual truth for information about those terms. Enlightenment mind is defined as two types. The fictional type is the conventional type: it is explained as consisting of love and great compassion within the framework of an intention to obtain truly complete enlightenment for the sake of all sentient beings. The superfactual truth type is the ultimate type: it is explained as the enlightenment mind that is directly perceiving emptiness.

Field, Field realm, Tib. zhing, zhing khams: This term is often translated "buddha field" though there is no "buddha" in the term. There are many different types of "fields" in both saṃsāra and nirvāṇa. Thus there are fields that belong to enlightenment and ones that belong to ignorance. Moreover, just as there are "realms" of saṃsāra—desire, form, and formless—so there are realms of nirvāṇa—the fields dharmakāya, saṃbhogakāya, and nirmāṇakāya and these are therefore called "field realms".

Five paths, Tib. lam lnga: In the Prajñāpāramitā teachings of the Great Vehicle, the Buddha explained the entire Buddhist journey as a set of five paths called the paths of accumulation, connection, seeing, cultivation, and no more training. The first four paths are part of journeying to enlightenment; the fifth path is that one has actually arrived and has no more training to undergo. There are a set of five paths that describe the journey of the Lesser Vehicle and a set of five paths that describe the journey of the Greater Vehicle. The names are the same in each case but the details of what is accomplished at each stage are different. Gampopa also mentions the five paths of Mahāmudrā, which is the same five paths but described according to the Mahāmudrā journey.

Floaters, Tib. rab rib: This term has usually been mistakenly translated as "cataracts". It is the medical term for eyes with a disease known as *Muscaria volante* in Western ophthalmology. The disease is common to a large portion of the world's population and has the common term "floaters" given to it by the medical profession. Almost anyone who looks out at a clear source of light will see grey threads, sometimes twisted, sometimes straight, floating in the field of vision. When an eye is moved, because the gel of the eye shifts, the floaters can seem to be like hairs falling through the field of vision and so are sometimes called "falling hairs". They seem to be "out there" when in fact they are shadows being cast on the retina by fissures in the gel inside the eye. The point is that they seem real when in fact they are an aberration produced by an illness of the eye.

Focus, foci, Tib. gtad so: A focus is a particular issue that rational mind is focussing on. Sometimes this term is used to infer the presence of dualistic mind.

Foremost instruction, Skt. upadeśha, Tib. man ngag: There are several types of instruction mentioned in Buddhist literature: there is the general level of instruction which is the meaning contained in the words of the texts of the tradition; on a more personal and direct level there is oral instruction which has been passed down from teacher to student from the time of the buddha; and on the most profound level there are foremost instructions which are not only oral instructions provided by one's guru but are special, core instructions that come out of personal experience and which convey the teaching concisely and with the full weight of personal experience. Foremost instructions or upadeśha are crucial to the Vajra Vehicle because these are the special way of passing on the profound instructions needed for the student's realization.

Fortune, fortunate person, Tib. skal ldan: To meet with any given dharma teaching, a person must have accumulated the karmic fortune needed for such a rare opportunity, and this kind of person is then called "a fortunate one" or "fortunate person". This term is especially used in the Vajra Vehicle, whose teachings and practices are generally very hard to meet with.

Generic image, Tib. spyi don: Generic image is the technical name for one type of conceptual structure used in the operation of conceptual mind. A generic image is a concept that conceptual mind takes and uses instead of having a direct perception of the actual thing. For example, a person can have a concept of a table, a complicated operation one aspect of which is a generic image, or can have direct sight of a table, which has no operation of concept with it. Thus, for example, the process of rational, dualistic mind with its generic images can never get at something like rigpa which lies outside the reach of dualistic mind.

Grasped-grasping, Tib. gzung 'dzin: When mind is turned outwardly as it is in the normal operation of dualistic mind, it has developed two faces that appear simultaneously. Special names are given to these two faces: mind appearing in the form of the external object being referenced is called "that which is grasped" and mind appearing in the form of the consciousness that is registering it is called the "grasper" or "grasping" of it. Thus, there is the pair of terms "grasped-grasper" or "grasped-grasping". When these two terms are used, it alerts one to the fact that a Mind Only style of presentation is being discussed. This pair of terms pervades Mind Only, Middle Way, and tantric writings and is exceptionally important in all of them.

Note that one could substitute the word "apprehended" for "grasped" and "apprehender" for "grasper" or "grasping" and that would reflect one connotation of the original Sanskrit terminology. The solidified duality of grasped and grasper is nothing but an invention of dualistic thought; it has that kind of character or characteristic.

Great Bliss, Skt. mahāsukha, Tib. bde ba chen po: "Great bliss" is a standard but not good translation of this key term. The phrase actually means "the great state of satisfactoriness" that comes with entering an enlightened kind of existence. It is blissful in that it is totally satisfactory, a condition of perfect ease, in comparison to samsaric existence which is totally unsatisfactory and always with some kind of dis-ease. As Thrangu Rinpoche once observed, if saṃsāra is thought of as "great suffering" then this is better thought of as the "great ease". Similarly, if saṃsāra is "total unsatisfactoriness" then this is the "great satisfactoriness".

Great Bliss Chakra, Tib. bde chen 'khor lo: The name of the chakra situated at the crown of the head.

Great Completion, Tib. rdzogs pa chen po: Two main practices of reality developed in the Buddhist traditions of ancient India and then came to Tibet: Great Completion (Mahāsanndhi) and Great Seal (Mahāmudrā). Great Completion and Great Seal are names for reality and names for a practice that directly leads to that reality. Their ways of describing reality and their practices are very similar. The Great Completion teachings are the pinnacle teachings of the tantric teachings of Buddhism that first came into Tibet with Padmasambhava and his peers and were later kept alive in the Nyingma (Earlier Ones) tradition. The Great Seal practice came into Tibet later and was held in the Sakya and Kagyu lineages. Later again, the Great Seal was held by the Gelugpa lineage, which obtained its transmissions of the instructions from the Sakya and Kagyu lineages.

It is popular nowadays to call Great Completion by the name Great Perfection, though that is a mistake. The original name Mahāsandhi refers to that one space of reality in which all things come together. Thus it means "completeness" or "completion" as the Tibetans chose to translate it and does not imply or contain the sense of "perfection".

Great Vehicle, Skt. mahāyāna, Tib. theg pa chen po: The Buddha's teachings as a whole can be summed up into three vehicles where a vehicle is defined as that which can carry a person to a certain destination. The first vehicle, called the Lesser Vehicle, contains the teachings designed to get an individual moving on the spiritual path through showing the unsatisfactory state of cyclic existence and an emancipation from that. However, that path is only concerned with personal emancipation and fails to take account of all of the beings that there are in existence. There used to be eighteen schools of Lesser Vehicle in India but the only one surviving is the Theravada of south-east Asia. The Greater Vehicle is a step up from that. The Buddha explained that it was great in comparison to the Lesser Vehicle for seven reasons. The first of those is that it is concerned with attaining the truly complete enlightenment of a truly complete buddha for the sake of every sentient being where the Lesser Vehicle is concerned only with a personal liberation that is not truly complete enlightenment and which is achieved only for the sake of that practitioner. The Great Vehicle has two divisions: a conventional form in which the path is taught in a logical, conventional way, and an unconventional form in which the path is taught in a very direct way. This latter vehicle is called the Vajra Vehicle because it takes the innermost, indestructible (vajra) fact of reality of one's own mind as the vehicle to enlightenment.

Ground, Tib. gzhi: This is the first member of the formulation of ground, path, and fruition. Ground, path, and fruition is the way that the teachings of the path of oral instruction belonging to the Vajra Vehicle are presented to students. Ground refers to the basic situation as it is.

Habituation, Tib. gom pa: Habituation is similar to but not the same as meditation (Tib. sgom pa). Where meditation is the process of creating then cultivating a certain quality which was not there before, habituation is the process of re-familiarizing yourself with a quality that is already present, even if it has become temporarily unavailable due to being covered over.

Ignorance: See under not-rigpa.

Innate, Tib. gnyug ma: This is a standard term of the higher tantras used to mean the inner situation of samsaric mind, which is its indwelling or innate wisdom.

Introduction and To Introduce, Tib. ngos sprad and ngos sprod pa respectively: This pair of terms is usually mistakenly translated as "pointing out" and "to point out". The terms are the standard terms used in day to day life for the situation in which one person introduces another person to someone or something. They are the exact same words as our English "introduction" and "to introduce".

In the Vajra Vehicle, these terms are specifically used for the situation in which one person introduces another person to the nature of his own mind. There is a term in Tibetan for "pointing out", but that term is never used for this purpose because in this case no one points out anything. Rather, a person is introduced by another person to a part of himself that he has forgotten about.

Kagyu, Tib. bka' brgyud: There are four main schools of Buddhism in Tibet—Nyingma, Kagyu, Sakya, and Gelug. Nyingma is the oldest school dating from about 800 C.E. Kagyu and Sakya both appeared in the 12th century C.E. Each of these three schools came directly from India. The Gelug school came later and did not come directly from India but came from the other three. The Nyingma school holds the tantric teachings called Great Completion (Dzogchen); the other three schools hold the tantric teachings called Mahāmudrā. Kagyu practitioners often join Nyingma practice with their Kagyu practice and Kagyu teachers often teach both, so it is common to hear about Kagyu and Nyingma together.

Kaya, Skt. kāya, Tib. sku: The Sanskrit term means a functional or coherent collection of parts, similar to the French "corps", and hence also comes to mean "a body". It is used in Tibetan Buddhist texts specifically to distinguish bodies belonging to the enlightened side from ones belonging to the samsaric side.

Enlightened being in Buddhism is said to be comprised of one or more kāyas. It is most commonly explained to consist of one, two, three, four, or five kāyas, though it is pointed out that there are infinite aspects to enlightened being and therefore it can also be said to consist of an infinite number of kāyas. In fact, these descriptions of enlightened being consisting of one or more kāyas are given for the sake of understanding what is beyond conceptual understanding so should not be taken as absolute statements.

The most common description of enlightened being is that it is comprised of three kayas: dharma, saṃbhoga, and nirmāṇakāyas.

Briefly stated, the dharmakāya is the body of truth, the saṃbhoga-kāya is the body replete with the good qualities of enlightenment, and the nirmāṇakāya is the body manifested into the worlds of saṃsāra and nirvāṇa to benefit beings.

Dharmakāya refers to that aspect of enlightened being in which the being sees the truth for himself and, in doing so, fulfils his own needs for enlightenment. The dharmakāya is purely mind, with-out form. The remaining two bodies are summed up under the heading of rūpakāyas or form bodies manifested specifically to fulfil the needs of all un-enlightened beings. "Saṃbhogakāya" has been mostly translated as "body of enjoyment" or "body of rap-ture" but it is clearly stated in Buddhist texts on the subject that the name refers to a situation replete with what is useful, that is, to the fact that the saṃbhogakāya contains all of the good qualities of enlightenment as needed to benefit sentient beings. The saṃbhogakāya is extremely subtle and not accessible by most sentient beings; the nirmāṇakāya is a coarser manifestation which can reach sentient beings in many ways. Nirmāṇakāya should not be thought of as a physical body but as the capability to express enlightened being in whatever way is needed throughout all the different worlds of sentient beings. Thus, as much as it appears as a supreme buddha who shows the dharma to beings, it also appears as anything needed within sentient beings worlds to give them assistance.

The three kāyas of enlightened being is taught in all levels of Buddhist teaching. It is especially important in Mahāmudrā and is taught there in a unique and very profound way.

The four kāyas usually refers to the three kāyas defined above with the addition of the svabhāvikakāya, the most essential body. This kāya is defined as the common emptiness of all three kayas, that is, the fact that the three kāyas collectively are empty. The four kāyas occasionally refers to the three kāyas defined above with the addition of the mahāsukhakāya, the body of great bliss; the three kāyas collectively are enlightened being and therefore collectively are a body of the great bliss of enlightenment.

Key points, Tib. gnad: Key points are the key issues in practice which, if attended to, cause one to move ahead.

Knower, Tib. ha go ba: "Knower" is a generic term for that which knows. There are many types of knower, with each having its own qualities and name, too. For example, *wisdom* is a non-dualistic knower, *mind* is the dualistic samsaric version of it, *consciousness* refers to the individual "registers" of samsaric mind, and so on. Sometimes a term is needed which simply says "that which knows" without further implication of what kind of knowing it might be. *Knower* is one of a few terms of that sort.

Latency, Skt. vāsanā, Tib. bag chags: The original Sanskrit has the meaning exactly of "latency". The Tibetan term translates that inexactly with "something sitting there (Tib. chags) within the environment of mind (Tib. bag)". Although it has become popular to translate this term into English with "habitual pattern", that is not its meaning. The term refers to a karmic seed that has been imprinted on the mindstream and is present there as a latency, ready and waiting to come into manifestation.

Lay aside, Tib. bshags pa: This term is usually translated as "confession" but that is not the meaning. The term literally means to cut something away and remove it from oneself. In Buddhism, it is used in the context of ridding oneself of the karmic seeds sown by bad karmic actions.

Buddhism is a totally non-theistic religion, so it is very important to understand that one is not confessing wrongdoings to anyone, including oneself. There is no granting of absolution in this system. As the Buddha himself said, he has no ability to purify the karmic stains of sentient beings, he can only teach them how to do so. The practice that he taught for ridding oneself of karmic wrongdoings is the practice of realizing for oneself that they hold the seed of future suffering, rousing regret, and distancing oneself from them. In doing so, one lays them aside.

There is a longer phrase that indicates the full practice of laying aside. The Tibetan phrase "mthol zhing shags pa" literally means "admitting and laying aside". Note that "admitting" also does not entail confession; it refers to that fact that one first has to admit or acknowledge to oneself that one has done something wrong, kar-mically speaking, and that it will have undesirable consequences. Without this, one cannot effectively take the second step of distancing oneself from the actions. Therefore, it is explained that the process of "laying aside" has to be understood to include the practice of "admission" because, without that acknowledgement, the laying aside cannot be done.

Lesser Vehicle, Skt. hīnayāna, Tib. theg pa dman pa: See under Great Vehicle.

Liveliness, Tib. rtsal: This is a a key term in Mahāmudrā. The term is sometimes translated as "display" or "expression" but neither is correct. The primary meaning is the ability of something to express itself but in use, the actual expression of that ability is also included. Thus, in English it would not be "expression" but "expressivity" but that is too dry. This term is not at all dry; it is talking about the life of something and how that life comes into expression; "liveliness" fits the meaning of the original term very well.

Luminosity or illumination, Skt. prabhāsvara, Tib. 'od gsal ba: The core of mind has two aspects: an emptiness factor and a knowing factor. The Buddha and many Indian religious teachers used "luminosity" as a metaphor for the knowing quality of the core of mind. If in English we would say "Mind has a knowing quality", the teachers of ancient India would say, "Mind has an illuminative quality; it is like a source of light which illuminates what it knows".

This term been translated as "clear light" but that is a mistake that comes from not understanding the etymology of the word. It does not refer to a light that has the quality of clearness (something that makes no sense, actually!) but to the illuminative property which is the nature of the empty mind.

Note also that in both Sanskrit and Tibetan Buddhist literature, this term is frequently abbreviated just to Skt. "vara" and Tib. "gsal ba" with no change of meaning. Unfortunately, this has been thought to be another word and it has then been translated with "clarity", when in fact it is just this term in abbreviation.

Mara, Skt. māra, Tib. bdud: The Sanskrit term is closely related to the word "death". Buddha spoke of four classes of extremely negative influences that have the capacity to drag a sentient being deep into saṃsāra. They are the "māras" or "kiss of death": of having a samsaric set of five skandhas; of having afflictions; of death itself; and of the son of gods, which means being seduced and taken in totally by sensuality.

Migrator, Tib. 'gro ba: Migrator is one of several terms that were commonly used by the Buddha to mean "sentient being". It shows sentient beings from the perspective of their constantly being forced to go here and there from one rebirth to another by the power of karma. They are like flies caught in a jar, constantly buzzing back and forth. The term is often translated using "beings" which is another general term for sentient beings but doing so loses the meaning entirely: Buddhist authors who know the tradition do not use the word loosely but use it specifically to give the sense of beings who are constantly and helplessly going from one birth to another, and that is how the term should be read.

Mind, Skt. chitta, Tib. sems: There are several terms for mind in the Buddhist tradition, each with its own, specific meaning. This term is the most general term for the samsaric type of mind. It refers to the type of mind that is produced because of fundamental ignorance of enlightened mind. Whereas the wisdom of enlightened mind lacks all complexity and knows in a non-dualistic way, this mind of un-enlightenment is a very complicated apparatus that only ever knows in a dualistic way.

The Mahāmudrā teachings use the terms "entity of mind" and "mind's entity" to refer to what this complicated, samsaric mind is at core—the enlightened form of mind.

Mindfulness, Skt. smṛiti, Tib. dran pa: A particular mental event, one that has the ability to keep mind on its object. Together with alertness, it is one of the two causes of developing shamatha. See under alertness for an explanation.

Mindness, Skt. chittatā, Tib. sems nyid: Mindness is a specific term of the tantras. It is one of many terms meaning the essence of mind or the nature of mind. It conveys the sense of "what mind is at its very core". It has sometimes been translated as "mind itself" but that is a misunderstanding of the Tibetan word "nyid". The term does not mean "that thing mind" where mind refers to dualistic mind. Rather, it means the very core of dualistic mind, what mind is at root, without all of the dualistic baggage.

Mindness is a path term. It refers to exactly the same thing as "actuality" or "actuality of mind" which is a ground term but does so from the practitioner's perspective. It conveys the sense to a practitioner that he has baggage of dualistic mind that has not yet been purified but that there is a core to that mind that he can work with.

Muni: See under capable one.

Noble one, Skt. ārya, Tib. 'phags pa: In Buddhism, a noble one is a being who has become spiritually advanced to the point that he has passed beyond cyclic existence. According to the Buddha, the beings in cyclic existence were ordinary beings, spiritual common-ers, and the beings who had passed beyond it were special, the nobility.

Not-rigpa, Skt. avidya, Tib. ma rig pa: Rigpa *q.v.* is a key term in these discussions. It refers to the enlightened kind of knowing. Its opposite, not-rigpa, which refers to the unenlightened way of knowing, is equally important. As it says in the *Abhidharmakosha*, "not-rigpa is not merely a discordance with rigpa but is its very opposite". Not-rigpa is usually translated as ignorance but this masks the all-important opposing relationship between rigpa and not-rigpa. Therefore, in this book, this term is usually translated as "not-rigpa" rather than "ignorance".

Not stopped, Tib. ma 'gags pa: An important path term in the teaching of both Mahāmudrā. There are two ways to explain this term: according to view and to practice. The following explanation is of the latter type. The core of mind has two parts—emptiness and luminosity—which are in fact unified so must come that way in practice. However, a practitioner who is still on the path will fall into one extreme or the other and that results in "stoppage" of the expression of the luminosity. When emptiness and luminosity are unified in practice, there is no stoppage of the expression of the luminosity that comes from having fallen into one extreme or the other. Thus "non-stopped luminosity" is a term that indicates that there is the luminosity with all of its appearance yet that luminosity, for the practitioner, is not mistaken, is not stopped off. "Stopped luminosity" is an experience like luminosity but in which the appearances have, at least to some extent, not been mixed with emptiness.

Offput, Tib. gdangs: Offput is a general term for that which is given off by something, for example, the sound that comes from a loudspeaker. In Mahāmudrā, it refers to what is given off by the emptiness factor of the essence of mind. Emptiness is the empty condition of the essence of mind, like space. However, that emptiness has liveliness which comes off the emptiness as compassion and all the other qualities of enlightened mind, and, equally, all the apparatus of dualistic mind. All of this is called its offput.

Outflow, Skt. āsrāva, Tib. zag pa: The Sanskrit term means a bad discharge, like pus coming out of a wound. Outflows occur when wisdom loses its footing and falls into the elaborations of dualistic mind. Therefore, anything with duality also has outflows. This is sometimes translated as "defiled" or "conditioned" but these fail to capture the meaning. The idea is that wisdom can remain self-contained in its own unique sphere but, when it loses its ability to stay within itself, it starts to have leakages into dualism that are defilements on the wisdom. See also under un-outflowed.

Own Appearance, Tib. rang snang: This is regarded as one of the more difficult terms to explain within Buddhist philosophy. It does not mean "self-appearance" in the sense of something coming into appearance of itself. Suffice it to say that it refers to a situation that is making its own appearances in accord with its own situation.

Poisons, Tib. dug: In Buddhism, poison is a general term for the afflictions. For samsaric beings, the afflictions are poisonous things which harm them. The Buddha most commonly spoke of the three poisons, which are the principal afflictions of desire, aggression, and ignorance. He also spoke of "the five poisons" which is a slightly longer enumeration of the principal afflictions: desire, aggression, delusion, pride, and jealousy.

Post-attainment, Tib. rjes thob: See under equipoise and post-attainment.

Prajna, Skt. prajñā, Tib. shes rab: The Sanskrit term, literally meaning "best type of mind" is defined as that which makes correct distinctions between this and that and hence which arrives at correct understanding. It has been translated as "wisdom" but that is not correct because it is, generally speaking, a mental event belonging to dualistic mind where "wisdom" is used to refer to the nondualistic knower of a buddha. Moreover, the main feature of prajñā is its ability to distinguish correctly between one thing and another and hence to arrive at a correct understanding.

Preserve, Tib. skyong ba: This is an important term in Mahāmudrā. In general, it means to defend, protect, nurture, maintain. In the higher tantras it means to keep something just as it is, to nurture that something so that it stays and is not lost. Also, in the higher tantras, it is often used in reference to preserving the state where the state is some particular state of being. Because of this, the phrase "preserve the state" is an important instruction in the higher tantras.

Rational mind, Tib. blo: Rational mind is one of several terms for mind in Buddhist terminology. It specifically refers to a mind that judges this against that. With rare exception it is used to refer to samsaric mind, given that samsaric mind only works in the dualistic mode of comparing this versus that. Because of this, the term is mostly used in a pejorative sense to point out samsaric mind as opposed to an enlightened type of mind.

The Gelugpa tradition does have a positive use for this mind and their documents will sometimes use this term in a positive sense; they claim that a buddha has an enlightened type of this mind. That is not wrong; one could refer to the ability of a buddha's wisdom to make a distinction between this and that with the term "rational mind". However, the Kagyu and Nyingma traditions in their Mahāmudrā and Great Completion teachings, reserve this term for the dualistic mind. In their teachings, it is the villain, so to speak, which needs to be removed from the practitioner's being in order to obtain enlightenment.

This term has been commonly translated simply as "mind" but that fails to identify this term properly and leaves it confused with the many other words that are also translated simply as "mind". It is not just another mind but is specifically the sort of mind that creates the situation of this and that (*ratio* in Latin) and hence, at least in the teachings of Kagyu and Nyingma, upholds the duality of saṃsāra. In that case, it is the very opposite of the essence of mind. Thus, this is a key term which should be noted and not just glossed over as "mind".

Realization, Tib. rtogs pa: Realization has a very specific meaning: it refers to correct knowledge that has been gained in such a way that the knowledge does not abate. There are two important points here. Firstly, realization is not absolute. It refers to the removal of obscurations, one at a time. Each time that a practitioner removes an obscuration, he gains a realization because of it. Therefore, there are as many levels of realization as there are obscurations. Maitreya, in the *Ornament of Manifest Realizations*, shows how the removal of the various obscurations that go with each of the three realms of samsaric existence produces realization.

Secondly, realization is stable or, as the Tibetan wording says, "unchanging". As Guru Rinpoche pointed out, "Intellectual knowledge is like a patch, it drops away; experiences on the path are temporary, they evaporate like mist; realization is unchanging".

A special usage of "realization" is found in the Essence Mahāmudrā teachings. There, realization is the term used to describe what happens at the moment when mindness is actually met during either introduction to or self-recognition of mindness. It is called realization because, in that glimpse, one actually directly sees the innate wisdom mind. The realization has not been stabilized but it is realization.

Referencing, Tib. dmigs pa: This is the name for the process in which dualistic mind references an actual object by using a conceptual token instead of the actual object. The term referencing implies the presence of dualistic mind and the term non-referencing or without reference implies the presence of non-dualistic wisdom.

Refuge, Skt. śharaṇaṃ, Tib. bskyab pa: The Sanskrit term means "shelter", "protection from harm". Everyone seeks a refuge from the unsatisfactoriness of life, even if it is a simple act like brushing the teeth to prevent the body from decaying un-necessarily. Buddhists, after having thought carefully about their situation and who could provide a refuge from it which would be thoroughly reliable, find that three things—buddha, dharma, and saṅgha—are the only things that could provide that kind of refuge. Therefore, Buddhists take refuge in those Three Jewels of Refuge as they are called. Taking refuge in the Three Jewels is clearly laid out as the one doorway to all Buddhist practice and realization.

Rigpa, Tib. rig pa: This is a most important term in Mahāmudrā. Rigpa literally means to know in the sense of "I see!" It is used at all levels of meaning from the coarsest everyday sense of knowing something to the deepest sense of knowing something as presented in the system of Essence Mahāmudrā. The system of Essence Mahāmudrā uses this term in a very special sense, though it still retains its basic meaning of "to know". To translate it as "awareness", which is common practice today, is a poor practice; there are many kinds of awareness but there is only one rigpa and besides, rigpa is substantially more than just awareness. Since this is such an important term and since it lacks an equivalent in English, I choose not to translate it.

This is the term used to indicate enlightened mind as experienced by the practitioner on the path of these practices. The term itself specifically refers to the dynamic knowing quality of mind. It absolutely does not mean a simple registering, as implied by the word "awareness" which unfortunately is often used to translate this term. There is no word in English that exactly matches it, though the idea of "seeing" or "insight on the spot" is very close. Proof of this is found in the fact that the original Sanskrit term "vidyā" is actually the root of all words in English that start with "vid" and mean "to see", for example, "video", "vision", and so on. Chogyam Trungpa Rinpoche, who was particular skilled at getting Tibetan words into English, also stated that this term rigpa really did not have a good equivalent in English, though he thought that "insight" was the closest. My own conclusion after hearing extensive teaching on it is that rigpa is best left untranslated. Note that rigpa has both noun and verb forms.

Samsara, Skt. saṃsāra, Tib. 'khor ba: This is the most general name for the type of existence in which sentient beings live. It refers to the fact that they continue on from one existence to another, always within the enclosure of births that are produced by ignorance and experienced as unsatisfactory. The original Sanskrit means to be constantly going about, here and there. The Tibetan term literally means "cycling", because of which it is frequently translated into English with "cyclic existence" though that is not quite the meaning of the term.

Satva and sattva: According to the Tibetan tradition established at the time of the great translation work done at Samye under the watch of Padmasambhava not to mention the one hundred and sixty-three of the greatest Buddhist scholars of Sanskrit-speaking India, there is a difference of meaning between the Sanskrit terms "satva" and "sattva", with satva meaning "an heroic kind of being" and "sattva" meaning simply "a being". According to the Tibetan tradition established under the advice of the Indian scholars mentioned above, satva is correct for the words Vajrasatva and bodhisatva, whereas sattva is correct for the words samayasattva, samādhisattva, and jñānasattva, and is also used alone to refer to any or all of these three satvas.

All Tibetan texts produced since the time of the great translations conform to this system and all Tibetan experts agree that this is correct, but Western translators of Tibetan texts have for last few hundreds of years claimed that they know better and have "satva" to "sattva" in every case, causing confusion amongst Westerners confronted by the correct spellings. Recently, publications by Western Sanskrit scholars have been appearing in which these great experts finally admit that they were wrong and that the Tibetan system is and always has been correct!

Secret, Skt. guhya, Tib. sang ba: This term is used in Buddhist texts in a specific way. It does not mean that someone has made something secret but that something has a nature which is hidden from the view of ordinary sentient beings, that it is not obvious to them.

With that meaning, it is used in this text in two ways:. Firstly, it is used to refer to the tantric or Vajra Vehicle level of teaching; this teaching is about profound subjects that are not immediately understood by ordinary beings. Secondly, it is used to refer to enlightenment; for example, "the supreme secret" mentioned in the very first line of the text is the most excellent of all hidden phenomena, which is enlightenment itself.

Secret Mantra, Tib. gsang sngags: Another name for the Vajra Vehicle or the tantric teachings.

Shamatha, Skt. śhamatha, Tib. gzhi gnas: The name of one of the two main practices of meditation used in the Buddhist system to gain insight into reality. This practice creates a foundation of one-pointedness of mind which can then be used to focus the insight of the other practice, vipaśhyanā . If the development of śhamatha is taken through to completion, the result is a mind that sits stably on its object without any effort and a body which is filled with ease. Altogether, this result of the practice is called "the creation of workability of body and mind".

Shine forth, shining forth, Tib. shar ba: This term means "to dawn" or "to come forth into visibility" either in the outer physical world or in the inner world of mind.

It is heavily used in texts on meditation to indicate the process of something coming forth into mind. There are other terms with this specific meaning but most of them also imply the process of dawning within a samsaric mind. "Shine forth" is special because it does not have that restricted meaning; it refers to the process of something dawning in any type of mind, un-enlightened and enlightened. It is an important term for Mahāmudrā where there is a great need to refer to the simple fact of something dawning in mind especially in enlightened mind but also in un-enlightened mind.

In the Tibetan language, this term stands out and immediately conveys the meaning explained above. There are words in English like "to appear" that might seem easier to read than "shine forth", but they do not stand out and catch the attention sufficiently. Moreover, terms such as "appear" accurately translate other Tibetan terms which specifically indicate an un-enlightened context or a certain type of sensory appearance, so they do not convey the meaning of this term. There will be many times where this term's specific meaning of something occurring in any type of mind is crucial to a full understanding of the expression under consideration. For example, "shining-forth liberation" means that some content of mind, such as a thought, comes forth in either un-enlightened or enlightened mind, and that, on coming forth, is liberated there in that mind.

State, Tib. ngang: This is a key term in Mahāmudrā. Unfortunately it is often not translated and in so doing much meaning is lost. Alternatively, it is often translated as "within" which is incorrect. The term means a "state". A state is a certain, ongoing situation. In Buddhist meditation in general, there are various states that a practitioner has to enter and remain in as part of developing the meditation.

Stoppageless, Tib. 'gag pa med pa: This is a key term in Mahāmudrā. It is usually translated as "unceasing" but this is a different verb. It refers to the situation in which one thing is not being stopped by another thing. It means "not stopped", "without stoppage", "not blocked and prevented by something else" that is, stoppage-less. The verb form associated with it is "not stopped" *q.v.* It is used in relation to the practice of luminosity. A stoppageless luminosity is the actual state of reality and what the practitioner has to aim for. At the beginning of the practice, a practitioner's experience of luminosity will usually not be stoppageless but with stoppages.

Stopped, Tib. 'gags pa: See under not-stopped and stoppageless.

Superfactual, Skt. paramārtha, Tib. don dam: This term is paired with the term "fictional" *q.v.* In the past, the terms have been translated as "relative" and "absolute" respectively, but those translations are nothing like the original terms. These terms are extremely important in the Buddhist teaching so it is very important that their translations be corrected but, more than that, if the actual meaning of these terms is not presented, the teaching connected with them cannot be understood.

The Sanskrit term literally means "the fact for that which is above all others, special, superior" and refers to the wisdom mind possessed by those who have developed themselves spiritually to the point of having transcended saṃsāra. That wisdom is *superior* to an ordinary, un-developed person's consciousness and the *facts* that appear on its surface are superior compared to the facts that appear on the ordinary person's consciousness. Therefore, it is superfact or the holy fact, more literally. What this wisdom knows is true for the beings who have it, therefore what the wisdom sees is superfactual truth.

Superfactual truth, Skt. paramārthasatya, Tib. don dam bden pa: See under superfactual.

Superfactual enlightenment mind, Tib. don dam bden pa'i byang chub sems: This is one of a pair of terms; the other is Fictional Truth Enlightenment Mind *q.v.* for explanation.

Superfice, superficies, Tib. rnam pa: In discussions of mind, a distinction is made between the entity of mind which is a mere knower and the superficial things that appear on its surface and which are known by it. In other words, the superficies are the various things which pass over the surface of mind but which are not mind. Superficies are all the specifics that constitute appearance—for example, the colour white within a moment of visual consciousness, the sound heard within an ear consciousness, and so on.

Suppression and furtherance, Tib. dgag sgrub: Suppression and furtherance is the term used to express the way that dualistic mind approaches the path to enlightenment. In that case, some states of mind are regarded as ones to be discarded, so the practitioner takes the approach of attempting to suppress or stop them, and some are regarded as ones to be developed, so the practitioner takes the approach of trying to go further with and develop them. Essence Mahāmudrā practice goes beyond that duality.

Tha mal gyi shaypa, Tib. tha mal gyi shes pa: See under common awareness.

The nature, Tib. rang bzhin: The nature is one of the three characteristics—entity, nature, and un-stopped compassionate activity—of the core of mind. Using this term emphasizes that the empty entity does have a nature. In other words, its use explicitly shows that the core of mind is not merely empty. If you ask "Well, what is that nature like?" The answer is that it is luminosity, it is wisdom.

Three kayas, see under kaya.

Unaltered or uncontrived, Tib. ma bcos pa: This term is the opposite of altered and contrived. It refers to something which has not been altered from its native state; something which has been left just as it is.

Un-outflowed, Skt. aśhrāva, Tib. zag pa med pa: Un-outflowed dharmas are ones that are connected with wisdom that has not lost its footing and leaked out into a defiled state; it is self-contained wisdom without any taint of dualistic mind and its apparatus. See also outflowed.

Upadesha, Skt. upadeśha, Tib. man ngag: See under foremost instruction.

Vacillatory focus, Tib. gza' gtad: This term is twice pejorative. The word "vacillatory" refers to a process of hovering around a subject, seeing it from this angle and that angle because of vacillating over how it really is. "Focus" means that rational mind takes one of the possible angles and settles on that. For example, in the process of resting in the essence of mind, there can be the fault of not leaving rational mind but staying within in it and thinking, "Yes, this is the essence of mind" or "No, this is not it. It is that". Each of those is a vacillatory focus. Any vacillatory focus implies that the practitioner has not left rational mind and so is not in rigpa.

Vajra Vehicle, Skt. vajrayāna, Tib. rdo rje'i theg pa: See under Great Vehicle.

Valid cognizer, valid cognition, Skt. pramāṇa, Tib. tshad ma: The Sanskrit term literally means "best type of mentality" and comes to mean "a valid cognizer". Its value is that is can be used to validate anything that can be known. The Tibetans translated this term with "tshad ma" meaning an "evaluator"—something which can be used to evaluate the truth or not of whatever it is given to know. It is the term used in logic to indicate a mind which is knowing validly and which therefore can be used to validate the object it is knowing.

Valid cognizers are named according to the kind of test they are employed to do. A valid cognizer of the conventional or a valid cognizer of the fictional tests within conventions, within the realm of rational, dualistic mind. A valid cognizer of the ultimate or valid cornier of superfact tests for the superfactual level, beyond dualistic mind.

View, meditation, and conduct, Tib. lta sgom spyod: This set of three is a formulation of the teachings that contains all of the meaning of the path.

Vipashyana, Skt. vipaśhyanā, Tib. lhag mthong: This is the Sanskrit name for one of the two main practices of meditation needed in the Buddhist system for gaining insight into reality. The other one, śhamatha, keeps the mind focussed while this one looks piercingly into the nature of things.

Wisdom, Skt. jñāna, Tib. ye shes: This is a fruition term that refers to the kind of mind, the kind of knower possessed by a buddha. Sentient beings do have this kind of knower but it is covered over by a very complex apparatus for knowing, dualistic mind. If they practise the path to buddhahood, they will leave behind their obscuration and return to having this kind of knower.

The Sanskrit term has the sense of knowing in the most simple and immediate way. This sort of knowing is present at the core of every being's mind. Therefore, the Tibetans called it "the particular type of awareness which is there primordially". Because of the Tibetan wording it has often been called "primordial wisdom" in English translations, but that goes too far; it is just "wisdom" in the sense of the most fundamental knowing possible.

SUPPORTS FOR STUDY

I have been encouraged over the years by all of my teachers to pass on the knowledge I have accumulated in a lifetime dedicated to study and practice, primarily in the Tibetan tradition of Buddhism. On the one hand, they have encouraged me to teach. On the other, they are concerned that, while many general books on Buddhism have been and are being published, there are few books that present the actual texts of the tradition. Therefore they, together with a number of major figures in the Buddhist book publishing world, have also encouraged me to translate and publish high quality translations of individual texts of the tradition.

My teachers always remark with great appreciation on the extraordinary amount of teaching that I have heard in this life. It allows for highly informed, accurate translations of a sort not usually seen. Briefly, I spent the 1970's studying, practising, then teaching the Gelugpa system at Chenrezig Institute, Australia, where I was a founding member and also the first Australian to be ordained as a monk in the Tibetan Buddhist tradition. In 1980, I moved to the United States to study at the feet of the Vidyadhara Chogyam Trungpa Rinpoche. I stayed in his Vajradhatu community, now called Shambhala, where I studied and practised all the Karma Kagyu, Nyingma, and Shambhala teachings being presented there and was a senior member of the Nalanda Translation Committee. After the vidyadhara's nirvana, I moved in 1992 to Nepal, where I

277

have been continuously involved with the study, practise, translation, and teaching of the Kagyu system and especially of the Nyingma system of Great Completion. In recent years, I have spent extended times in Tibet with the greatest living Tibetan masters of Great Completion, receiving very pure transmissions of the ultimate levels of this teaching directly in Tibetan and practising them there in retreat. In that way, I have studied and practised extensively not in one Tibetan tradition as is usually done, but in three of the four Tibetan traditions—Gelug, Kagyu, and Nyingma—and also in the Theravada tradition, too.

With that as a basis, I have taken a comprehensive and long term approach to the work of translation. For any language, one first must have the lettering needed to write the language. Therefore, as a member of the Nalanda Translation Committee, I spent some years in the 1980's making Tibetan word-processing software and high-quality Tibetan fonts. After that, reliable lexical works are needed. Therefore, during the 1990's I spent some years writing the *Illuminator Tibetan-English Dictionary* and a set of treatises on Tibetan grammar, preparing a variety of key Tibetan reference works needed for the study and translation of Tibetan Buddhist texts, and giving our Tibetan software the tools needed to translate and research Tibetan texts. During this time, I also translated fulltime for various Tibetan gurus and ran the Drukpa Kagyu Heritage Project—at the time the largest project in Asia for the preservation of Tibetan Buddhist texts. With the dictionaries, grammar texts, and specialized software in place, and a wealth of knowledge, I turned my attention in the year 2000 to the translation and publication of important texts of Tibetan Buddhist literature.

Padma Karpo Translation Committee (PKTC) was set up to provide a home for the translation and publication work. The committee focusses on producing books containing the best of Tibetan literature, and, especially, books that meet the needs of practitioners. At the time of writing, PKTC has published a wide range of books that, collectively, make a complete program of study for those practising Tibetan Buddhism, and especially for those interested in the higher tantras. All in all, you will find many books both free and for sale on the PKTC web-site. Most are available both as paper editions and e-books.

It would take up too much space here to present an extensive guide to our books and how they can be used as the basis for a study program. However, a guide of that sort is available on the PKTC web-site, whose address is on the copyright page of this book and we recommend that you read it to see how this book fits into the overall scheme of PKTC publications. In short, given that this book is about Kagyu Mahamudra and the Kagyu view, other books of interest from PKTC would be:

- *Gampopa's Mahāmudrā, The Five-Part Mahāmudrā of the Kagyus*, a set of several texts showing the view of Mahāmudrā and how to practise it;
- *Drukchen Padma Karpo's Collected Works on Mahamudra*, the entire writings on Mahāmudrā of one of the most important Kagyu authors, with many details of the non-dual view;
- *The Bodyless Dakini Dharma: The Dakini Hearing Lineage of the Kagyus*, with several very early teachings on the view;
- *A Juggernaut of the Non-Dual View, Ultimate Teachings of the Second Drukchen Gyalwang Je*, a set of sixty-six teachings on the ultimate view by one of the early masters of the Drukpa Kagyu;
- *Maitrīpa's Writings on the View*, several teachings on the view from the "father of other emptiness";
- *Theory and Practice of Other Emptiness Taught Through Milarepa's Songs*, a complete explanation of the view of other emptiness given through two songs of Milarepa which are famous for their expositions of the non-dual view;

- *Dusum Khyenpa's Songs and Teachings.*

We make a point of including, where possible, the relevant Tibetan texts in Tibetan script in our books. We also make them available in electronic editions that can be downloaded free from our website, as discussed below. The Tibetan texts for this book have not been included because of size constraints. However, PKTC has prepared a digital edition of the Derge Edition of Gampopa's *Collected Works* which contains all of the texts presented in this book and which is available from PKTC.

Electronic Resources

PKTC has developed a complete range of electronic tools to facilitate the study and translation of Tibetan texts. For many years now, this software has been a prime resource for Tibetan Buddhist centres throughout the world, including in Tibet itself. It is available through the PKTC web-site.

The wordprocessor TibetDoc has the only complete set of tools for creating, correcting, and formatting Tibetan text according to the norms of the Tibetan language. It can also be used to make texts with mixed Tibetan and English or other languages. Extremely high quality Tibetan fonts, based on the forms of Tibetan calligraphy learned from old masters from pre-Communist Chinese Tibet, are also available. Because of their excellence, these typefaces have achieved a legendary status amongst Tibetans.

TibetDoc is used to prepare electronic editions of Tibetan texts in the PKTC text input office in Asia. After that, they are made available through the PKTC web-site. The electronic texts can be read, searched, and even made into an electronic library using either TibetDoc or our other software, TibetD Reader. Like TibetDoc, TibetD Reader is advanced software with many capabilities made specifically to meet the needs of reading and researching

Tibetan texts. PKTC software is for purchase but we make a free version of TibetD Reader available for free download on the PKTC web-site.

A key feature of TibetDoc and Tibet Reader is that Tibetan terms in texts can be looked up on the spot using PKTC's electronic dictionaries. PKTC also has several electronic dictionaries—some Tibetan-Tibetan and some Tibetan-English—and a number of other reference works. The *Illuminator Tibetan-English Dictionary* is renowned for its completeness and accuracy.

This combination of software, texts, reference works, and dictionaries that work together seamlessly has become famous over the years. It has been the basis of many, large publishing projects within the Tibetan Buddhist community around the world for over thirty years and is popular amongst all those needing to work with Tibetan language or deepen their understanding of Buddhism through Tibetan texts.

INDEX